◉ THE MAD MOTORISTS ◉

D1493285

THE MAD MOTORISTS

THE GREAT PEKING–PARIS RACE OF '07

by Allen Andrews

MOTORACES BOOK CLUB
GEORGE G. HARRAP & CO. LTD.
London 1966

TO
THE LADY
WITH WHOM I MOTOR

This Motoraces Book Club edition was produced in 1966
for sale to its members only by the proprietors, Readers
Union Ltd, at Aldine House, 10–13 Bedford Street,
London W.C.2 and at Letchworth Garden City, Herts.
Full details of membership may be obtained from our
London address. The book is set in Linotype Caledonia
and has been reprinted by Western Printing Services Ltd,
Bristol. It was first published by George G. Harrap & Co.
Ltd.

◎ ◎ Preface

It is a bold claim to suggest that in this book the fair truth is told for the first time about an adventure that is still, after fifty years, to my mind, the greatest feat in motoring outside the laboratory of the track circuit. I make that claim.

"As long as a man has a car he can do anything and go anywhere—*anywhere*." That was the boast of the infant automobile industry, and a team of cars set out to prove it by starting at Peking and stopping in Paris, on a route later calculated to stretch 10,000 miles. The cars were called on to overcome obstacles for which men later designed the tank. The scream of low gear was their morning chorus. Their crews hauled them through mountain gorges, hitched them like gun-carriages to half-wild horses to ford the broad Siberian rivers, dug them out of deserts, bogs, and quicksands all over Asia. They sent camel caravans out in advance across the Gobi Desert to lay down petrol dumps; they travelled with silver ingots, knives to shave them with, and scales to weigh the shavings as payment for the chicken they bought from Mongolian nomads; they entertained without loss of face the Grand Lama in Urga, the Siberian Cycle Club in Irkutsk, and an intoxicated countess in the Urals. Both their organization and their improvisation were superb. "This is a real Jules Verne undertaking," observed the Marquis de Dion before the start. But Phileas Fogg never had to cope with a burnt-out magneto 6000 miles from base.

I called this expedition an *épreuve* by a 'team of cars.' In one sense the description is the wildest irony. They certainly were not a team of crews. They were by degrees, grudging, jealous, selfish, and ruthless in their dealings with each other—and then, in duress, capable of the decent magnanimity that man gives to man as long as woman is not involved. There was nothing to hold them together as Captain Scott's team were held—to his spirit and their flag. These men were rivals pretending to be companions. The prestige of three nations was at stake; the commercial future of three automobile manufacturers was strongly affected by the outcome of the *raid*; and it cannot be ignored that every jockey, whether he pushes horses or cars, expects a 'present' from the owner proportionate to his position at the finish—and this affects his comradeship. That is a list of incentives in descending order. But above them all—I do not think it is false heroics to say it—these men knew, as gourmets, the appreciation of endurance and the satisfaction of achieving their end. It may seem profane to have mentioned Captain Scott in comparison with any aspect of this expedition. But these men, in the way they fought their personal duel with death, played out the comedy of "hardihood, endurance, and courage," just as Scott, to my mind, played the transcending tragedy.

Why has it taken so long to tell the truth? Four writers, of varying merit, rode on the *raid* from Peking to Paris, and with admirable publishing enterprise they produced long books, in French or Italian, within three months of its finish. Each writer was partisan. Each not only gave a naturally biased account, but also—it must be concluded—told solid lies, either in the interests of self, or employers, or to 'cover up' incidents that may have seemed unpleasant.

The one man who said nothing—though nowadays his very raffish disreputability would have ensured him a newspaper contract—had the best story to tell. He was Charles Godard, driver of the Dutch car, the Spyker, the most brilliant automobilist of them all in terms of sheer driving nerve and endurance, though not from the point of view of rally organization. He alone was backed by no manufacturer, sponsored by no angel, unable to use private means to compete as a gentleman rider. When this story starts he is performing in a Paris fairground. When it ends he is shrugging shoulders in a Paris nick. A historian should have no favourites, but all the world loves a rascal. The classic hero of the *raid* was the meticulous planner and polished executant Prince Scipione Borghese. The sympathy of romantics is still reserved for the motoring Macheath, Charles Godard.

The truth about the Peking–Paris *raid* rests on the truth about Godard. I could not find it in any published reference until one afternoon in Amsterdam, when the spotless offices of *De Telegraaf* newspaper billowed with the paper-dust of old files, I think I got as near as possible to it. One man survives who knew Godard well, the distinguished engineer Bruno Stephan, famous for his association with Fokker aircraft, who rode with Godard for part of the *raid*. Heer Stephan's memory—he is seventy-seven—has been invaluable for the details of his personal contact with Godard. I have had to disagree with his stoutly defended reconstruction of Godard's movements during one sequence in Siberia, because wherever Godard *told* Stephan he had been at a particular time, his French friends had *seen* him somewhere else. And in Paris at the final point of high drama, as Heer Stephan has told me, "I was practically out of the game." I have used the contemporary account of Godard's remarkable deceptions received direct from Heer Jacobus Spijker (the man who was principally deceived) and set down by John Coucke, the sporting correspondent of *De Telegraaf*. John Coucke is also a survivor.

This book is a chronicle. There are six main sources—none of which entirely matches—and innumerable subsidiary springs of description and comment. I have had to make hard decisions about fact, and this book is not the work for comment on discrepancies to be noted in scholarly footnotes about folio A and quarto B. I have hazarded some direct quotations, the verbal accuracy of which I do not guarantee, but I have good evidence for their sense. The great majority of the 'conversations' are authenticated.

I enjoyed writing this book. The people who made it more enjoyable were the host of enthusiasts who clarified research on the details, especially Heer C. Poel junior of Westzaan, Holland. They include the staff of my dear, indulgent London Library, the British Museum Library at Bloomsbury and at Colindale— through the latter I must acknowledge by implication the acquiescence of the publishers of the *Daily Telegraph, Daily*

Mail, and *Times,* of London, and the periodicals *The Automobile, Automobile Times, Automotor Journal, Car, Motor, Motor Car Journal, Motor Car World,* and *Motor Times,* of London and Coventry, with the *Corriere della Sera* of Milan, *Le Figaro* and *Le Gaulois* of Paris, the *North-China Herald and Supreme Court and Consular Gazette,* of Shanghai, and *Lloyd's Weekly Shipping Index;* the Bibliothèque Nationale, of Paris, for access to the files of *Le Matin;* the Editor of *De Telegraaf,* of Amsterdam; Henriette Bardell, Sam Bardell, Ronald Barker, Luigi Barzini, John Coucke, Capitano di Vascello Luigi Donini, Generale Pier-Luigi Donini, Derek Forsyth, Bas Goedhardt, Ellen de Haart, Sten Huygens, B. Stephan, Bart van Veen, Dr J. P. Veening.

The principal contemporary sources are: Luigi Barzini, *La Metà del Mondo vista da un'Automobile* (Milan, 1908); Georges Cormier, *Le Raid Pékin–Paris* (Paris, 1907); Edgardo Longoni, *Da Pechino a Parigi* (Milan, 1938); Jean du Taillis, *Pékin-Paris Automobile en Quatre Vingts Jours* (Paris, 1907); and the files of *Le Matin, Corriere della Sera, Daily Mail,* and *Daily Telegraph.*

I am grateful to Juliana Forte for the preparation of the maps.

I acknowledge the illustrations as follows: Luigi Barzini, Plates one to eight and Plate eleven; C. Poel junior, Plates nine and ten; "Radio Times" Hulton Picture Library, Plate 12.

A.A.

◎ ◎ Contents

Contents

◎ ◎ Illustrations

Plates in half-tone between pages 128 and 129

ERRATUM SLIP

Illustration No. 11 should read as follows :
A verst pole on the Siberian tract.

Illustrations

1 ◉ ◉ The Stupendous Challenge

Paris, the 2nd of February 1907. Spring hovered behind the green-flecked skies of the final frosts. Paris was noticeably colder than London, observed King Edward VII, arriving for a week's stay in his spiritual capital. He came incognito as the Duke of Lancaster, a veil which obscured his personality about as effectively as Irving's make-up when the actor played Othello. It did nothing to dispel the crowd of welcoming Parisians at the Gare du Nord, nor to discourage the busy Press photographers. Queen Alexandra, Duchess of Lancaster, gasped as an unexpected magnesium flash startled her. She quickly recovered herself. "How ridiculous!" she said. "I really ought to be accustomed to it by this time."

The boulevardiers read all about it as they sprawled amid the crimson and leather of the café interiors. They preened themselves a little in reaction to the royal visit. They guffawed at the disrespectful ditty about Edouard d'Angleterre being sung to the tune of *La Petite Tonkinoise*. Then they tossed into the roulette-round of knowledgeable gossip the topic Paris–Peking. De Dion had accepted; Contal, too. What else did anyone know?

On the morning of the 31st of January, 1907, the newspaper *Le Matin* of Paris had appeared with a bold announcement displayed on its front page. It read:

PARIS–PEKING AUTOMOBILE
A Stupendous Challenge

People are busy nowadays organizing automobile events and races on selected small circuits. These shows have their entertainment value as long as they are under sufficient control not to be a public danger.

But they are small-scale efforts, and their small scale lessens their practical value.

The organizers of these diversions seem to lag behind their industry. The supreme use of the automobile is that it makes long journeys possible. Its effect is to make man the master of distance. Its appeal is that it opens up to us journeys hitherto undreamed of. But all we have done is make it go round in circles.

What would we say if the railway companies descended to pitting the noble locomotives of, say, the Orient Express and the Nord Express into a dash round the Inner Circle? When the trains which go to Constantinople and St Petersburg had finished 150 circuits of Paris what progress would have been registered?

The whole *raison d'être* of cars is that they make possible the most ambitious and unpremeditated trips to far horizons. For this reason the general public fails to see the logic of making motor-cars chase their tails in tight circles.

We believe that the motor industry, the finest industry in France, has the right to claim a wider field in which to demonstrate its potential. Progress does not emerge from backing mediocrity or routine.

What needs to be proved to-day is that as long as a man has a car he can do anything and go anywhere.

Anywhere. Yes, anywhere.

That is what the makers tell us. That is what the buyers want to know.

All right! We ask this question of car manufacturers in France and abroad:

Is there anyone who will undertake to travel this summer from Paris to Peking by automobile?

Whoever he is, this tough and daring man, whose gallant car will have a dozen nations watching its progress, he will certainly deserve to have his name spoken as a byword in the four quarters of the earth.

A member of our staff will follow this stupendous expedition, and readers of *Le Matin* will be able to share day by day the triumphs and disasters of this fantastic journey.

The challenge was hardly uttered before it was accepted. With a promptitude that was not taken at the time to indicate foreknowledge, the Marquis de Dion, president of the de Dion-Bouton Motor Corporation, founder of the Automobile Club of France, and undisputed king of French motoring, had a letter delivered by special messenger:

> I have read in *Le Matin* of a challenge trial from Paris to Peking. The roads are abominable, and often exist only as lines on a map. However, it is my belief that if a motor-car can get through, the de Dion-Bouton will get through.
>
> This being so, and this trial having such great interest from the point of view of the world-wide significance of the motor-car, I take up this challenge here and now, provided that I have one other car against me as competitor and travelling companion.
>
> This is a real Jules Verne undertaking, a Mayne Reid adventure. But nothing is impossible.
>
> DE DION

The Marquis's stipulated rival announced himself within a few hours in a letter which arrived in time to be printed along with de Dion's in the next issue of the paper. It came from an unexpected source. A cheeky little *mototri*—a three-wheeler not much bigger than an ice-cream tricycle, with a 6-h.p. motor—had captured the affection of sportsmen by its performance in *Le Matin's* recent contest for the "Coupe du *Matin*," in which it had been driven by a young enthusiast named Auguste Pons. A couple of these Contal *mototris* were nonchalantly tossed into the rally by their maker:

> A moment ago I received your newspaper, and I very cheerfully accept the challenge you issue—to complete the trip from Paris to Peking this summer in a creditable time. I should be willing to set on the grid one or two of my gallant little *mototris*, which will not buck at this run, however terrible it is. I propose to come and see you first thing to-morrow to discuss it. . . .
>
> C. CONTAL

By Saturday the 2nd of February boulevard gossip had it that more entries had joined the two so far published. Already there was a very high degree of general interest in the Paris–Peking *raid*—the French term which became universally adopted in connexion with the event. This was the Paris of *Gigi*, the most highly cultivated society any Renaissance had yet produced, if 'culture' may be rescued from a purely cerebral orientation. Colette was an intellectual music-hall mime, writing when she was resting, germinating *Gigi*. The real Maurice Chevalier was singing in the suburbs. The real Marquis de Dion was propagating 'automobilism' in every social and commercial gesture this captivatingly active man could make. Women and *voitures* were accepted enthusiasms. The Parisian men, who expertly assessed—and occasionally kept—the high-class courtesans of the day, applied the same fine connoisseur's appraisal to cars as they did to women and racehorses.

Motoring was a sport, in spite of *Le Matin*'s hint that it might finish as a convenience. This was the Golden Age of motoring, and the French were the heroes of the age. The Tour de France was already an institution, having been first won at an average speed of thirty-five miles an hour over 1350 miles—a performance which few tourists in France can maintain sixty years later. Frenchmen were not solely confined to circuit racing. They were dashing between Paris and Bordeaux, Marseille, or Menton at speeds that continually erased old records. Occasionally they braved the restrictive Customs barriers of the Continent, and chased each other right round Europe or even round the Mediterranean, from the gorges of the Balkans to the deserts of North Africa. The French automobile industry was supreme in Europe, and raced wing to wing in technical originality with the Americans, both on the ground and in the air. (The Wright brothers and Blériot were already 'airborne,' but 1908 and 1909 were to see their significant progress accomplished, all three working *in France*.) French newspapers, with disarming enterprise, were skilled in promoting the *épreuve*, or trial, which was more than a stunt. Men responded to the adventure of endurance that demanded virility, planning, intelligence, and skill. The Marquis de Dion likened the Paris–Peking *raid* to a Jules Verne adventure, and the newspaper said it was comparable to a polar expedition. Jules Verne was only two years dead. Peary had not yet reached the North Pole. Scott was still dreaming of the South, and anxious for any trial by which he could assess the performance of motors in rough country. The world was cornered with adventure, and the motor-car was not a bore.

Within a week of the publication of the challenge there were ten acceptances, all 'works entries.' Under the chairmanship of M. Dubail, former French Minister in Peking, a committee of men with experience of China and the Far East had been convened to formulate the route to be followed. There were considerations of geography and terrain, seasonal variations in the climate, the width of mountain gorges, self-defence, and even politics to be examined: some Asiatic tribes were reputed to murder strangers on sight; Russia was in an extraordinary state of turmoil, even by Russian standards. Its usual revolutionary unrest was exacerbated by frequent mutinies among garrisons whose morale had been annihilated by defeat in the recent Russo-Japanese war, and uncounted escaped political prisoners were on the run in Siberia. As the *Matin* committee gathered for its second sitting the Military Governor of Penza, 300 miles south-east of Moscow, was assassinated while leaving the theatre by a young man who had introduced the ingenious refinement of packing his revolver bullets with cyanide.

But Paris moved gaily on towards *mardi gras* and the spring. King Edward, on his usual theatre-round, saw plays with Sacha Guitry and Sarah Bernhardt, amid a number of lighter entertainments. The visit to Bernhardt in *Les Bouffons* was characteristically arranged. Bernhardt's maid reported at breakfast-time that there was a telephone call from some one who would not give his name. "Allo, qui est là?" demanded the great Sarah. "C'est le Roi d'Angleterre," answered the monarch, who was clearly not stressing his incognito. He asked if a box could be obtained for that evening. Bernhardt managed to get a box cleared, and had the theatre programme specially printed on silk, and the King graciously visited her in her dressing-room between the acts. The King was speeding about Paris in his own automobile, shipped from Britain. But his English chauffeur was highly affronted when, after a virulent altercation with the Paris police, he was forced to carry registration number-plates like more plebeian drivers.

The endless warfare, *Motor-drivers* v. *the Rest*, was already in progress, and the loudest and saltiest abuse among the Rest came from the rugged horse-cab drivers of Paris. These had lately been joined by two women drivers, reputed to be able to hold their own in any war of words, who had passed their knowledge-of-Paris tests, and were tailoring the short jacket, knee-breeches, and hose which the police ordained that they must wear "with a view to the possibility of falls."

By *mardi gras*, the great Parisian carnival before the comparative rigours of Lent, the *Matin* committee had reversed the route of the *raid*. Paris-to-Peking was now to be Peking-to-Paris, the cars being sent by sea to the Chinese capital "after being admired before their departure." The reason for this decision was the intelligence that the rainy season began in China about the 20th of July, and it was considered undesirable to inflict the mud of the Chinese mountain passes on competitors at the end of their arduous journey. The fearful mountains between Mongolia and Peking—gorges where even pack-camels were said to rip their loads against the narrow walls of the defiles—had always been accepted as the most destructive section of the route. By contrast the Trakt, or cart-track, across Siberia was believed to be comparatively easy, although it was known to be badly kept since the Trans-Siberian railway had captured most of the Continental traffic after 1899. "The Trakt across Siberia seems to be in a good state of preservation and not too grossly neglected," reported the committee. Events proved that in this and other judgments the committee was optimistic. Though the competitors did not expect a beaten track through such stretches as the Gobi Desert, many parts of Siberia—across steppes, marshland, and forest country—were equally tractless, and offered little but mud. For the weather intelligence was mistaken too. Not only did the Chinese rain-season begin six weeks earlier than forecast, on the actual day the drivers set out from Peking; an 'unprecedented' bad summer in Siberia (though bad summers are given this label the world over) brought continuous rain, serious enough to impede even the sowing through that agricultural subcontinent, apart from turning the motor course into a morass. The hoods of the screenless cars used then were no protection at any speed over five miles an hour, and were eventually thrown away as jetsam.

Such prospects, which, though they were not known, might be intelligently guessed, did not deter the mad motorists of Europe. Entries continued to come in. "Your plan for a motor *raid* between Peking and Paris is tailor-made to seduce me," wrote the Baron Duquesne, "and I write as one who has done thousands of kilo-metres in the Sahara with my various cars, from the little 3-horse job to the 18-h.p. Panhard, which is the machine I intend to submit to the admiration of the Sons of Heaven in their own capital."

A more restrained and businesslike entry came from Prince Scipione Borghese, one of the most formidable and practical men of action of the day. Writing from Rome, before news of the reversal of route reached him, he confirmed, "The car I am entering for your Paris–Peking trial is an Itala. I should be much obliged if you would give me more details at your earliest con-venience so that I may make adequate planning decisions." Imme-diately he read the *Matin* challenge Borghese had telegraphed the Itala works in Turin ordering a new 40-h.p. 'racer'—really a touring car—with a chassis of girder-steel to be made to his own specifications, thicker than usual. As soon as he was informed that the quick delivery he demanded could be fulfilled—he was actually driving the car within two months—he wired Paris with his final acceptance. Count Gropello, another Italian enthusiast, had a stable of Fiats, which were his pride, but also ordered another to his specifications. It was Prince Scipione Borghese's entry, however, that hardened the image of the *Matin* challenge from a stunt to an expedition. The Prince, trained in the diplo-matic service, had abandoned career diplomacy for scientific exploration, and had, in addition, an imposing record as an Alpine mountaineer and as a motorist. His reputation was of an assiduous planner with an iron nerve, which he brought into action only after the most detailed study of his obstacle. He was known among the Roman nobility—where he was not popular—as "the English officer," partly for his lean, clean-shaven face in an epoch of luxuriant moustaches, but mostly for his cool and undemon-strative reserve. It was felt in Rome and Paris that if Borghese entered for the Peking–Paris *raid* the event was not only possible: its entry in the record-books was assured.

On Monday the 11th of February, 1907, at four in the afternoon, thirty manufacturers, trading agents, and professional drivers met in the offices of *Le Matin* to make certain *raid* decisions final. Prince Scipione was not there. Apart from the fact that the day was his thirty-sixth birthday, he was too busy planning ever to find the time to come to Paris. He asked Fournier, president of the French Automobile Club and a famous winner of the Paris–Bordeaux race, to watch over his interests. At this early stage, only eleven days after the announcement of the *raid*, it was necessary to make a hard schedule for embarkation to Peking. The entrants agreed to ship their cars from Marseille on the 14th of April. They themselves could follow overland in May to receive their cars in China in early June.

Apart from Borghese, all the principals who were eventually to drive out of Peking were there. Georges Cormier, a stolid, cautious man, with a high forehead, hooded eyes, and a vast dark-chestnut moustache drooping in the Balkan fashion, was a motor-car dealer retained by de Dion-Bouton for driving in endurance trials. He had competed in the Circuit Européen and the Circuit Européen-Africain, was a devotee of light cars, and had been engaged to drive the de Dion-Bouton 10-h.p. *voiturette* from Peking to Paris. It was also likely that he would be relied on, with his experience of practical planning for long-distance events, for the organization of petrol dumps along some part of the long route of the *raid*.

Victor Collignon, big, fat, and ruddy, and with the full moustache of the period, was another experienced de Dion-Bouton driver, with less personality and authority than Cormier, to whom he habitually tended to yield. He was engaged to drive a de Dion-Bouton 15-h.p. machine. De Dion had originally entered three of his cars, all of different power, but he finally shipped only two, both 10 h.p.

Auguste Pons was a good-looking young man, with an attractively audacious personality, who was known only for his dogged demonstration of the capability of the Contal tri-car. Contal had by now varied his entry of two *mototris*, and had put in only one three-wheeler and a more orthodox 8-h.p. *voiturette*. In the event, it was only the three-wheeler that was put aboard the ship at Marseille.

The fourth in the quartet of professional drivers who started had a less solid reputation than the de Dion stalwarts, but was known to the more observant students of form as potentially the most outstanding of them all, both for brilliance and endurance. Charles Godard was a jockey who had just not had sufficient mounts to be taken too seriously in automobilism, and his attitude to daily life prevented him from being taken seriously in any other sphere. He was, sometimes a little too conscientiously, the life and soul of the party wherever he went. His quick repartee, his amusing boastfulness, his apparent ignorance of the details of practical planning or even the mechanical working of the machines he drove so stylishly, veiled from most of his companions his quite fanatical devotion to motor-driving. No one knew quite how he lived between races, and Charles Godard did nothing to enlighten them; he was new enough in this professional circle for it not to have become common gossip that even Godard's fast talking had not been fast enough to save him from one monitory spell in prison for false pretences.

He was a fair man of medium height, hailing from Burgundy, though his temperament was considered pure Mediterranean. He had the india-rubber face of the true mime, and seemed able to wash it clean of all expression with a pass of his hand. Then one heavy drooping eye would open, the corner of a lip would twist, and with a quick glance to make sure that he held attention he would register the expression of the moment and back it with an appropriate joke.

Godard at the *Matin* offices, quipping, leg-pulling, poohpoohing practical difficulties, was delirious with happiness. Against the run of his luck he had catapulted through the scores of drivers and mechanics clamouring to compete in the *raid*, and had been engaged to drive a heavy car, a 40-h.p. Métallurgique. Métallurgique was a Belgian firm which had entered three cars, a 30 h.p. and two 40's. Godard had secured the last place in their list of drivers. As the noisy meeting broke up and his new companions reluctantly detached themselves from the vivacious

Godard the driver walked along the Boulevard Poissonnière, meditating how best he could squeeze an advance on his retaining fee from Métallurgique. Then he strode briskly out for the fairground sited in the middle of the vast boulevard below Montparnasse. To-morrow was *mardi gras*, and there was money to be made. Godard was booked to ride a motor-cycle in the fairground's Wall of Death.

Unfortunately, Godard had taken too little notice of the very serious hazards entailed in the race, which were now being revealed as reports came in from St Petersburg, Peking, and the string of branches of the Russo-Chinese Bank spaced across Siberia. Hard facts about the rigours of the route began to emerge through the haze of early enthusiasm as inexorably as five months later the great cliff-face of Tuerin was to solidify out of the luminous mirage of the Gobi Desert. It seemed certain that many cars must break down at a distance from their base that would render major repair impossible and the safety of their crews a heavy liability. Even more disconcerting facts about expense were also beginning to be realized. An entrance-fee of 2000 francs (about £400 by present standards) had been agreed. Estimates of the outlay for the trip were running at up to 100,000 francs (£20,000 now) for each car. Firms which had lightly entered one car decided, on consideration, to abandon the project. Among them was the only British entry, a C.V.R. motor put in by the St. James Motor Company, Ltd. Firms which had put in up to three cars began to think very seriously about an expense of perhaps a quarter of a million francs. De Dion withdrew one car. Métallurgique made a preliminary retreat by scratching the duplicate 40 h.p. run by their third man, Charles Godard. When the intrepid motor-cyclist finished his stint on the Wall of Death he discovered that he was no longer listed among the intrepid automobilists.

Godard reacted with amazing speed. With his carnival wages in his pocket he sought out a man called Subardie, Paris agent for the Spyker cars, and had a long and useful conversation with him. Then he bought a train ticket to Amsterdam, and presented himself at the Trompenburg factory of Spijker Brothers, automobile manufacturers. He could not have arrived at a less opportune moment.

Jacobus Spijker, then aged fifty, and his younger brother Hendrik had been running the biggest motor-car factory in Holland. Employing a fine designer, Joseph Laviolette, they were producing an impressive range of Spyker cars—deliberately spelt thus as an aid to the foreign market. Hendrik was a keen sales director, spending most of his time abroad—in Europe, America, and in the Dutch East Indies. Jacobus, the managing director, was an irrepressible enthusiast—far too lively and unconventional a character, many in Amsterdam thought, to face the routine of the large commercial and administrative responsibilities which were remitted to him. The Spijker brothers were making good cars, but not selling them as fast as they wished. In France the native manufacturers had ringed up round them very effectively, and Subardie was having great difficulty in making sales. Britain was the only market in which they had made a break-through, and the Elsworth Automobile Company of Bradford took nearly all the Spyker output from 1903 to 1905. In 1906 Jacobus Spijker took his chief mechanic, Hautekeet, his chief electrician, van Asselt, and a crew which included a nineteen-year-old apprentice, Bruno Stephan, to compete in the prestige Hill Climb of the Birmingham Motor Club. He won, in a six-cylinder, four-wheel-drive model, and the Spyker under-body guard achieved fantastic results in the dust trials—grim events, where the amount of dust thrown up by a car had to be judged by a suffering jury, who measured how dirty they got as it passed. Spijkers laid the foundation of a good order-book, not only for sporting cars, but for Spyker taxis, which were familiar in London throughout the First World War. Charles Godard had solid grounds for the new-found enthusiasm for Spyker cars, which he constantly confessed to Jacobus Spijker in Amsterdam. But he could not know how bloodless was the body to which he became self-appointed leech. In the autumn of 1906 a hurricane financial crisis had hit Spijker Brothers with extraordinary speed. In a vigorous effort to raise a loan from the beneficiaries in his solid British market, Hendrik Spijker finally went to England to see his old friends at Elsworths and his new agents, the British Automobile Syndicate. Elsworths, though they had lost the general agency, were well inclined towards the Spijkers, and it seemed that something might well be arranged. A trip to Amsterdam was agreed for the final checks before a decision was made.

On the 20th of February, 1907, Hendrik Spijker and his friend old Mr Elsworth embarked at Harwich in the steamer *Berlin* for the overnight voyage to the Hook of Holland. At six on the following morning the south-west gale, which had blown all night, flung the *Berlin* ashore on the granite North Pier, at the entrance to the Maas River. The ship broke up with horrifying speed. Within sight and even sound of thousands on the shore, as tugs and lifeboats stood helplessly by, men, women, and children were swept off the wreck and battered against the blocks of the pier, which was submerged by the high seas. Among the 129 passengers drowned were the almost complete singing cast of the German Opera Company. Among the missing were the Dutchman Hendrik Spijker and the Englishman J. Elsworth.

Jacobus Spijker hurried to the Hook, and lingered there desolately for days, cherishing the hope that his brother might somehow have survived. Finally he had to admit the fact of his loss. But while he waited, searched the sandy dunes, visited hospitals, and walked through the morgues improvized in railway waiting-rooms and quayside sheds he was dogged by a disconsolate Frenchman, with sensitive eyes drooping like a spaniel's ears, but with one mundane thought fixed in his eager mind—to drive a Spyker car in the *raid* from Peking to Paris.

Business had at some stage to be considered. The arguments of the persuasive Frenchman had to be weighed. They had, indeed, already been advanced by Subardie in Paris, who was shrewdly aware of the publicity value of the Peking–Paris *raid*. Jacobus Spijker had been keen to enter his car. He had already tested a four-cylinder open tourer on some difficult hill-country near Arnhem, with his daughter Annie and his principal test-driver Frijling as crew. The tests convinced him that a fairly light car with a low-geared rear axle was greatly to be preferred to a heavier model. Having made this decision, he found he could do no more without an independent backer. The firm had no money to spare for exploitation in such a costly venture as the Peking-Paris *raid*. Mr Elsworth was coming over from England. If his enthusiasm could be aroused, then an entry might be possible. But within days Elsworth was dead.

This man Godard, however, kept assuring Jacobus Spijker that a reputable and possibly winning performance in the *raid* could be put up by the Spyker at no cost at all. At no cost? ... well, hardly any. Even Godard could not eventually conceal the entrance-fee of 2000 francs, but he assured Spijker that that was the only outlay and, moreover, it was returnable at Peking. It seems fantastic that Spijker, a canny businessman with an agent in Paris, with whom he could check the details of the *raid*, allowed himself to be convinced that not only would *Le Matin* defray all expenses of transport to Peking and subsequent organizing and provisioning, but also that a substantial prize was to be the reward of the winner, and above all that Godard would win. Spijker even agreed to give Godard a personal prize of 10,000 francs after his victory, with proportionately smaller sums for lower places. Such an *entente* would have been incredible but for one fact of sheer coincidence: Jacobus Spijker was of a very similar psychological nature to Charles Godard. He was full of vitality, a most ingenious man, and very persuasive. He was not a trained engineer, but he was full of ideas, and though some of his minor inventions were practical, many of his grander ideas were, for the time, ludicrously impossible. Half a century before the introduction of fibre glass he suggested to his designer that they should produce a car body pressed out of the roots of tropical trees, which, after pressing in the mould, was to be entirely nickel-plated. When Laviolette demonstrated that these and many other suggestions could not be put into production Spijker persisted in canvassing his dreams to other departmental heads in the factory, and many of his experiments cost the firm a great deal of money. Jacobus Spijker was, therefore, a man who could first catch Godard's enthusiasm, and then overlay it with his own. He did not care if Godard was lying about the sponsorship by *Le Matin*. He did not want to know the truth. He would give Godard a car, and trust in the intuition of a kindred genius to get the car across Asia and Europe. And with the same unrealistic confidence he would offer Godard 10,000 francs prize money. Of course, he did not have it now—but if the Spyker won he would have it, probably. So these two men, drugged with confidence, blithely worked a confidence trick on each other. And on the 22nd of February, even before Hendrik's body had been found, the Spyker car was an official entry. Spyker was among the signatories (who still included Métallurgique) to a declaration by the Peking–Paris entrants agreeing the conditions of the *raid*.

This declaration is an interesting document, not only for the details of the contract of mutual assistance between the competitors—which was never kept, particularly by the winners—but also as an illustration of the very high degree of organization along a route of between 9000 and 10,000 miles which had been achieved in the space of three weeks.

The entrants agreed:

1. The journey will be made in convoy, the drivers promising each other mutual assistance as far as the German frontier.
2. Every driver is forbidden, on pain of disqualification, to take the railway anywhere between Peking and Paris.
3. Fuel supplies for the stages across China will be provided by the Asiatic Petroleum Company, transporting special supplies from Sumatra to Tientsin, and relaying them to the stations of the Trans-Manchurian Railway.

In the event, the competitors did not take the Manchurian route, but the Mongolian, where there was no railway.

Fuel supplies for the Siberian and Russian sections will be provided by the monopolists of fuel in Russia, the Nobel Company, who have already telegraphed to the Paris committee that they will deliver these stocks. Since this company already maintains depots along the line of the Trans-Siberian Railway it can send stocks of petrol to the horse-relay stations of the postal service along the route, according to the requirements of the competitors.

Decisions on the relay stations where this petrol is to be stored will be left to the agents of the competitors, and will be continually signalled by telegraph to all the drivers in the *raid*.

4. The entrants note that they have received sixty-two requests from mechanics and drivers to take part in the Peking–Paris *raid*, many offering to compete at their own expense.

5. Since *Le Matin* declines to levy any sum as entrance-fee the entrants bind themselves to deposit with the race committee of the Automobile Club of France the sum of 2000 francs for each car entered. This money will be returned to each entrant at Peking at the moment of departure. The fee will not be refunded to those cars which fail to start from Peking, but it will be shared among the starters.

This rule will not be enforced for those owners who have entered cars under their personal names and without specifying the make of the car engaged.[1]

Finally the contestants underlined the serious doubts then entertained that anyone would finish the race at all:

The entrants have decided to publish the following declaration in order that it may be appreciated what, in their opinion, the Peking–Paris challenge really entails:

The difficulties of this extraordinary trial seem to us, on searching examination after several weeks of study, as grave as we envisaged them on the first day. Peking–Paris! Perhaps it is an endeavour that cannot be realized. Certainly it provides an opportunity for the pioneers of automobilism to demand new progress in mechanical traction, and to show the way by which manufacturers should advance in order to create cars of global function, automobiles which can cross at need deserts, mountains, steppes . . . half-way across the world.

(*Signed*) De Dion, Contal, Werner, Metallurgique, Sider, Edmond Levi, Swinehart, Spyker

It may be significant that neither Prince Scipione Borghese nor his agent Fournier signed this document.

Le Matin published the declaration, and encouraged the now somewhat wary entrants with a roll of the drums of *la gloire*:

The trial is comparable to an attempt to travel to the Pole. What a rare chance of glory awaits our modern heroes! Ahead of them lies a journey half-way across the world, through primitive lands and changing climates. . . . Eighty days of extraordinary adventure.

[1] It may be noted that no one took advantage of this clause since the fruits of victory in the shape of public prestige and advertising were worth far more than the 2000 francs involved.

This was a most remarkable forecast of the time to be taken for the *raid*. It was far shorter than the estimate of most of the entrants. The cautious Cormier and other veterans read the journalistic guess with a scepticism they did not trouble to conceal. To one competitor, busy at his desk with maps and tables and a diminishing pad of telegraph forms, eighty days seemed an outrageous overestimate. He was Prince Scipione Borghese, actively planning the campaign from his study in the Palazzo Borghese in Rome.

Scipione Luigi Marcantonio Francesco Rodolfo, Prince Borghese, Prince Sulmona, Prince Bassano, Prince Aldobrandini, the holder of four ancillary Italian Dukedoms and four Marquisates, a Duke in the Peerage of France, a Grandee of Spain of the First Class, a Noble Roman and Conscript, a Patrician of Naples, Genoa, and Venice, was descended from the brother of the Prince Camillo Borghese who became Pope Paul V, and who passed his titles and many more—with the revenues of the acquired estates—on to his brother's heirs. After the term of military service that was considered part of a nobleman's education Prince Scipione entered diplomacy, but resigned from full participation in this field also. He was not considered a dilettante in these matters, however, and he led important politico-military missions to Russia in the spring of 1917, when the Tsarist régime first collapsed, and in 1918, at the height of the Bolshevik revolution.

Prince Scipione had the means and the temperament to become an independent explorer. In 1900 he crossed Asia from the Persian Gulf to the Pacific, penetrating a number of virtually unexplored areas in Northern Persia and Turkestan, travelling by horse, camel caravan, on foot, and not disdaining the Trans-Siberian Railway, whose spine was then completed. He wrote a classic account of this journey, not traveller's jottings, but a technical explorer's handbook, as cold and precise as the man himself appeared to be. He had taken his wife, Princess Anna Maria, former Duchessina de Ferrari, on the Persian journey and on many of the others with which he now occupied himself.

Princess Anna Maria—a pretty and supremely adaptable

woman then, and a formidable *grande dame* of Rome, Paris, and London later—was not to be deterred from the trip to Peking.

Prince Scipione reserved for himself, however, two occupations which could not be shared. One was horse-breaking. He was re-nowned throughout Europe for his skill in subduing the wildest mount. The other, which he preferred to retain for the winter, was the solitary diversion of mountain-climbing. He had a magnificent record in the Alps for skill and endurance, and was remarkable for never using the services of a guide. There seemed some need in him to test himself, to see how far a man could go and how much strain he could take. But his exploits did not appear to be directed by merely clinical curiosity about the limits of tolerance of human flesh. It was the performance of the body controlled by intelligence and will that seemed to fascinate him. He despised recklessness, though his course of life had made him superbly fit to meet the unforeseen crisis. *Anticipation* was his war cry, and planning his most characteristic occupation.

The man who sat so calmly in the Palazzo Borghese on his thirty-sixth birthday, calculating, scribbling, and unrolling huge military maps, was tall, lithe, and elegant enough in the unself-conscious way his clothes sat on his thin, hard body. Blue eyes looked, slightly mercilessly, out of a clean-shaven face. His smile was quick but not deep; even a short career in diplomacy had increased the tendency for that smile to come a little too often and not last long enough. There was something peculiar about his nose, the end of which seemed to protrude in a fleshy triangle beneath the fine, narrow, patrician bridge, and to be a little whiter than the surrounding flesh. The nose was a legacy from his way of life. While breaking in a horse one day he was heavily thrown and lay unconscious in the dust, with blood pouring from his head. When they turned him over they saw that his nose was almost severed from his face. A surgeon was quickly sent for, and the tip promptly stitched back. But the emergency had not allowed time for the attendance of the best cosmetic specialist, and plastic surgery was not then so commonplace. The nose healed firm enough, but a little askew and outstanding. Indeed, Borghese swore that its principal use was barometic, since it changed colour according to the weather.

The Prince was relying on a little more than his nose at the moment, for he had the seasonal reports for 5000 miles of Asia spread on his desk. Borghese was working on a network of acquaintance and interest which was open to none of the other competitors. With kinsmen spaced throughout Europe, from Spain through Hungary to Imperial Russia, he had ready springs of influence at his command. His diplomatic connexions increased his reach. His brother Livio, for example, was then chargé d'affaires at Peking and an invaluable holder of the bridgehead, passing back information, advice, and alternatives on the hundreds of details which Borghese shot on to telegraph forms from the files in his head. To be fair, it is doubtful if the other entrants —who were less entranced with planning as a sheer intellectual exercise—wanted the sort of co-operation which Borghese was able to obtain; and they were used enough in those days to accept, on the actual route of the *raid*, the entertainment of the Prince by local aristocracy or military commanders, while they were occasionally consigned to the barns of the village post-house. The organization which *Le Matin* had laid on for the jockeys was adequate, practical, and fluid enough to be adapted by intelligent men, which the drivers unquestionably were.

This organization was, of course, available to Prince Borghese, and he used it when it suited him. There were a number of men and corporations who had a keen concern for the outcome of the challenge, which had been perhaps a little lightly thrown out by *Le Matin*. A widely publicized motor-run through Asia and Europe suited their own interests admirably. These parties were anxious to make available to the 'raiders' all the influence at their command. The petrol companies were obvious examples. The principal use of petrol throughout Russia—and almost its sole use in Siberia—was for dry-cleaning. There were a few stationary engines, and agricultural 'machinery' was beginning to be imported into Siberia from America; but the possibilities of power had hardly been realized. There were not half a dozen towns in the East where a motor-car had ever been seen. Any prospect of the development of the automobile to the French or American level was a chance not to be missed by the Nobel Company, which, holding mineral concessions all over the Russian Empire and entire ownership of the Baku oilfields, monopolized the oil market in Russia. On a smaller scale the Asiatic Petroleum Company could expect substantial advantage if sales of refined oil could be stepped up from supplying the present motoring requirements of a few sporting merchants in Batavia or Shanghai. The wonder is not that these petroleum companies eagerly arranged dispatch and storage through China and Siberia, but that they expected to be paid for it. They were getting priceless mention in an age when neither editors nor readers had hardened their hearts against free editorial publicity, and 'plugs' were not only frequently given in the text of news stories, but also digested without resistance by the readers.

To open up Asia to the motor-car: that was the object of many people. Some of them were pure automobile enthusiasts, like Prince Khilkoff, who as Russian Minister of Roads and Railways not only ran cars himself, but had begun the establishment of motor-truck freight services in the Crimea, until the disastrous war with Japan killed the scheme—and many others. After the war he still planned the construction of wooden motorways through the swamps of Siberia as spurs connecting with the Trans-Siberian Railway. When the Peking 'raiders' finally got through to Moscow from the East Prince Khilkoff told the *Matin* representative (who was himself no mean hand at shaping a plug for *Le Matin*), "The great thing lacking in this country is a means of communication. You have given us a golden lead, which must not be abandoned. Thanks to *Le Matin* the legend of the automobile solely as a distraction for sportsmen has vanished. The small car which can run from Peking to Paris by the most frightful roads is something more than a costly toy. I have here"—and he indicated a sheaf of papers on his desk—"the draft of a plan for motor transport on wooden tracks. I have worked out the cost of a plank-road for automobiles at a maximum of 5000 roubles per verst, dropping to 500 roubles in forest areas. The normal cost of a rail-track is 20,000 roubles per verst. I have made tests on my own estate, and with a small 3-h.p. engine consuming little petrol I can haul loads of up to 100 poods (about 1600 kilograms, or over 30 cwt.). Now your *raid* has proved what the murderous speed races on prepared enclosed roads could never do."

All over Siberia the 'raiders' met practical men assessing their achievement in these terms. Could the China tea trade be diverted from the sea route via Vladivostok to a truck service across the Gobi Desert? Could the English goldminers of Krasnoyarsk improve on the river route to Yeniseysk? Could the communication-centre of Tomsk be linked with the mines of the Altai Mountains? How best could motor transport be used to develop the chain of industry in the wild Urals or the vast dairy country of Western Siberia, where Danes and Norwegians, Englishmen and Germans were all involved in the export of millions of tons of butter to Europe each year and the massive importation of agricultural machinery? And at the heart of all this interest lay the alert and throbbing pulse of the Russo-Chinese Bank, which sprawled in a vast chain of offices across Asia.

Prince Borghese used the local managers of the bank particularly as an intelligence network to answer queries on local conditions. What were the roads like here? What was the attitude of the tribesmen there? How much to pay for food, hardware, or even distilled water at another place? The *Matin* committee in Paris had made comparable inquiries, sending a duplicated telegram to every likely staging-post. But they had concentrated mainly on track conditions and Siberian bank managers, who had never seen a car in their lives, had little idea of optimum mud conditions necessary for fairly heavy machines—which had not the advantage of four hooved feet pushing down through the slime to firmer soil, to drag the vehicles along. Consequently the preliminary road reports for the whole of the route came in consistently tinted with optimism.

Borghese divided his planning operations into three main heads —the route, replenishment of supplies, and the car. For the route he relied on the mass of information from his local agents, Russian war maps and the detailed charts of Asian territory prepared in Germany, his personal experience of part of the route, and the additional experience he intended to gain—for he had decided to travel early to Peking to reconnoitre the nightmare mountain gorges around the Great Wall of China.

The main supply problem was the provision of oil and spare parts. By building special tanks on to his car Borghese was able

to carry 300 kilograms (84 gallons) of petrol and 100 kilogram
(35 gallons) of oil. This stock was sufficient to take the 40-h.p
Itala only 600 miles. He ordered enough fuel and oil for a com
plete refill to be dumped at every stage. In Mongolia, where th
stages could be established only at certain relay telegraph-station
in the desert, the dumps were up to 450 miles apart. They had t
be supplied by a camel caravan, which the committee in Pari
had arranged to go out from Peking on a thousand-mile trek o
behalf of all the competitors. Within Siberia, where the service
of the railroad and the busy river boats were available, the dis
tances between the depots were shortened, sometimes down t
150-mile stages. Since Borghese carried the wherewithal for 60
miles aboard his car, his stocks laid down were always in excess o
his needs, a fact which could not help being of some assistance t
Godard, who had made no refuelling arrangements at al
Borghese carried a large fitted tool-case, crammed with spar
parts, and ordered a complete set of spares to be sent by railwa
to Omsk, which he calculated he would reach after 4000 miles c
mainly trackless country. He carried a dozen tyres and inne
tubes, which he thought should last at least as far as Irkutsk, i
Central Siberia. At Irkutsk, and at subsequent stages never mor
than a thousand miles apart, he ordered Pirelli to send furthe
consignments of tyres.

The car, on which most enthusiasts would be inclined t
lay the greatest emphasis, was characteristically dismissed b
Borghese as a comparatively unimportant factor in the ventur
compared with his organization. He did concede that it was a
"excellent machine." But it was, he declared, "only the tool b
which success was achieved, the chisel used by the artist to shap
the statue which the inspiration of his own mind had create
Controlled by intelligence the hand directing the chisel is th
important factor in a work of art, just as it is in the meticulo
planning of an expedition."

Tool or master-key, the car was a 40-h.p. 1907 Itala, four-spee
model, right-hand drive, with four double-block cylinders
130-mm. bore by 140-mm. stroke. It had L.T. magneto ignitio
conical clutch, transmission by Cardan shaft (universal join
leaf-spring suspension and axle-trees. Its petrol consumption

ormal conditions was three kilometres to the litre (under eight
nd a half miles per gallon), and in sand or mud heart-rendingly
ess. The body behind the front seat was almost entirely devoted
o the big wing tanks for petrol, the tool-chest for spare parts, and
ear tanks for oil and water. A third seat had been installed be-
ween the tanks, but it was generally piled with baggage. The
wheels were wooden, of artillery type. The tyres were from
irelli's normal stock, wider than was customarily used on a car
f this build, being all the same size—935 by 135 mm. or some
in. wide, and flat in shape. Their life was around 2500 miles—
ainly not on metalled roads—though two tyres ran 5000 miles
ach.

The car was ordered in February and delivered in April, with
e few modifications that could be incorporated in the time. The
ala firm were so doubtful of its prospects over a course of such
tremes of terrain and temperature—they were particularly
xious about the efficiency of the radiator—that at one point
ey begged Borghese to withraw his application. But the sculp-
r did not consider changing his chisel. He turned it over to his
ry competent mechanic Ettore Guizzardi, and got on with his
ganization.

Ettore (Hector) Guizzardi was a fine example of the New Man
hom Bernard Shaw had already sketched in the character of
raker, the chauffeur in *Man and Superman*: "Very nice sort of
ace, Oxford, I should think, for people that like that sort of
ace. They teach you to be a gentleman there. In the Polytech-
c they teach you to be an engineer." In another age Guiz-
rdi would have been a careful peasant in Romagna. Now he
d gone to work on the railway, and at fifteen was firing his
her's engine when it crashed off the rails and over an embank-
nt near Borghese's villa at Albano. Ettore came round from
consciousness to find his father was dead, and he himself was
talled in one of Borghese's beds. The Prince kept him on as an
prentice mechanic, and sent him to factories and polytechnics
 further training. Ten years (and eleven cars) later he was
dy at the age of twenty-five to nurse the Itala machine from
king to Paris. It was not his place to do the driving.
But the engine was his concern, the gearbox, differential, and

transmission, every bolt in the chassis and every leaf in the springs
Luigi Barzini, the *Corriere della Sera* correspondent who joined
the Prince's crew at Peking, reported how he first met Ettore: "He
was flat on his back under the Itala, lying quite still, with his arms
folded. My first thought was that he was busy working. But he
was relaxing. I discovered later that he was in his favourite place
of off-duty pleasure. When there is nothing else to do he simply
lies on his back under his motor-car and observes it, contemplates
it item by item, every bolt and screw, in mystic communion with
his machine."

On Wednesday the 10th of April, 1907, Ettore was safely in
stalled with the Itala car aboard the Norddeutscher Lloyd line
Gneisenau, bound for the Far East, having joined the ship at
Genoa. Prince and Princess Borghese were in Rome, making their
last farewells before they travelled that night to Naples to join
the *Gneisenau* there. Borghese noted that Count Gropello, the
Fiat enthusiast, was not listed among the passengers, and drew
his own conclusions. The Norddeutscher Lloyd line called at Italy
fortnightly, and the next sailing would reach Shanghai only on
the 29th of May, which gave precious little time to tranship the
Fiat and get it the thousand miles to Peking, either by coaster or
by river-steamer and the Hankow Railway. For the start of the
raid was scheduled for the 10th of June. But there was no reason
why the voyage should be governed by the Norddeutscher Lloyd.
Seaports then cleared as many passengers a day as comparable
airports now. Mail liners were calling every day at one of the
Italian ports, and Gropello could get a passage. But he would
need to hurry.

It was while he was thinking in this strain, with his car already
bound for China, that Borghese received a cable from Paris. It
was signed by the competitors he most respected, and it informed
him that the Peking–Paris *raid* was cancelled. The entrants had
retired, and the plan was abandoned.

Nothing had gone sensationally wrong in Paris. The committee
had toiled on as hard as ever, and the newspaper had puffed the
project every four or five days. It is true that some of the original
entries had quietly dropped out. Métallurgique now talked of only
one car—a 40 h.p., to be driven by Nielsen. But others were

:oming in, and the total was kept above twenty. The committees were active, not only in Paris, but in St Petersburg and, it was reported, in many towns on the Siberian route, where Russian gentlemen had caught the excitement of the enterprise. Even the Wai Wu Pu, the Imperial Grand Council of China, had at last taken official cognizance of the request for facilities made through the French Minister at Peking, and had cabled to the French Foreign Office to ask, with a certain lack of enthusiasm, "What is the number of motor-cars in the caravan which may set off from Peking for the destination Paris? The route by Manchuria is likely to be bad." The reply announced that the route out of China had been changed from the northern way by Manchuria to the north-west passage through Mongolia, which was unpleasant news to the Chinese—extremely sensitive to any Western familiarity with the gateway to China used by Genghis Khan and many invaders after him. The French reply, sent in the last days of February, also revealed officially the first indication of uncertainty on the part of the competitors. "Twenty-two entries have already been accepted," said the telegram, "but it is possible that the competitors will limit the maximum number of starters to eight cars, to be chosen according to expert assessment of their performance."

The Russo-Chinese Bank reported from Peking in answer to a query about the actual width of the gorges in the dreaded first hundred miles after the exit from Peking. The message declared that the passes were wide enough for cars, but they were steep and rocky. This seemed to dispose for the moment of the suggestion that the cars might have to be hauled through the beds of mountain torrents, though even that prospect, at that distance, did not daunt the de Dion driver Cormier. "Only recently," he declared, "I have encountered in Hungary and Spain bridgeless rivers, sandy deserts, and foul tracks that have gone on for hundreds of kilometres. And I have beaten them in my little 8-h.p. de Dion. Eight horses—eight horses are all I need."

Heart-warming accounts came in of the enthusiastic activity of the Committee of Honour in St Petersburg, to which the highest in the Empire had been proud to be co-opted. M. Kokovtzoff, Minister of Finance, General Chaufus, the new Minister of Com-

munications, M. Izvolsky, the Foreign Minister, and Prince Khilkoff were all delighted to serve, and it was said that the *raid* had
the warm interest of the Tsar himself. It was true that Colonel
Novitzky, a member of the Russian Geographical Society, had
put in a disconcerting report on the passes between Peking and
the Great Wall, which was not quite as vague as the laconic
assurance of the Russo-Chinese Bank. "The rock is worn into deep
ruts by the wheels which have passed along the same path for
centuries. Some of the descents are so steep that the Chinese have
to hang on to ropes trailing behind their carts to stop them from
falling into the ravines. But," he concluded inconsequently, "the
automobiles will pass."

Official concessions by the Russians included the remission of
all Customs levies due on the cars when they arrived in Siberia
and exemption of duty on spare parts and tyres being sent in
from France to meet the requirements of the 'raiders.' If any
section of the route developed unexpected difficulties reports on
the emergency would be signalled by telegraph to every staging-
post that the oncoming drivers might use. Access to the telegraph
service was available at all times to the competitors. And finally,
as rather doubtful comfort to the motorists, anyone who broke
down irretrievably would be granted free travel on the Trans-
Siberian Railway.

The enthusiasm of the Russian official class was completely
sincere, yet more than their support alone might be necessary for
a successful crossing of the unquiet Empire. Russia had been
experiencing an unadmitted revolution since the military disaster
of 1905. Daily the newspaper headlines read: Russian Crisis,
Russia's Anarchy, Increasing Trouble in the Provinces, Terrible
Outrage. On one day alone it was reported that an attempt had
been made to assassinate the Grand Duke Nicholas by placing
a bomb on the railway; that in Kazan, one of the cities on the
'raiders'' route, famine was so bad that hungry parents were
selling their daughters for 100 roubles; and that at Krasnoyarsk,
another city on the route, the town commandant had been shot
and killed. The commandant, General Kozloffsky, had taken his
afternoon walk through the town, stopping to show his friends
letters announcing that he would be assassinated at five o'clock.

"The scoundrels have deceived me," he guffawed. "It is already five o'clock, and yet I am alive and well." The general had paid insufficient attention to Russian unpunctuality. At 5.45 a voice cried "Halt!" Three revolver shots were fired, and Kozloffsky lay dead.

At the end of March, after the French Foreign Office had received a telegram from its Minister in Peking declaring, "The Peking–Paris race is authorized by the Chinese Government," a wave of pessimism swept over the entrants, though it was carefully concealed from the *Matin* public. There was only a fortnight to the date of embarkation at Marseille. The stakes of 2000 francs had to be deposited irrevocably. Passage money for cars and crews had to be found, and the orders for petrol placed. Some firms had had a good run of publicity for the expenditure of nothing but words, but somehow the prize of final victory, though it glittered more entrancingly than ever, did not seem so attainable as before. The expected stake money was not paid in to the race committee of the French Automobile Club. When the final acceptances were counted they totalled six. Even the Baron Duquesne, who had declared the project "tailor-made to seduce him," finally declined seduction. The bottom fell out of the market, and in a final ebbing of confidence the survivors of the grand project sent their telegram to Prince Borghese announcing their withdrawal from the contest. Borghese merely replied, "I sail from Naples to-morrow"; and he sailed—with Princess Anna Maria and her friend Countess Nora Salzani, and with his car and mechanic already on board. Jules Madeline, the managing director of *Le Matin*, and the Marquis de Dion were set in a maddening situation. The Paris–Peking challenge had been engineered to boost the French car industry, but the only entrant on the starting-line was to be an Italian car driven by an Italian prince and crewed by an Italian newspaperman. De Dion would have to reconsider his misgivings. De Dion had reconsidered them as soon as he had learnt of the telegram, for Borghese's decision committed them all. And on Sunday the 14th of April, very early in the morning, the cars based on Paris were at the Marseille quayside. And Charles Godard was talking very fast to an official of the Messageries Maritimes shipping line, explaining why it was inconvenient to pay the freight-charges for the shipment of the Spyker car to China.

Godard had had little to do with the recent attack of nerves among the promoters of the works-entered cars. The Spyker was not works-entered. Jacobus Spijker had not even paid the 2000 francs entrance-fee, which had been finally found by Subardie, Spyker's agent in Paris, who could not let the chance of participation slip from the firm.

Spijker kept strictly to the promise Godard had persuaded him to make, and went no farther. He would provide the car and reasonable spares. The rest was up to the Frenchman. And the 10,000-franc prize was still to be claimed if he won. Regarding financial matters the relationship was rigid, but over the car itself the atmosphere was much more cordial. The manufacturer had faith in his machine, and he soon saw that Godard was a fine driver, though a poor mechanic. The car was a standard 15-h.p., four-cylinder model, but adapted with low gears and large wheels to raise the chassis higher off the ground to avoid the boulders and other obstacles that were expected on the journey.

The technical specifications were: *Engine*, four-cylinder, two double blocks with T-formed heads, 90-mm. bore by 110-mm. stroke, output 15–20 h.p. at 1000 r.p.m. Lubrication of the engine by the Spyker patent system of forced circulation with wet sump and external oil-pump. *Carburettor*, Longuemare, the main jet having six outlets to diminish the chance of hold-up by a choked jet, with adjustable air-valve to cope with different qualities of petrol. A 45-litre brass *petrol-tank* was under the front seat. *Ignition* by Bosch H. T. magneto. Oil-tight *gearbox*, three forward speeds and reverse, ball-bearing supported, gate change. The leather-lined *clutch* was incorporated in the flywheel. The *steering-pillar* was spring-suspended by another Spyker patent, isolating the driver from road shocks. *Brakes:* the footbrake was worked by a contracting band around a pulley, fixed on the transmission shaft just behind the gearbox. The handbrake worked with expanding shoes on the rear-wheel brake-drums. When either the handbrake or the footbrake was applied the clutch was automatically disengaged. It was intended that the brakes could be adjusted within five minutes. *Back axles* and Cardan shaft were of best nickel-steel of exceptional diameter, as were the main driving-bevels. *Wheels,* artillery type, with fourteen wooden spokes set in steel rims and the front wheels on ball-bearings. The wheelbase of the standard model was 8 ft. 9 in. and the wheel track 4 ft. 8 in. The honey-comb *radiator* was attached to the frame by a Spyker shock-proof patent. The *frame* was riveted throughout, all frame-members being hydraulically pressed from best boiler-sheet steel. Godard took delivery of his Spyker with only candles in the side-lamps, but in Paris he was given a complete set of carbide headlamps with built-in generators and oil side-lamps, and he used these throughout the *raid*.

Jacobus Spijker superintended the Spyker's preparation with great care, and took Godard off for further trials on the sand-dunes along the North Sea. The car behaved beautifully, and after final adjustments was ready for Godard to pick up.

Godard arrived jauntily at the Trompenburg factory, and immediately instructed the coach-painter to paint the sides of the body and even the radiator with the vertical red, white, and blue stripes of the French flag. The Dutchmen considered these colours to be an inauspicious decoration for the only Dutch car in the race. On the stripes Godard ordered to be superimposed the words PEKIN and PARIS, with details of the intended route —*la Sibérie, la Russie, l'Allemagne.* Godard then checked the spare parts with Spijker, declared that he had not been given enough parts or tyres, and demanded more. When he was at last persuaded to leave the factory he drove into the centre of Amsterdam with J. G. Stegwee, a Spyker foreman. He stopped at the showroom of Leonard Lang, on the Stadhouderskade, and ordered as many spare tyres as the loaded car could carry, instructing Lang to send the account to Spijker. Lang was the Spyker sales agent in Amsterdam, and held the Michelin general agency for Holland. It was Monday the 1st of April. Unfortunately for Lang, it was not only All Fools' Day but Easter Monday. When Lang tried to check by telephone with the Trompenburg works he found that the office was closed for the holiday.

Godard and Stegwee drove in a day from Amsterdam to Reims in the low gear specially fitted for the desert and the swamps. In an evening session there Stegwee was treated by the Frenchman to a conducted tour through the wine-list, in which Godard displayed exquisite taste and inordinate capacity, and retired to bed none the worse for wear. Next day they reached Paris. Stegwee made a final check on the car, and returned by train to Amsterdam.

Though Godard found a mood of deep gloom among the survivors of the entrants for the *raid*, he was unaffected by their low spirits, and seems to have given no consideration at all to the possibility of not making the voyage to Peking. He had already bought his ticket to China. True he had been able to pay for it only by selling the spare parts and tyres he had extracted so painfully from Spijker, but when measures were necessary they had to be taken. "I want to get there; therefore I must start," was his attitude. Jean du Taillis, the blond bearded foreign correspondent of *Le Matin*, who had been assigned to go to Peking with the crews and cover the *raid* in transit, got to know Godard very well in Paris and even better in the desert. He watched the tyres and spares disappear, the money from their sale mount, until Godard was able to buy himself a first-class ticket on the ship. Nothing but the best could be tolerated. As for the car, it would have to go carriage forward to Tientsin.

"And then?" asked du Taillis.

"Then? Oh, something will turn up."

"But you can't set out on a journey like this without a sou. The *Matin* organizer and each of the entrants have gone to enormous trouble to arrange fuel dumps, and stocks of tyres and spare parts to be held in depots. But you have done nothing about it at all. You've not only not bothered, but you've even disposed of the tyres you did have and could have taken with you. You can't tempt fortune. You can't run these risks over such a long trip with the resources you've got. You can't do it!"

To which Godard simply replied, "Why not?"

He laughed, and hit one fist in the other hand. "Either I shall never see Paris again, or I shall come back to it in my Spyker, hot from Peking."

And Charles Godard was serious.

He was serious too on the quayside at Marseille when the shipping officials refused to accept his Spyker aboard the liner

Océanien shipped carriage forward. Godard could not persuade
them to swing the crate aboard. The officials wired Spijker in
Amsterdam asking him to guarantee the money. Jacobus Spijker
wired back that no money would be laid out for Godard. The ship
was due to sail at noon. Finally the company relented and
accepted the crate. Godard had won a respite of thirty-six days.
But the supercargo of the *Océanien* was a worried man. The crews
and cars had to be transhipped to a smaller vessel at Shanghai,
which would mean that the final payment would have to be made
at Tientsin. The task of tackling Godard would be the responsibility of another man, which lifted a certain load off the supercargo's mind. But would the money ever get back to Messageries
Maritimes?

The matter was certainly not troubling Godard. He was happy.
The passengers were happy at the jokes he made, the tricks he
played, and the captivating evenings he organized. The ship's
captain was happy to have him at his table. The ship's purser
was happy to oblige him with orders to have the pianos moved
from the second-class saloons to the promenade deck, to request
those members of the crew who could play the accordion to form
a ship's band, and to announce yet another gay evening for all
with, as Master of Ceremonies, our very own Mr Charles Godard.

Some five days behind the *Gneisenau*, the *Océanien* steamed
fast and south. With the ringing pianos and throbbing accordions
she left a wake of gaiety. Charles Godard led the lively cotillion,
swept the timid into a waltz, joked with the Colonial Governor's
wife, paired off the young and flattered the elderly, and found
time to compose an eloquent cable to be dispatched from the next
port requesting a small advance on his prize-money from Heer
Jacobus Spijker.

The man had charm.

3 ◎ ◎ The Globe-trotters muster

The line Messageries Maritimes maintains an excellent table. The Peking–Paris passengers attacked their meals as if they were building up winter blubber and with a gaiety that made them the darlings of the passenger-list. Their moral leader and universal uncle was the writer from *Le Matin* who had been assigned to cover the *raid* as a reporter, and also to handle the field organization. Jean du Taillis, in his early thirties, plump, and with a trimmed blond beard giving shape to his rosy face, was a man of courage, talent, and wit. To watch him going through his habitual blundering motions of writing a dispatch, from the moment when he had to request from a colleague first the date, then a share in his ink-bottle, then the loan of his pen, and finally a few sheets of paper, was to gain an uncompensated view of his character. When the gold-rimmed pince-nez came off, and the bright eyes could be seen shining with a sort of dancing malice, while the nostrils quivered at the scent of mischief to come, another characteristic aspect of du Taillis presented itself. It was confirmed as the great red mouth opened, with its two reefs of white teeth standing out strong as a shark's, and an elemental laugh tore from his frame like a thunder-clap. Constantly the first-class passengers flinched as the first shock hit them, then turned round smiling to see what lark the *Matin* party was up to.

Du Taillis was a skilled newspaperman of proved resource in an age when there was enough colonial and international tension and even war to keep a first-rank special correspondent very busy. He had served in many parts of the world, very happy in his job. In his own words, "All I am and all I want to be is a modest globetrotting reporter." The word globe-trotter, like the word reporter, was then an accepted French noun, and was a title claimed mainly by gentlemen tourists, though more justifiably by the international tramps who were an attractive example of the restlessness of the period. One of the last interviews du Taillis conducted before the Peking–Paris event was with globe-trotter Laurent Revel, who arrived in Paris after a ten-year absence, having walked through every country in every continent in the world except Australia. He had lived by selling picture-postcards of himself, giving occasional lectures on his experiences, and appearing in travelling shows. He had started off with a friend, but the companion was reported missing in Upper California, believed to have been murdered by cowboys for his money. Revel had been sent to prison in five countries as a suspected spy, and was not going home to his village in Savoy until he had completed his travels in Australia.

Du Taillis, Borghese, Cormier, Barzini, were all accounted globe-trotters, and now by train or ocean liner were converging on Peking.

Aboard the *Océanien*, if du Taillis was the leader, the anchor man of the *Matin* party was Jean Bizac, an employee from the de Dion-Bouton works, who had been drafted to serve as mechanic on the second de Dion-Bouton car, driven by Victor Collignon. Bizac, a quiet, imperturbable southerner, had served seven years in the engine-rooms of the French Navy, and had never yet conquered an inclination to seasickness. He sat all day, apart from meal-times, dozing in a deck-chair, fully clothed in a blue flannel suit buttoned over a woollen jersey, while his companions, nervously changing into successively lighter weights of white tropical linen, seemed to sweat all the more profusely. Bizac broiled in his flannel and dozed on. A wizard with engines, Bizac had, incredibly enough, never travelled in a motor-car in his life. The prospect of undertaking his baptism on a hard seat in a light car bucking across the boulders of Asia did not seem to preoccupy him.

Bizac was the only man of the de Dion team travelling out by sea with the cars. The drivers Cormier and Collignon were to go by rail to Peking on a faster journey, which would give them time to send out the camel caravan laying down fuel depots across Mongolia. The other mechanic was engaged on a more arduous trek eastward from Irkutsk reconnoitring the actual ground of the first 1200 miles of the route from Peking into Siberia by direct observation from a jogging ox-cart. But the crew of the Contal tri-car was aboard the *Océanien*. Young Auguste Pons, handsome, daring, and incurably optimistic, was accompanied by his mechanic Octave Foucault, who quickly acquired the nickname "Apache" from the supposed sinister cast of his features. Edgardo Longoni was also a member of the party. He was an Italian journalist, a member of the staff of *Il Secolo* of Rome, also retained to report the *raid* for the London *Tribune*, who was to travel in Count Gropello's Fiat.

The cruising party was completed by the gay Charles Godard, who quite literally had no idea where he was going, but knew he could rely on the others to see that he got there. He had only the vaguest idea of geography and could not read a map. Peking–Paris had been proposed by people who were more knowledgeable than he, and even if it did seem necessary to start by sea he presumed that the two capitals must be connected by land—why, otherwise, should the *raid* be suggested? If there was a land link he would find it. It was only necessary to start, and one would arrive. For the rest—and the skin beneath his jawbones began to inflate like a frog's as the intoxication of success suffused him— the Spyker was a magnificent car, and Godard was an incomparable driver, and nothing could possibly daunt this formidable combination. Du Taillis listened to these declarations with charmed wonder, and promptly dubbed Godard "Tartarin du Gobi," after Daudet's captivating larger-than-life character Tartarin de Tarascon.

Bickering, joking, planning, and boasting, the spirited Peking 'raiders' sailed towards the tropics with the impact of a kennel of high-bred puppy hounds held together by the bark of their leader's laugh, with only the veteran Bizac mute, sagely nodding at the table, and sleeping for the rest of the time. At Port Said Godard went ashore to send the first of his confidential cables requesting the favour of an advance on his prize-money from Jacobus Spijker. Du Taillis went with him to pay the charges. The journalist, who was a truly generous man, was peculiarly sensitive to the suspicion—probably well founded—that he was consistently cheated in bargains struck in foreign countries. On the trip back to the *Océanien* he became so incensed in his protest at the fare being charged by the bumboatman that he fell into the harbour, to the delight of the rest of the team. Through Suez the khamsin blew for two full days—the passage was prolonged because the gale stranded the *Océanien* in the canal—injecting the sand of the desert into every cranny in the ship and every crevice in the passengers' anatomy: the Peking team accepted it joyfully as training for the Gobi Desert. In Jibuti Godard threw his remaining small change delightedly into the water for the Somali divers, who trapped the coins fathoms deep, and came up singing *La Petite Tonkinoise* in pidgin-French. In Ceylon Tartarin du Gobi shinned up coconut-palms like a monkey and threw the nuts down to his companions. In Singapore they all went ashore to a reception given in the Raffles Hotel by a rich rubber-exporter named Lewin, who had travelled out with them. Longoni was delighted to hear some good Italian music as a change from the waltz and the cake-walk. The team, who had tirelessly discussed their *raid* on board with the long-service French Army officers travelling from home leave back to colonial service—and gained much first-hand information from men who had served in China during the Boxer revolt—now had fresh opponents to argue with them.

"You don't know what you're up against. You will not be able to drive six miles out of Peking."

"It makes no difference. We shall get through even if we have to put the cars on the camels' humps."

"You shouldn't even try. It will be wasted labour."

"Jamais de la vie!" The attack was being held by Godard. "If we don't find roads we shall build them, but the cars will get through."

"Do be serious." The speaker was a French merchant now based on Bangkok. "I know the roads of China and the route to Kiakhta which you will have to take, and the one is as bad as the others. Isn't that so, General?"

A Chinese general, Chin-Kao, who had said nothing until then, spoke hesitantly in a pure French accent. "You automobilists have undertaken a very hazardous enterprise. Your machines are very heavy and, in my opinion, too wide for the cart-tracks of Mongolia."

Even Bizac had an answer to this objection. "But for that very reason we have put in two little de Dions."

"In any case," interrupted Pons, "if the roads are really like that the first to get through, and perhaps the only one to get through, will be the Contal. Whenever you are stranded you can pick it up in your arms like a toy."

Jean du Taillis pulled his team together again, patiently re-iterating the hope, which was never fulfilled, that all the cars would work together. "It isn't a question of heavy cars or light cars. We shall all go in convoy, heavy and light." He touched the arm of the slim Longoni. "The little Italian and me, the colossal Itala and the tiny Contal. Stick to that understanding, and we shall all get through. Waiter, more champagne!"

It was champagne all the way. In Saigon the Peking 'raiders' were fêted with two days of receptions, banquets, and fervent toasts. On the night before Shanghai the captain of the *Océanien* gave a party for the guests who had made the voyage memorable. Next morning, the 16th of May, when the anchor chains rattled out into the broad estuary of the Yangtze Kiang, du Taillis, Godard, Bizac, Pons, and Foucault said good-bye, and were ferried ashore to the clubs of the French Concession. There they were all made honorary members, the wine was ordered, and the arguments started again.

"Do you know what Chinese roads are like? Do you know what Chinese people are like? Don't you realize you will never reach Nankow, and the pass beyond that is insuperable. . . ."

"The bridges over the Cha Ho are heaps of ruined battlements. There is as much water above them as below. . . ."

"You are simply *too wide* for the gorges. . . ."

Pons and Godard, Bizac and Foucault, merely countered with a phrase of race-track slang, "*Faut pas cherrer*"—no line-shooting. And du Taillis summed up again, "We have strong cars, sturdy engines, tough tyres. Why shake our confidence? Fortune favours the brave. Waiter, more champagne! *Vive Pékin–Paris!*"

The *Océanien*, anchored off Woosung, had discharged the cargo of crated motor-cars into lighters, which had to be towed ten miles to the quays of Shanghai proper, where there they were reloaded into the coaster *Admiral von Tirpitz* for shipment to Taku, the port for Tientsin. The crews were not making the twelve-day journey by way of the Yellow Sea and the Gulf of Chihli, but cut inland on a steamer up the Blue River to Nanking, and then went on to Peking by the Hankow Railway.

There were now no fewer than six 'expeditions' making towards Peking for the start of the race.

Prince and Princess Scipione Borghese, with Anna Maria's friend Countess Nora Salzani, had arrived at Shanghai in the *Gneisenau* four days before du Taillis. Without staying for the social encounters which the French party savoured in Shanghai they came north the next day to reach the Hankow Railway, bringing the crated Itala car and their mechanic Ettore Guizzardi with them.

A few days behind them du Taillis, Godard, Bizac, Pons, and Foucault were travelling to Peking while the four cars came by sea.

Cormier and Collignon, the de Dion drivers, had left Paris on the 25th of April on the Nord Express for St Petersburg, and from there went by rail to Moscow. They took the Trans-Siberian Railway to Kharbin, some 400 miles from Vladivostok, and then came south through Mukden on the Japanese line, through the battlefields of the recent war in Manchuria, down to Tientsin, and back on the Chinese line to Peking. They arrived in Peking on Friday the 17th of May, at seven in the evening, when the Borghese party was coming north by rail, and du Taillis and his charges were relaxing with a little club refreshment after touring the gardens of Shanghai in smart two-wheeled tilburies.

Lelouvier, Cormier's mechanic, was making painful progress by ox-cart after being decanted from the Trans-Siberian Railway at Irkutsk, on the western side of the great Lake Baikal, with some five weeks' rough travel ahead of him. At the time his chiefs arrived in Peking, as the sun was getting low, he was beginning his 'day's march' across the Gobi Desert, a seventeen-day stretch which was attempted only at night in the summer months.

Luigi Barzini, special correspondent of the *Corriere della Sera* of Milan and the London *Daily Telegraph*, was in Japan, reporting on that country's recovery from the war with Russia. His editor in Milan, who had 'bought him in' on Borghese's attempt at the *raid*, had sent Barzini round the world in the reverse direction first—to New York for the notorious Thaw trial (the most famous of the rather numerous *crimes passionels* in America that year, when husbands or fathers killed to avenge the lost honour of women in their families), on to San Francisco to report on its rebuilding after the earthquake of 1906, and to Japan by way of Hawaii.

Edgardo Longoni, of *Il Secolo* and the *Tribune*, was also on his way to Japan, having remained on board the *Océanien* bound for Yokohama to give his own impressions on the surprise victors of the recent war.

When du Taillis bade him good-bye he reminded Longoni that the *raid* was due to start on the 10th of June. "Be punctual; we shan't wait for you." Longoni arrived in Peking on the 3rd of June. Every one was now there except Prince Borghese, who had gone on a week's reconnaissance trip over the dreaded first 160 miles of country. From the railway-station near the legation quarter Longoni took a rickshaw to the Hôtel de Pékin. His French shipboard companions hurried towards him blurting out, before even asking how he was, that the *raid* was cancelled.

Since its first announcement the Peking-Paris project had been an irritatingly unwelcome intrusion on the peace of mind of the Chinese Empress and the considerations of the Imperial State Council.

China in 1907 was ruled by an unscrupulous but failing Dowager Empress, aged seventy-one, who had deposed her nephew nine years before, but still kept up the façade that he was Emperor. The enormous Empire, with provinces as large as European countries, ruled by viceroys, who were frequently not only corrupt but incompetent, was administered by a hugely branching civil service, centralized in Ministers sitting in an executive council. These Ministers were subject to no control save that of mutual intrigue and the vagaries of the Empress. They were the supreme decision-makers in the Empire—the only decision-makers as far as the outside world was concerned. They were the members of the Wai Wu Pu, the Grand Council of the Celestial Empire.

When the French Minister in Peking, Monsieur E. V. E. Bapst, was first required by his foreign office to request from the Wai Wu Pu permission for a motor-car rally starting in Peking he considered the matter a slight affront to his dignity, but duly carried out his orders.

The department clearly affected by a request to run a motor-race out of Peking was the Ministry of the Interior. If public order in the capital were hazarded there would also be a call on the Peking Gendarmerie. Since the proposed motorists were foreigners there was some case for surveillance by the Chinese Foreign Ministry. If, as was immediately darkly hinted, the motorists were really spies the matter also became the concern of the War Ministry. Since the cars intended to follow ancient caravan trails reference would have to be made to the Ministry of Posts and Communications. And the general principle of consent to any automobile excursion would need approval by the Imperial Grand Council.

The departmental channels involved certainly seemed complicated. But there was a ray of light for M. Bapst in the fact that in all this administrative maze only two men were concerned. One was Na Tung, Grand Secretary of State, Manchu President of the Grand Council, Acting President of the Department of the Interior, and General Commandant of the Peking Gendarmerie. The other was Yi K'uang, Prince Ching, uncle of the Emperor, President of the Grand Council, Comptroller General of Foreign Affairs, Comptroller General of the War Ministry, and Chief Minister and Prop of the Throne.

Any civil service influence not directly open to Prince Ching was available through his son, Prince Tsai Chên, President of the Ministry of Agricultural Works and Commerce, and hotly tipped as the next Minister of Finance, Comptroller of the China Merchants' Steam Navigation Company, and Minister of Posts and Communications.

The struggle for the Ministry of Posts and Communications— which controlled all the Chinese Railways—had been severe since a successful court intrigue had secured the removal from office of Shih Shao-chi, Acting Junior Deputy Assistant Vice-President of the Ministry of Posts and Communications prior to his dismissal by Imperial edict. Though the position of Acting Junior Deputy Assistant Vice-President seems minor, it carried with it the re-munerative directorate of the Peking–Hankow Railway. The undermining of Shih Shao-chi meant that the Minister at the top was insecure. And Tsai Chên, Prince Ching's son, thought he might offer the shaky Minister a worth-while bargain by pro-posing a direct swop, an exchange of offices whereby Tsai Chên became Minister of Posts and Communications and the then Minister, who had already complained to Prince Ching that he knew nothing about Posts and Communications, took over Agri-cultural Works and Commerce. Unfortunately for Tsai Chên, the Minister died suddenly before the exchange could be effected.

M. Bapst began to see that the proposed motor *raid* out of Peking ran into most serious opposition from the Grand Council as soon as the Paris committee changed the proposed route from an exit through Manchuria to an exit through Mongolia. For it was this change that united both Na Tung and Prince Ching in attempting to veto it.

Na Tung was an old supporter of the Boxers in their uprising against the Western Powers in 1900. Indeed, his execution after the rising had been demanded by the Western Powers and pro-mised by the Court. Instead he had survived, and risen to great eminence in the Grand Council. Na Tung, fiercely suspicious of the West, was convinced that the proposal to send motor-cars out of China was merely a necessary mask for bringing motor-cars *into* China. He considered that the invasion of China by a sort of fœtal tank warfare was imminent, and that even if the cars entered Peking without specifically dominating the capital by the artillery they doubtless carried they would certainly use the opportunity of their exit, through the gateway in the Great Wall, to spy out the terrain in preparation for a future invasion by Russia. For Russia had recently lost to Japan control of the route into China by Kharbin and Mukden. The fact that the expedition was 'led' by a princely soldier-diplomatist only deepened Na Tung's suspicions.

Prince Ching, on the other hand, felt that the dark plot behind the façade of the *Matin* challenge was a project of commercial domination. The West intended to open up China's communications. If anyone should open these communications it must be China. The means must not be motor-cars, of which there were none in China, but railways. Hitherto Chinese railways had been built and operated by foreign *concessionnaires*. But now, at long last, the Chinese were building a railway of their own, and building it, moreover, towards Nankow and Kalgan and on to Russia via Mongolia, on the very route on which the Westerners had announced they were running what was obviously their pilot motor service. The motor exit through Kalgan and Mongolia must be blocked. The Ministry that could best block it was Posts and Communications. And not the least reason for making that block effective was the fact that the principal shareholder in the Kalgan Railway was Prince Ching.

Prince Ching and Na Tung therefore had no alternative but to advise the Grand Council to refuse the French request for permission to run a motor rally from Peking to Paris.

As soon as the refusal was conveyed to M. Bapst the French Minister became enthusiastic over a project which had formerly been but a tiresome chore. There must be a *reason* for the refusal. He discussed the motor *raid* with the Russian Minister, and discovered that the Russian Government was surprisingly keen on the *raid*—principally reflecting the enthusiasm of the Russian Minister of Communications. But apart from practical objectives a refusal was a blow to the prestige of the Western Powers. It was more than a loss of face, it was a direct abnegation of the treaty rights of the Western Powers as agreed after the Boxer rising. The Chinese Government simply *had no right* to forbid the request of Western nationals to pass in simple transit across Chinese territory. Permission must be granted at once, and the requisite passports issued.

As soon as the French and Russian Ministers raised the pressure the Grand Council was convinced that there must be a *reason* for this unexpected obstinacy. The suspicions of Na Tung or of Prince Ching—it did not matter whose—must be correct. There *was* a plot against the Chinese Empire, and they were correct to have opposed the project from the first. Thus in a very few weeks a full-scale diplomatic incident was created. It started over a Western machine, which the Court of Peking had never seen, and for which the Chinese had no name. At least the menace had to be defined. The Grand Council therefore coined a word for motor-car. They called it *chi-cho*, meaning oil chariot, on the analogy of their word for railway engine, *huo-cho*, or fire chariot. The slogan of the political campaign immediately suggested itself: "The *chi-cho* must not pass."

Prince Ching saw that the occasion had arisen for him to perform his last significant patriotic duty. He had just passed his seventieth birthday, smarting under the stricture of the English-language *North China Herald and Supreme Court and Consular Gazette* that he had "done nothing of any use either for his country or people during the last decade." He had been denounced to the Empress by the censor Chao Ch'i-lin as having received 100,000 taels as a bribe for appointing as Acting Governor a man from whom his son Prince Tsai Chên had recently accepted singing girls; and he had only been able to secure a judgment that the charge "cannot be established," while his son's connexion with the owner of the singing girls was declared a "culpable association." Now he could do something glorious for China. The *chi-cho* must not pass.

The Wai Wu Pu saw that it was undesirable to force an early show-down by a blanket refusal of facilities. Instead, having established that the motorists found the Manchurian route via Kharbin impracticable, they offered every aid for an exit in this direction. After the necessary time had been expended in considering, referring, and rejecting this offer the French Minister repeated the request for passports for Mongolia. The Grand Council deputed Prince Ching to give humanitarian reasons why the transit of Mongolia was most undesirable. "Mongolia is inhabited by savages," the Prince assured M. Bapst. "The tribes there cannot be expected not to be terrified by your horseless carriages. They will consider them as invaders, and will very possibly screw themselves up to attack the caravan. We cannot expose your countrymen to such a fate."

The French Minister, caught up fully in the struggle now,

replied that the motorists would take the risk, that passports for Mongolia must be issued for them, and that it was against all treaty rights to withold them.

After a few days the Wai Wu Pu issued passports made out for Manchuria. They were rejected.

Further precious time passed. Finally the passports arrived. They were made out for Mongolia. They seemed very adequate personal passports. Unfortunately, there was no reference to any passage without let or hindrance and with all necessary assistance and protection for the motor-cars. Without such cover the 'raiders' were helpless against the action of local mandarins. The passports were rejected.

After three weeks of further negotiation Bapst received a letter saying that the Chinese Government were definitely opposed to the passage through Mongolia. If the Ministers insisted the Wai Wu Pu not only declined all responsibility, but would give no order assuring the safety of the travellers.

It was at this point that the final wave of defeatism engulfed the competitors in Peking, and Longoni arrived to learn that the *raid* was cancelled.

It was Cormier, de Dion's professional driver, who had collapsed, as he had done once before over the telegram to Prince Borghese in Rome. He was an admirable man in a practical emergency, but without the mental stamina for a war of nerves. He was irritable and forceful. He habitually carried Collignon along with his decisions, but normally he had no effect on the resolution of Pons and Godard. Why, then, did Cormier's impulsive reaction override them in the absence of Borghese? The reason is to be found in their financial standing. Pons was genuinely awaiting the arrival of a draft of money, and was very seriously worried that it was so long delayed. Godard had no money at all, though he too announced that a remittance was due any day. If the works-backed de Dion-Boutons started the race the refuelling organization would work as planned, and there should be some pickings of surplus fuel for the others. If de Dion's withdrew, and Cormier telegraphed to the depots along the route that they were not starting, the supplies now being moved up the line might be frozen where they were. Godard, a student of life, knew Cormier's character well enough to let the first explosion of frustration flash unchecked. There was still a week to work on him if only the hardening of his decision could be avoided.

Cormier had worked well at the special tasks assigned to him. He collected the oil and petrol which had been shipped in from Sumatra via Shanghai and the Hankow Railway. He got it loaded on to a camel caravan, which took the cans to the four telegraph relay-stations spaced across Mongolia, the only possible stages in the route across the desert into Siberia. The farthest point he supplied, Urga, was a thousand miles from Peking. He had then sent Collignon out on a mule to make a close study of the 160 miles of mountain country to Kalgan. Since he had the advantage in time over Prince Borghese, the de Dion organizer had almost completed this part of his reconnaissance when the Prince reached Peking and also set out for Kalgan.

Prince Scipione took with him his wife Anna Maria and her friend the Countess Nora. The three went out on horses to survey the passes, and each rider carried a bamboo-cane which was exactly the width of the Itala car. Where the cane could pass the car would pass. Where the cliffside path overhanging a ravine could be estimated to hold the car except at a few tight corners the rock could be dug out with pickaxes to get the Itala by. Where there were too many narrow places the cliff path must be rejected, and a way sought at the bottom of the ravine, through the bed of the torrent if necessary. The surveying party completed its task and returned to Peking in six days. The feature which appalled Borghese, because his maps had given him no hint of it, was that the construction of the railway, which Prince Ching and his fellow-investors were so feverishly pushing out to the northwest, had seriously changed the terrain. A vastly increased cart-traffic had churned up the route in some places; earthworks, tunnelling, rock-levelling, and all the litter of a series of construction sites had narrowed the track in some parts and blocked or destroyed it in others.

Riding back to the capital, the Prince summarized his survey before discussing it with the rest of the Peking–Paris entrants, none of whom he had yet met, but whom he expected to have arrived by the time he returned to Peking.

The French party had indeed arrived, and were installed in the old one-storey Hôtel de Pékin, facing the legation quarter. The Prince's party was at the Italian Legation. Barzini, who had also arrived during the surveying trip, was in the newer, two-storey Hôtel des Wagons-lits, built since the siege of 1900, and actually within the legation quarter. Du Taillis and Barzini had both been in Peking before in times of previous troubles. The first bitter reminder experienced by du Taillis was the acrid taste of the yellow dust constantly swept into ears and eyes and nostrils by the petulant whirlwinds of summer.

Yellow dust overlaid, but could not extinguish, the lacquer and painted wood of shop-fronts, the gilt pillars and glazed green roofs of temples, the rich, irrepressible gleam of printed silk on the clothes of the women, constantly guarded as they promenaded or shopped. Amid the dust flew the banners and mottoes and the almost permanent bunting of a city that seemed to be always celebrating. Peking was an ochre canvas of feudal poverty and feudal unconcern, on which were built up in great heavy blocks of extravagant colour the humming establishments of rich men and the warehouses whose treasure was carefully leaked into the market so that the whims of rich men could be satisfied.

Architecturally Peking was a nest of Chinese boxes in a walled and moated city that had kept the same aspect for three centuries. Within the walls Peking was five miles square, an immense and insanitary area for an ancient centre of habitation, though the spacious grounds of some temples in the south gave a certain breathing-space: the gardens of the Altar of Heaven, for example, were roughly a mile square, but they were still bounded by the city wall. The centre of the nest of boxes was the Forbidden City, an area of spacious colonnades, decorated palaces, and high pagodas, a Ming Versailles, where the Gate of Supreme Harmony led by way of five marble bridges over the Golden Water River, past huge bronze lions and carved marble ornaments, and over dragon pavements to the halls of harmony beyond. There were fifty pavilions and palaces within the Forbidden City, enclosed by its very high, broad, crenellated wall, pierced only by four gates. Around the Forbidden City was grouped the Imperial City, whose Government offices and imposing residences were contained by a high red wall of brick, running in a square for six miles, and again with only one gate in each side. Surrounding the Imperial City was the Tartar City, another square, whose walls were forty feet high, sixty-two feet thick at the base, and half as wide at the top. Every sixty yards along this wall huge stone buttresses projected fifty feet out. Tacked on to the southern wall of the Tartar City was the sprawling Chinese City, about five miles across and two in depth, which was also enclosed by a wall.

Apart from the palaces and some legations and an occasional

modern building like the Hôtel des Wagons-lits, Peking was a one-storey city. In the legation quarter, which, in addition to having its own wall since the Boxer rising, was squeezed between the high walls of the Tartar City and the Imperial City, there was a lack of perspective that could induce claustrophobia. From anywhere else, and particularly from any of the unforbidden walls, the view of the city looking south gave the impression of a remarkably mean capital, a humble, squared-off assortment of cardboard houses, with an occasional far temple breaking the line of the strangling walls. Yet northward the prospect changed completely to a fantastic silhouette of curving eaves and roof-lines, with the green glazed tiles always gleaming.

And, only twenty miles away, the Western Hills formed a splendid backcloth—and added the reminder to the visitors that they formed only the gateway to 160 miles of the most discouraging touring ground.

Since the last visit of du Taillis the drains seemed more extensively dug, the roads better laid out, and many avenues had been made into tree-lined boulevards. At times the dust was briefly conquered by a rudimentary municipal water-sprinkling service. The streets were continually thronged with the traffic of carriages and rickshaws or the cavalry escort, in unmilitarily flowing robes, of a high functionary being swiftly borne in by mule-litter from administrative service in Mongolia.

Near the open workshops, where for centuries craftsmen had fashioned objects of beauty in jade and enamel and porcelain, and carved and painted wood, rickshaws waited. Light, curtained carriages in varnished wood, with the ornamental wheels decorated with huge enamel-headed nails, drew up. The gross eunuchs, bald under their scarlet cone-shaped hats, guarded their occupants as the delicate women, teetering on their tiny mutilated feet, alighted to shop. In the legation quarter, at Kierulfs, for long the only Western shop allowed in Peking (for the capital was not a treaty port), Manchu princes wandered through the store followed by the day's choice of their concubines and singing girls and the appropriate eunuchs. And as the girls passed du Taillis he noted the enamelled effect of the thick paint on their faces and the elegance of their rich silk robes, brightly embroidered, the hems of their skirts disclosing loose silk trousers gathered at the ankle.

The French party devoted little time to sightseeing, though the truth was that there was nothing else to do. They could take no part in the final savage duelling between the legations and Prince Ching. But they were restless without their cars. And on Friday the 31st of May they all took the train to Tientsin, where the *Admiral von Tirpitz* was due to unload the crated motor-cars. They arrived too early, and had to waste time again in the clubs of the British Concession, a well-laid-out quarter, with big hotels, spacious villas, and expensive shops—and even the English luxury of a town hall and a Victoria Park. The *Tirpitz* was held up beyond the Taku bar, the reef at the mouth of the Peh Ho, which was covered by only three feet of water at low tide. The 'raiders' sat in the centre of the usual circle of club raillery until midnight, and were about to go to bed when a pigtailed Chinese, who had been engaged to wait on the quays as a courier, ran in to say that the coaster was coming in.

Laughing with relief, the party hurried to the quay. The *Tirpitz* was just tying up. The party swept aboard like children out of school, and bombarded the good-natured German officers with inquiries about the cargo. How had it travelled? Had there been rough weather? Did they suspect any damage? Above all, how soon—how soon could they discharge the crates?

Godard was mad with excitement. He had brought along some of his admirers from the Club, and was whipping up their enthusiasm with the promised perfection of engineering that they would be glimpsing any moment, and the cunning driving tricks that could be demonstrated even on a dark dockside at two in the morning. But the officers of the *Tirpitz*, with the greatest regret, could not accommodate him. There was no dockside labour available at that time. The cars were at the very bottom of the hold, beneath the rest of the cargo. They would naturally begin to unload in the morning, but the soonest they could promise access to the cars was within forty-eight hours.

Gloom hit the whole company, and not only Godard. They left the ship. Some one proposed a cinema in the arcade, but no one was in the mood for it. They went back to their hotel, where du

Taillis, sharing a room with Godard and cheerfully paying for it, had to endure all night the savage snoring of Tartarin du Gobi.

Next morning they were up before daybreak, and on the quay-side by five o'clock. Godard whipped aboard the *Tirpitz*, and was immediately lost to sight. He was already in the hold. It took all the patience of the ship's officers to tolerate him. He was giving his orders, with the utmost coolness, direct to the stevedores. Lift these cases. Shift those sacks. Get a rope round here. Fix your tackle there. And in no time at all—or two hours at the most— he had forced a path through the hold to the crate holding his Spyker, and was making professional movements of his hand to direct the crane-driver.

The great mass of the crated car rose in the air, hovered over the deck, and sank gently to the quayside. Godard was already immersed to the depth of his persuasive soul in another opera-tion. He had the Dutch Consul in Tientsin by the elbow. He was selling him faith in the performance of the car. It was quite unnecessary, for the fair, thickset Consul was beaming with enthusiasm that a Dutch car should be engaged in this historic race. He was full of goodwill, and amiably accepted Godard's passionate declaration of delight at seeing the emissary of the Netherlands present at such an inconvenient hour, when the car that was to carry all that was best of Dutch aspirations took possession of the soil of the Celestial Empire.

The Consul was a man of goodwill, but not quite so willing to be fooled by eloquence. He mentioned that he had attended the quayside not only for the honour of the occasion, but at the request of the shipping company. He had been informed that there was a matter of a bill for 3000 francs to settle for freight-charges. Godard warmed to him even more. It was indeed a fact that the car had been sent carriage forward. Godard's own remit-tance had not yet arrived, though he had made every inquiry at Peking. It would be a most profound tragedy if the car were impounded now, when there was such short time to service it, for a mere matter of 3000 francs carriage. Would Monsieur le consul? . . . Oh, he understood! What sympathy, what honour was already evident. A guarantee—that was all that was needed. Everything would be straightened out very shortly.

And the Dutch Consul gallantly walked to the agent's office and guaranteed payment of the freight-charges. Godard was at his elbow again. In the circumstances, could another small guarantee be given, and the trifling cost of rail transit to Peking also be covered?

Discharge of cargo over forty-eight hours was certainly a cautious estimate by the officers of the *Tirpitz*, who had never had a Godard to deal with before. By eight in the morning the crate containing the Contal tri-car was safe on the quay, and the two de Dions followed. Du Taillis, the organizer, had received excellent co-operation from the French forwarding house of Olivier in Shanghai, and had extended it as far as taking two of their men to supervise transhipment both in Tientsin and Peking. These agents, Heitz and Charlot, began to form a gang of porters to get the extremely heavy and bulky crates from the quayside to the railway station Tientsin Settlements.

The cases had to be manhandled, up-ended, carried, inevitably dropped, and heaved over the edge of platforms. At a critical stage the men struck. The freight entries had just been completed in the railway office, and the gang had learnt from the spy they had posted there that the charges made, and now paid, had not included the cost of manual haulage between ship and freight-truck. The ball was in their hands. Unless the payment was now settled, at a necessarily favourable rate, the crates would stay right where they were. The negotiations were conducted between the Olivier agents and the men's *comprador*, a sort of self-employed overseer, who took commission from the principals who engaged him and from the men whom he employed. With his fan in one hand and a little sparrow hopping sadly in a wicker cage held in the other, he signed a satisfactory treaty with the Oliviers, and, using the same manual properties, quietly gave his orders to the gang, and got the cars, with their crates of spares, lashed on to two flat railway wagons.

Heitz, of Olivier, posted his Chinese personal servant to guard the trucks all day and through the night, for they would be made up in the same passenger-train that was to take the 'raiders' back to Peking the next day, Sunday. Meanwhile the jubilant Frenchmen reverted to club life to celebrate a glorious Saturday night.

The two goods-trucks were pushed ahead of the engine which drew the passenger-train next day. The faithful Chinese kept a careful watch, until at a station half-way through the journey he saw with horror the foremost freight-truck, on which the Contal and Collignon's de Dion had been loaded, detached and hauled away out of sight. His anguish was extreme, but he dared not leave his post to get the message through to the passenger section for fear that in his absence the devils would whip away the truck on which he was standing. But the weight of guilt slowly forced him to a state of nervous collapse, so that by the time the train arived at Peking he could make no coherent explanation to his employer, or even speak words, but only emit the most soulful wails usually reserved for the extremes of personal bereavement.

Cormier immediately got in touch with the French Minister Bapst, who fired a short burst of protests, and soon discovered that the wagon had been taken out of service because of an over-heated axle, and would be brought in to Peking that evening. Accordingly on Sunday the 2nd of June the motorists were at last able to gaze on their machines. Major Laribe, commanding the French garrison in Peking, lent a squad of his men from the 18th Colonial Regiment. They attacked the crates with vigour and within minutes the Spyker was on show.

Godard had merely driven his car on to a set of planks in Marseille, and had a crate built round it. The Spyker had travelled all the way with its wheels attached. The end of the crate made a perfect slope from the truck to the ground, and with Godard at the helm the car glided smoothly down. The driver's face lit up as if he were the source of solar energy.

"One swing of the handle and we're away," he shouted. "One swing . . . oh—petrol!"

Victor Collignon, who was in no mood to spoil Godard's triumph, obligingly passed him a can of de Dion petrol. Godard lifted the driving-seat, filled the tank, and gave his boasted one swing. And he was right! The engine roared. Godard, intoxicated with the success of the moment, put the car in gear, and, with little idea where he was going, shot straight off the platform and up the ash road by the side of the legation quarter, until he was stopped at the Gate of Heavenly Peace, at the entrance to the Imperial City. Na Tung, as General Commandant of the Peking Gendarmerie, had slipped into circulation an order that no *chi-chos* were to proceed under their own power in Peking, but could proceed only if drawn by mules—and a maximum of two mule-power at that. Charles Godard became the first to defy this ordinance.

He was speedily followed by the two de Dion-Boutons, which had first to have their wheels attached, and then showed that they were in as good a condition as the Spyker. The Contal was completely dismantled in a flat crate, and there was no possibility of assembling it at the railway-station. The soldiers of the 18th Regiment simply picked it up and carried it to the legation quarter, where it was deposited in the courtyard of the French barracks.

The next day, while Pons and Foucault rebuilt their machine, while the de Dion-Bouton men examined every part of theirs, while Ettore Guizzardi, in supine reverie on the flagstones of the Italian Legation, gazed contentedly at the gearbox of the Itala, which he had already dismantled and reassembled three times, and while Godard took every one from the Dutch Minister downward on joy-rides through the city—the Grand Council of State threw its carefully prepared bombshell to M. Bapst declaring that no safe conducts could be issued for Mongolia. And Longoni arrived from Japan to take the shockwave of the explosion.

Prince Borghese was still away on his survey expedition. No final decision was reached until he returned. Then, on Wednesday the 5th of June, five days before the *raid* was scheduled to start, all the competitors met in the large board-room of the Russo-Chinese Bank, which had been put at their disposal by Willpart, the bank's Peking director.

The text of the Wai Wu Pu's note was briefly given. Cormier, who until that moment had been speaking in terms of postponing the event for a year (since any serious delay after that week would push the race into the rainy season), now unexpectedly broke in to propose that the event should be abandoned altogether. "There is not even a garage in the city where the cars can be safely kept until next year," he said; "and the only possibility that I can see is that we sell our cars and go." It may be mischievous to point out that Cormier, whose basic business was as a de Dion-Bouton dealer in Paris, was always a little more interested than the rest in selling cars. He made a strong attempt to force a sale to the Grand Lama at Urga, in Mongolia. Collignon, as had been expected, backed his leader in his pessimism. He declared that passports were essential for the journey, and without them they would run the most intolerable risks.

The first to protest was Godard. He was spluttering with indignation. "Whether I have a passport or not, whether I go alone or in company," he said, "I intend to drive the Spyker out of Peking on the day agreed, the 10th of June." Du Taillis, presiding over the meeting as the *Matin* representative, heard him indulgently, but could not help reflecting on the impossibility of Godard's tacking the *raid* alone, without money to pay his bills in Peking, not to speak of the heavy expenses of the journey.

Pons jumped into the argument. "Foucault and I are determined not to go back to Europe without at least making the effort to start," he declared. "We came out here with the object of showing that the motor-car is the machine of the future, and nothing can stop its progress. We should make ourselves ridiculous if we went back the way we came, by the Trans-Siberian or by ocean liner, with all our gear packed just as we set out."

Pons had made his point. But du Taillis knew that he too was by misfortune also extremely short of money, and might not have the means to accomplish the trip without support. He turned to Prince Borghese.

The Prince summed up the situation drily. He outlined the preparations, the unrebuttable hazards of the first stages, and the luck as well as the courage that might be necessary in the wilds of Mongolia and Siberia. But he concluded in the same level tones as he had started, "Gentlemen, whatever conclusion you come to, my own decision is made, and nothing can change it. I shall start on Monday."

There was really nothing more to be said. Du Taillis ascertained that the 'sense of the meeting' was that they should start on the due day with or without passports, and the de Dion-Bouton drivers grunted acquiescence. The decision was reported to

Bapst, who reported it to Prince Ching, and awaited diplomatic developments.

The *raid* was on. There was still a great amount of preparation to do.

Cormier's first action was to dismiss his mechanic. Lelouvier had arrived in Peking with an accurate report on the state of the route from Irkutsk, and his pessimism about the wretchedness of the Peking-Kalgan link tallied with the reports of Collignon and Borghese, who had both inspected this section. No one among the competitors ever mentioned a reason for dissatisfaction with him. But, from any practical consideration, it was enough that Cormier did not get on with him. It was Cormier who had to endure his company for a trip up to 10,000 miles. Lelouvier was told to make his way back to Paris, and Cormier had a word with steady Jean Bizac, the mechanic who had still never made a journey in a motor-car.

"Well, Bizac, this is how it is. Will you agree to service both cars by yourself on the stages through the Gobi Desert while telegraph to Paris for another mechanic to be sent immediately to somewhere where we can pick him up from the railway—Irkutsk for example? Will it be too much for you to look after the two machines until he joins us?"

Bizac thought for a moment, and then committed himself to speech. "I can take care of the two cars. There is no point in telegraphing Paris. If I can do part of the route I don't see any reason why I shouldn't do it all." He was silent again, riding the impact of words.

Cormier smiled his thanks. "Well, it's not a bad start for you as a passenger," he said. "For a baptism of fire Peking–Paris is not a bad battle."

Bizac shrugged his shoulders.

The arrangement left a vacant place in Cormier's de Dion. The Frenchmen looked at each other, and nodded towards Longoni. The Italian journalist had heard the day before that Count Grospello's specially ordered Fiat could not reach Peking by the 10th of June, and would have to be listed a non-starter. Longoni had dived into inconsolable gloom. Every day there seemed to be a crisis, but this, for him, was the end. "It's terrible! If only I could cross the Gobi and Mongolia with you, and get as far as Irkutsk. It would be child's play to follow you from stage to stage after hat and get my dispatches in."

Godard was genuinely warm to him. "Everything will sort itself out. We haven't started yet. There is plenty of time for something o happen. Be patient and keep your hopes up."

And, again, comment may be mischievous. But Gropello's cratching meant that his stake-money would be divided between he starters. Two thousand francs between five promised the prospect of 400 francs hard cash. It was not to be paid until the very morning of the start, but in Godard's negotiations it represented solid credit. Credit alters a man's mood, and makes him reer with his sympathy.

Cormier came to an understanding with Longoni that if he ould get to the Kalgan Pass by his own means, and preferably n company with the cars, he could have a seat on the first de Dion rom there on. Until the pass Cormier was going to carry Goubault, a member of the Legation staff lent to the French team s interpreter.

There was no difficulty about this at all from Longoni's point of iew. Prince Borghese had already estimated that it would take up to eight days to get the cars through to the plateau above the Great Wall. A man on horseback could do it in almost half the ime. Longoni went off happily to inquire about a tough Mongol oony.

It had fallen to him by this chance to have the most comfortable ide of them all. For Borghese had now convinced all the competitors that it was impossible for the cars to drive through the Nanow range of mountains. The lowest speed that engines could give for any substantial period would be too fast to prevent the ars from fracturing themselves to pieces on the rocky ground. And the ground where engines could work was rare. Soon after he outskirts of Peking the 'road' to the north-west simply anished by any motoring standards. There was no permanent rail through the rocks because the pack-animals and draught oxen vhich used it were being continually diverted by landslides, and imply picked another path. In those gorges which the Prince had elected as wide enough for cars the ascents among the boulders were dangerous, and the descents were suicidal. No brakes could hold a car back from the rush down slopes which cornered over precipices. Men and beasts must drag them up, and men alone must hold them back—for animals were not adaptable enough for the emergencies of descent. Large companies of porters would therefore have to be hired.

Prince Borghese, with his usual efficiency, had immediately applied to a transport agency which specialized in the supply of porters. A gang of labourers arrived at the Italian Legation, and followed the procedure already familiar to the French party. The *comprador* gave them their instructions. The band advanced on the Itala, bearing tough bamboo-poles, planks, and crowbars to lift the machine bodily, testing its weight before they fixed the rate. They raised the car. After a few paces, during which they had been prepared to counterfeit the utmost distress, they found that the reality of the task made no demands on their acting. They collapsed. Borghese was not surprised. With its thick steel chassis the Itala weighed two tons. The *comprador* declared that his gang could not even consider towing the Itala unless it were considerably lightened. Borghese therefore decided to take the whole of the body off, including the great wing tanks and the tool-chest and to replace it when the car had finished its first week's slow progress. It was a decision that aroused great controversy among the rest of the 'raiders.' For they were starting out from Peking with the same load and the same equipment which they intended to take to Paris. Borghese filled three carts with the gear he removed from the Itala and bolted back later.

The prestige problems raised by haulage could be discussed later. The mutilating difficulty at the moment was the price that Borghese had agreed to pay his porters. The rate was set at no less than 3000 francs. It was an entirely unexpected expenditure for the starters, equivalent to the freight-charges from Marseille to Tientsin, and an item which the unbacked men had not the means to pay.

The price might have been brought down if there had been time to bargain. There was no margin, and the figure stayed at 3000 francs per car, amid the explosive yelps of an outraged du Taillis. The situation was eased by the manager of the Russo-

Chinese Bank, who advanced credit to those he considered most worthy, and therefore permitted a certain amount of private trans- action afterwards. The bank backed the de Dion crews, and du Taillis, of the indestructible *Matin*. Collignon, in turn, lent 3000 francs to Pons, whose letter of credit was now five weeks late from France, owing to the uncertainties of the Russian postal service in an age of revolution. Du Taillis lent 3000 francs to Godard to pay for porters, partly because he could appreciate that the haulage fees would have been an unscheduled charge on even the most conscientious planner, partly because the performance of the Spyker even on its little show-off runs round Peking had so im- pressed him that he was convinced that the Spyker had a far better chance of finishing than the light de Dions, which were beginning to look extremely frail under the heavy load of equip- ment they were being stacked with. Indeed, du Taillis's first enthusiastic reports on the Spyker in *Le Matin* before the start of the race were read by Jacobus Spijker in Amsterdam, and significantly changed his attitude of resentful recalcitrance to- wards the jovial Godard. The banked fires of sympathy for a fellow-optimist began to burn through again.

Meanwhile, backing his faith in the Spyker car, and at the same time keeping an eye on his investment, Jean du Taillis arranged to travel as passenger with Godard. The most constructive act the journalist could perform in automobilism was to swing the starting-handle—he could not even drive—and once the bonnet was up Godard was almost as mechanically helpless as he, so their prospects in a serious breakdown were poor, unless the rule of travelling in convoy was strictly operated. Cormier, in any case, now had vested interest in the convoy rule, for the only mechanic available to him was riding on the other de Dion.

The cars now certain to start were, therefore:

1. The 40-h.p., four-cylinder Itala, driven by Prince Borghese, with Ettore Guizzardi as mechanic and Luigi Barzini as passenger. Its laden weight without crew was 2000 kilograms.

2. The 15-h.p., four-cylinder Spyker, driven by Charles Godard, with Jean du Taillis as passenger. Its laden weight was 1400 kilograms.

3. The 10-h.p., two-cylinder de Dion-Bouton, driven by Georges Cormier, with Edgardo Longoni as passenger. Its laden weight was 1400 kilograms.

4. An exactly similar de Dion-Bouton driven by Victor Collignon, with Jean Bizac as mechanic.

5. The 6-h.p., one-cylinder two-stroke Contal tri-car, driven by Auguste Pons, with Octave Foucault as mechanic. Its laden weight was 700 kilograms.

On the journey through the Kalgan pass the Itala was stripped down to under 1500 kilograms, and at first carried five on board—Prince and Princess Borghese, Don Livio Borghese, Guizzardi and Barzini, though all but Guizzardi walked or rode on horseback for most of the way.

On Friday the 7th of June Barzini cabled the London *Daily Telegraph* with the confirmation of the agreement among the entrants that the convoy rule would be observed as far as Irkutsk. The message read:

PEKING, *Friday*

To-day the participators in the great race met together and drew up the general regulations as far as Irkutsk. If any car is so badly damaged as to be obliged to remain *en panne* the other competitors will lend all possible assistance, but if the means at their disposal should not permit complete repair the car shall be towed to the next stage or even abandoned, as the owner chooses. Should one of the chauffeurs be taken ill he will be conveyed to the next place where a doctor can be found and if his sickness should be judged to be curable within three days the invalid may claim to be waited for.

This clear understanding was ignored by Barzini's crew during the first clear day's run under the car's own power. It was afterwards claimed on behalf of Prince Borghese that he was not bound to observe rules of the contest which had been voluntarily agreed between factions of the competitors in Paris. But this definite pronouncement of agreement at Peking, published as the race started, but never later referred to by Barzini, invalidates this plea.

The final preparations and checks of preparations were made. For Borghese the last of the jigsaw slotted into place with the message from Willpart relayed from the Russo-Chinese Bank, at Kalgan, that the Itala's fuel had been securely dumped. For the Prince, doggedly independent by nature, had made no claim on the fuel sent out by Cormier as agreed by the Paris committee, but had made his own arrangements through the Russo-Chinese Bank for nineteen camels to leave Kalgan on a separate caravan delivering fuel to the same locations as Cormier's camels. Borghese was also given letters from Dr Davidoff, the energetic director of the Russo-Chinese Bank in St Petersburg, addressed to a long list of contacts through Asia, and desiring them to give the bearer the full resources of their aid. The bank seemed, in effect, to be issuing its own passport.

Godard's principal problem, which had none of the thrill of novelty, was lack of money. There was no panic, but the situation demanded action as precise, delicate, and finally as forceful as a safe-breaker's. As a result of his operations Godard emerged with a loan of 2100 dollars from the Dutch Minister, lent on the under-standing that Godard's letters of credit would soon arrive. The dollars current in China were Mexican, not United States, coin, but the Dutch Minister's advance was worth all of 5000 francs. Part of the money was used to settle for supplies of petrol and oil to be picked up at staging-points as far west as Irkutsk. This still left some 8000 miles of route unprovided for, but Godard was not anxious to pay in advance for petrol which might be obtained at less cost by the exercise of his native persuasiveness. He was hamstrung by language difficulties until he was out of Mongolia, but once in Siberia he was sure to be understood in French, the second language of Russia, and there would be a chance for the exploitation of charm. The rest of the Dutch loan seems to have gone on good living, with the last few dollars expended on a little Pekinese dog picked up in the market, which Godard named Pékine. He certainly started the journey quite penniless.

Godard had now obtained credit for the load of tyres lifted on the Spyker account from the garage in Amsterdam, 3000 francs from the Dutch Consul at Tientsin, 5000 francs from the Dutch Minister at Peking, 3000 francs from du Taillis to pay for porters, and he was about to take over 2400 francs starting money from the Russo-Chinese Bank, of which certainly 2000 francs was the

property of Subardie, the Spyker agent in Paris, who had actually
entered the car. The 10,000 francs prize-money which Jacobus
Spijker had promised if he won was, therefore, completely en
tailed. Godard did not know it, but a sequence of events wa
already in train which would block his ever handling any prize
money. The Dutch officials in China were cabling Jacobus Spijker
to confirm Godard's credentials, and to get the transfer of credi
authorized. Spijker, penniless himself, cannily replied that none
of Godard's actions was any concern of his. The car was not his
entry, but a private venture by Subardie from Paris. Spijker
declared that he was greatly surprised that Godard had started
the *raid* at all, having been convinced that Godard would sell the
car in China. In the face of this stonewalling, the Dutch official
in China instructed a Paris lawyer to lay an information against
Godard for false pretences, and to attach any prize-money due to
him to recoup them for their advance.

Unaware of this ultra-legal attitude to his enterprise Godard
was happily participating in the warmest co-operation from the
French garrison. Major Laribe was finding no request for assist
ance too trivial, and though the Spyker was officially quartered in
the Dutch Legation, it spent most of its time, between joy-rides
in the French Voyron Barracks, where Laribe impartially stocked
it with provisions, by the side of the two de Dions. In fact, since
the Spyker was the roomier car, it was stacked with the greater
part of the French Army gifts of canned soups, concentrated
vegetables, and cases of bully beef, which the French soldiers
called *singe* (monkey), but which the travellers declared was
excellent. Laribe also had specially cooked 200 kilograms of hard
biscuit-bread, which were laid down behind the front seats of
the Spyker, and he made over to the drivers useful equipment like
soldiers' desert water-bottles.

Room also had to be found for the cases of twenty-four bottles
of champagne, which the firm of Mumm had requested permission
to present to each starter in the race. It seemed that no expedition
in history had ever been so strongly supported by the bubbly as
the Peking–Paris *raid*. The French contestants had all but lived
on the wine on the voyage out and at the gay receptions in Singapore, Saigon, Shanghai, and Tientsin. They had been given a hint

of the banquets already awaiting them in the many cities of the Russian Empire which had set up committees of honour to welcome them as they passed. This last gift from Mumm seemed to assure them that the arid gap which might threaten them through the first inhospitable fortnight in Mongolia would be dissipated. But the sheer weight of the Mumm beneficence defeated the firm's generosity. Twenty-four bottles of champagne, cased, weighed nearly fifty kilograms—over 100 pounds. The travellers were being forced to cut down feverishly on personal luggage— Borghese restricted each of his crew to fifteen kilograms maximum. Most of the cars retained a bottle in the back for the most essential celebration, and the travellers dispensed the rest at the many farewell parties which were now being given. Godard alone determined to take a crate with him. But, before the crossing of the Gobi, an impulsive generosity caused him to abandon it. He started the journey without even one reserve bottle, a fact which brought him near to death.

Festivity demands decorations. Laribe ordered his men to bring out more flags, and to deck with bunting the barrack square, which was to witness the start of the *raid*. Even an ancient Chinese cannon in the courtyard was decorated with flowers. General Sucillon, commanding the French occupation forces from Tientsin, was pleased to favour du Taillis's request for music, and at noon, on Sunday June the 9th, the headquarters band of the 18th Regiment arrived by train from the coast. The Tientsin train was crowded that day. Officers, diplomatists, merchants, and their ladies were flocking into Peking for the send-off, even from Shanghai, hundreds of miles away. The regimental band played nobly at an afternoon reception at the French barracks and later at a soirée given by the French Minister. At the Legation that night, as the toasts of success were proposed and the visiting notables were announced, there was a sudden, excited silence as the major-domo cried, "His Excellency the Mandarin Kwo Kia-ki!" The Mandarin was a member of the Wai Wu Pu, who had been appointed Grand Council liaison officer to the 'raiders' in a letter received by Bapst on the 13th of May. This was his first appearance. It indicated as graceful an acceptance as possible by the Imperial Court of the Peking–Paris *raid* as a *fait presque accompli.* The Wai Wu Pu had sat through the whole of the previous day in a session devoted solely to the urgencies of the 'raiders'' decision to go at all costs. In the evening, the night of the 8th, they sent passports to the French, Italian, and Dutch Legations. The documents were more like criminal indictments than safe conducts. "The *chi-cho* is completely foreign to China," they declared, "and the Chinese Government will hold the drivers responsible for any injury or shock caused by these machines to Chinese subjects, their beasts, or property. Local mandarins are empowered to seize funds or goods as surety against any misconduct on the part of the *chi-chos* or their drivers."

The passports were promptly returned. On the Sunday evening fresh passports were delivered granting simple safe conduct for the travellers through Mongolia. The Wai Wu Pu had made merely one last gesture as a reminder of the privileges of oligarchy. The passports were written only in Chinese; they could not be understood in Mongolia; and, except in the bureaux of the highest officials in Mongolia, they were quite useless. Na Tung followed up the passports with a polite request for information on the route to be taken out of the city confines so that the streets could be watered, and finally the Mandarin Kwo Kia-ki arrived at the reception, radiating bland goodwill, to wish the 'raiders' *bon voyage*.

It was a brilliant evening. The ladies from the coast vied with the consorts of the Diplomatic Body in the splendour of their gowns. Every one crowded round the French, Russian, Italian, and Dutch Ministers to congratulate them on their heartening victory. These envoys were the heroes of the hour, but the reception was also marked by the fact that it was attended even by the Ministers of the United States and Austria-Hungary, who were reputed never to go anywhere. The band played, the champagne flowed, the toasts were announced. And the Russian Minister brooded on his latest précis of the state of the Empire: "The internal condition of Russia is growing more serious. Murder is common, pillage has become a means of livelihood, incendiarism is the common expression of the peasants' dissatisfaction with the landowners. During the week ending yesterday eighty civilians were killed and seventy-eight wounded."

Perhaps the unpleasant duty of withdrawing the motorists' safe conducts through Siberia would be better left to the authorities in Kiakhta. The 'raiders' were enjoying themselves so whole-heartedly. They would need all the sleep they could get for there was to be an early start in the morning. They had had enough problems for one week.

"Waiter, champagne!"

5 ◎ ◎ The Wine in the Dust

Peking, Monday the 10th of June, 1907. The fireworks had soared from the garden of the French Legation into a clear and cloudless sky, but the dawn broke grey. Barzini, awakened by a servant in the Hôtel des Wagons-lits, asked him the weather prospects.

"It will rain this morning."

"This morning?"

"This afternoon too."

The season had broken. In the Hôtel de Pékin, all meteorological auguries apart, clouds of temperament were beginning to gather over the proprietor. Godard could not pay his bill. For the last time the Frenchman told the story of his delayed remittance. The hotelier merely suggested that Godard should stay until it arrived. Jean du Taillis hurried to the Dutch Legation. The Minister had risen early for the ceremonial departure, and agreed to cross over to the hotel with du Taillis. He signed the account, ordered it to be sent in to the Legation, and determined that he had contributed his very last subsidy to the cause of automobilism. Godard, full of thanks and beaming with enthusiasm, accompanied the Minister to his Legation, and went on to the Russo-Chinese Bank to draw Subardie's 2000 francs deposit and the Spyker's share of the forfeited stake of Count Gropello.

The cars lay in rival camps, retaining to the last the impression that this was the dawn of a battle between them rather than the sharing of a festive departure. The Italian Legation had echoed early with the tramp of heavy boots as a detachment of sailors was sent off on the train to Nankow. Guizzardi fussed around the Itala. Princess Anna Maria held court from the rough plank chest which was the only seat left on the stripped chassis. Borghese chatted with Army officers, whose air of suppressed excitement contrasted with his own seemingly exaggerated coolness. Barzini bustled in with his meagre luggage, making no effort at all to brush the air of elation from his lean, brown features. The garrison chaplain cantered in like a bersagliere, field-boots protruding from his brown monkish habit. He joked for a moment, proceeded direct from his laughter to give the expedition his blessing, and broke the sudden silence with another joke. A soldier ran to say that the French cars were at the Voyron Barracks. Ettore Guizzardi swung the starting-handle, and ran to the platform on the back of the car, disappearing immediately from knees to armpits as he sat in a high stack of spare tyres. Borghese took the wheel. His wife, his brother Don Livio, and Barzini sat upright at his side like toys. The car ran slowly to the Legation gate, and the guard presented arms.

Borghese characteristically stopped the Itala outside the French barracks, where the other cars stood inside, in the square, and took his passengers inside to join the farewell gathering. The regimental band, standing in an unmilitary but graceful semicircle before their bandmaster, set a Parisian air by making mad dashes at Offenbach. The square was packed. Nobody had ever seen so many Europeans above the rank of private soldier up so early before. And every moment another rickshaw driver, catching the excitement of the occasion, raced to the barracks entrance with another distinguished guest. Outside the gates there was a good number of curious Chinese. But the majority of the spectators were the soldiers of the ten European nations besides the French who kept garrisons in Peking. The French walked unconcernedly into their own barracks, with an air of conscious proprietorship that it had never occurred to them to assume before as they hurried back for duty. The rest—Austrian, Belgian, German, Japanese, Russian, and Spanish, as well as the prouder nationals of the countries involved directly in the contest—stood around taking everything in on a day that was outstanding in their dull garrison round. The Americans, who man for man knew more about automobiles than any of the others, were indulging in a little compulsive gambling—not only about the result, where the bets would take a long time to be settled, but about the weight, horsepower, and petrol consumption of the cars, and even the number of swings necessary to start them. The British, rather shamefaced that there was no final entry from what every one down to the smallest drummer boy believed to be the supreme sporting nation, looked on, uninvolved, at the circus which would move off somewhere else to-morrow. Every one gazed at the women, who had arrived in Peking in undreamed of numbers. A surprising number of the ladies had brought sheaves of flowers, which they presented to the crews or laid on the cars. The barrack buildings were bristling with the clustered flags of the contestants, many of them decorated with evergreen.

It was a garden party at 7.30 in the morning, with the ladies in their prettiest dresses, their fresh complexions unmarred by afternoon heat or dust. Diplomatists and officers chatted with animation. Sir Robert Hart, Inspector-General of the Chinese Imperial Maritime Customs, well over seventy, bald, white-bearded, and with a face sallowed by fifty years' service in China, moved delicately among the guests, and paused long to appreciate the music of the band. Until the siege of 1900 he himself had supplied the instruments and instructions for a Western-style band of Chinese instrumentalists, who had given weekly concerts in the Customs Compound. The orchestra and instruments had been scattered during the Boxer rising. The Mandarin Kwo Kia-ki was again in attendance. His palankeen bearers waited by the gate as he proceeded amiably through the gathering, making quick, automatic movements with his fan and wishing a smiling good-bye to anyone who looked like a 'raider.'

The densest groups were round the cars. The two de Dion-Boutons, packed to their flat half-hoods with equipment, looked as pitifully frail as perambulators. Their colour was a utilitarian grey. Two French soldiers who understood Chinese script were painting in white the characters for Peking–Paris on their honey-comb radiators. In a momentary hardening of the patriotic emotion that was half-realized by every contestant Major Laribe presented a small French flag on a bamboo-stick to Cormier. "I want you to take this back to France," he said thickly, and as the crowd clapped and cheered, his adjutant, Bouton, fixed the flag to

he front of the first de Dion. The car was already bristling with
planks to ease its passage through mud, with spades and pickaxes
o cut away rock, and with ropes and pulleys and stanchions
forming tackle capable in emergency of hauling the car along
inclines or even lifting it bodily—an operation that was to become
necessary within five hours.

By comparison the Contal tri-car looked as neat as a bullet, and
as comfortless as a girder. The shape was peculiar. The passenger
sat in front on a hard bucket seat over the axle of the two front
wheels, as if he were the luggage in a delivery boy's tricycle. The
driver sat behind on a cycle saddle, poised over the engine and
the single driving-wheel, and had to steer the heavier front section. As an apparatus, the tri-car looked serviceable enough for a
short speed course, but useless for an expedition because it was
impossible to stow anything bulky on it. They carried no gear at
all for surmounting obstacles: it was true enough that the machine
could be lifted by hand, but for very short spells only. Pons and
Foucault carried no beds, no serious supply of rations. Effectually,
in order to accomplish the *raid* at all, they needed a 'mother
craft,' and Godard had good-naturedly assumed this responsibility. He carried on the Spyker one small bag of their personal
luggage, their blankets, and their provisions.

The Spyker was a bobby-dazzler. Painted in vertical stripes of
red, white, and blue from stem to stern, its after part, behind the
driving-seat, was crowned by a stiff canvas dome, shaped like a
four-sided Chinese bell. On the green canvas were pasted labels,
some of which advertised Spyker excellence, and some of which
gave details of the distance to various points on the route which
the car was, by implication, soon to reach in triumph. The words
SIBERIA, RUSSIA, GERMANY had been smartened up in fresh
paint over the tricolour along the body. Du Taillis had packed a
camp bed and a tent beneath the dome, and the general appearance of the car was remarkably smart—in the tradition of the fairground rather than the *concours d'élégance*.

Outside the barracks the Itala stood—a functional, stripped
racing chassis, with a workshop of tools strapped on to it. The
body, seats, spare tanks, and vast tool-box had entirely disappeared, and were at the moment rattling in ox-carts along the

road to Kalgan. One long locker replaced the driving-seats. It was filled with ropes and tackle, and a mattress was tied to the lid on which four people had to sit side by side. Instead of mud-guards it had four straight steel tracks, some six feet long, one end of each being lashed to the low, square carriage-step bracketed to the centre of each side-girder, while the other end sloped upward at an angle to connecting brackets over each of the four wheels. Viewed from the side, each pair of tracks made a shallow V following the rough line of mudguards. These detach-able tracks were designed for flinging down in sand under the spinning wheels of the car. The Itala carried over the first stage, like a *chevaux-de-frise* system that would have stopped the storm-ing of the Bastille, a formidable array of iron tools, crowbars, and picks, and a most pessimistically calculated stock of spare tyres. Borghese, like many a general, seemed to need three times the necessary armour before he would go into battle. Lashed to the batten of the dashboard was a staff, bearing a large Italian flag with the royal arms of Savoy.

The band had switched to military marches, and now, obedient to the peremptory double-beat of the big drum, stopped at the end of the bar. The mechanics swung their engines, and ran round to board their cars, and the Americans checked their bets. The first tentative roars of the exhausts settled into a rough, idling rumble. All the animated chatter had stopped when Major Laribe, a magnificent organizer, nodded to the bandmaster, and the brass cut shrill through the bourdon, with the trumpets tonguing an infinitely stirring tune. It was the Italian national anthem, not *La Marcia Reale*, but the passionate call to action sung more in the south—Garibaldi's hymn *All'armi, all'armi, si scopron le tombe*. It took Prince Borghese by surprise, and he stumbled awkwardly to his feet, standing over the steering-wheel, with his brother and his wife beside him, and his other friends still and solemn. The Itala was remote, outside the barrack gate. The crowd of private soldiers and nondescript Chinese around the Prince was not his class. The Italian soldiers and sailors stood very proudly, but the scene seemed to emphasize the isolation of Borghese.

The band began the Dutch hymn *Wilhelmus van Nassouwe*, the oldest tune of all among the national anthems. Then, with a fervour and familiarity it could not disguise, it played *La Marseil-laise*. And the French sang. The moment meant much to the company in the square of the Voyron Barracks. They were touched by friendship, moved by a manifestation of youth and adventure, which some of them knew had passed beyond their own reach for ever. They were far from home, and not ashamed to reveal that a single tune, an inimitable trumpet phrase, brought them a communion they desired; and words, even old words sung through tears, could be of comfort.

The band stopped, then marched outside the barracks. Many officers who intended to accompany the starters called to the orderlies holding their chargers, mounted, and came through the gates. The horses side-stepped into the crowd as the roaring motor-cars followed and lined up with the Itala. The gay assembly swept after them, and all the flowers lay on the ground where the cars had been. Madame Boissonnas, the wife of the First Secretary of the French Legation, was to be the starter. With an attractive lack of expertise she broke a bottle of champagne over the bonnet of the Itala. The wine foamed over the brass and disappeared into the dust, the last of all the toasts that had been offered over nineteen weeks to the Peking–Paris gamble. From now on the speculation was a reality. Madame Boissonnas raised a flag, then lowered it, and held it in her two hands, smiling to see the cars pass her. The band marched first, and then came the Spyker, Prince Borghese courteously declining to precede the car of the *Matin* organizer. Painted like a hoarding and topped with its green dome the Spyker moved slowly forward behind the sweating musicians. And all the Chinese sutlers, legation servants, and barracks hangers-on—the outcasts or stateless of the population of Peking, who alone among the Chinese warmed to the venture as something they could joyfully give allegiance to—let off squibs and threw fireworks in the conventional local formula for good luck. Above the crack of gunpowder and the thick melody of the euphoniums rose a high, excited yapping. It came from the front seat of the Spyker, where a tawny little bitch was joining in the fun. It was the lion-dog Pékine, the only loot that Charles Godard was removing from the capital of the Celestial Empire.

The procession passed up the narrow Rue Marco Polo, and

swung right at the corner, by the Italian Legation. The Legation roofs and walls were manned by the naval garrison, white suited, blue collars flying, standing formally as if they were dressing ship. As the Itala passed they doffed their wide-brimmed straw hats and gave three quick naval cheers, "Hurrah, hurrah, hurrah!" Borghese removed his solar topee in acknowledgment. The Italian crew looked at one another with limpid eyes. The march continued. In the wider boulevard the Army officers edged out their horses, and more ceremonially escorted the column of motor-cars, whose engines were now extremely hot owing to the slow speed they had to keep behind the band. They passed the Examination Halls, where for centuries before any Western country had a civil service 6000 graduates used to sit writing their papers, solitarily confined for three days in cells which were literally sealed, and could not be prematurely opened even after suicide or death from exhaustion. Farther in the same street they came to the von Ketteler Memorial, an imposing marble arch on the site of the murder of the German Minister in 1900. The Allies had compelled the Chinese to build it after the Boxer rising as a monument of expiation for the crime, though it was generally considered in Peking as a triumphal reminder of what, in the right circumstances, could be done with foreign devils. At the arch the band drew to one side, played its last, lively version of *Sambre et Meuse*, and let the cars accelerate. Most of the pedestrians had kept up with the march till then. They stopped and cheered. The bandsmen threw their caps into the air. This was the real farewell.

The mounted officers began to gallop. The cars increased their speed. The Peking Gendarmerie had stopped all traffic on the northern route out of the city, and the rickshaws stood with fretting passengers at the crossroads, restrained by the wands of the police, until the party had passed along the carefully watered road. The officers, outdistanced, pulled up their horses, and shouted a last farewell. The mildly curious Chinese stood in front of the lacquer and gilding and silk-fringed signs of the shops. The line of motors, elongated now, and led by Cormier, approached the high, fortified wall of Peking, and roared out of the city through the Gate of Virtue Triumphant. A curtain of fine rain began to fall. The road had changed in an instant to a track of ill-fitting blocks, which at speed hit the wheels like boulders. The cars ground down into low gear. After little more than a quarter of a mile Goubault, the French Legation interpreter, who was travelling with Cormier, stood up, apparently on his driver's instructions, and peered over the top of the hood. Cormier signalled that he was stopping, and the Spyker and the Itala drew up near him. No one else was in sight except an official who had been waiting on horseback at the gate. Cormier got out of his car and walked over to du Taillis with a broad gesture of resignation. It was clear that Collignon and Pons were already lost.

Prince Borghese, sitting at the end of his locker-seat like a charabanc driver, was acidly furious. Du Taillis, unwilling to create early difficulties, invited him to continue his course, and the Itala roared on. The Spyker and the first de Dion-Bouton waited in a country road crisscrossed by the spreading branches of fruit-trees. Time passed. The official, who apparently had orders to keep the 'invasion-spies' under observation, waited patiently. Cormier and Godard tossed to see who should go back to look for the missing cars, and Godard lost. Philosophically he turned back, leaving du Taillis, who eventually wandered along to a tea-garden, where he gloomily drank several glasses of tea as the rain hissed down. The walls of Peking were still in sight.

It was about three hours later, towards noon, that the Spyker was heard leading the other two cars along the road to Nankow. They had taken the wrong turning while still in the city, and gone far to the east, towards the Summer Palace. The Contal tri-car was in difficulties already, once the fairly level surface of the city roads had ceased. The blocks and ruts were forcing its heavier front downward, and lifting the single driving-wheel from the ground. The four cars went on, the Spyker and the two de Dions always leading, but waiting at intervals for the Contal to catch them up. They were keeping their convoy agreement, but their progress was far slower than they had calculated. They were already perturbed that they had not yet measured themselves against the first serious obstacle which they had charted in their reconnaissance of the route—the "heaps of ruined battlements" of the bridges over the Cha Ho, which they had first been warned about at Shanghai.

The crew of the Itala had already had to deal with these bridges. The road was an irregular ribbon of soft sand, under which lay a hard core that rose to within inches of the surface at some points, and emerged from the surface at others, like a chain of rocks occasionally rising from the sea. Since most of the floor-boards of the Itala had been removed to save weight the flywheel span the sand up in a spray over the passengers, and the hard underlay threw their bodies about like dummies on the wooden seat. The speed had to be kept low, and the radiator was constantly boiling. But, since they were passing through the well-watered plain of Peking, it was comparatively easy to find a well or stream to tap for the water they first threw over the radiator and then used to refill it. Both Borghese and Barzini had a smattering of Chinese and were able to communicate with the villagers.

After a slow but comparatively steady journey they came to the first of the bridges over the Cha Ho. These were pure ancient monuments, beautifully designed, and built entirely in white marble, with most elegant balustrades. Unfortunately, it was clear that they had never been repaired during the first centuries of their existence, and it had become completely impossible to mend them during their later life. The actual surface of the bridges consisted of blocks of marble of a minimum width of about three feet and often twice as long. But the blocks had fallen away from one another. There was no cement holding them. In some cases the complete upper block had vanished, leaving a cistern of water, and there were great gaps and differences of level between all the blocks. That was the bridge proper. But the greatest ravages of time had been wrought against the approaches. The run-up to the bridges had entirely disappeared, and the bridge level was between twelve and fifteen feet above the road. The difference in level had been made up in strips by tenuous mud pathways, which pack-animals could manage, and possibly carts, with the encouragement of human heaving. There seemed no means at all of getting the heavy automobile on to the upper stretch.

Borghese had already taken his car through a number of shallow streams, and he hoped he might find a ford even through this considerable river. But after exploring the bank to right and left of the bridge for some distance he was forced to return to the monument of masonry.

The steel tracks over the Itala's wheels were unshipped and placed over the first slabs of the bridge proper, at the top of the muddy approach. Ettore backed the car fifty yards to prepare a flying start, and on Borghese's orders he eased in the clutch, and roared towards the bridge. The car slowed with a shudder as it felt the effect of the steep incline, but did not stop, and uneasily continued, until its front wheels were on the beginning of the steel tracks. But the front wheels could not grip, and the back wheels, whirring noisily, merely dug the car into the mud. Guizzardi cut the engine, and let the car fall back. This time they set the tracks under the back wheels, still on the slope. But as Guizzardi put the car in gear again the tyres made such firm contact with the tracks that the iron lengths merely slipped through the mud like grease, and were thrown with alarming force backward behind the car.

"Let me try it my way," said Guizzardi. He backed the car again, shot forward up the slope, gained the first stone slabs with his front wheels, and set them spinning uselessly on the marble. "Push!" he yelled, and the men heaved behind the car, showered with mud and stones from the back wheels, and blistering their leggings with the exhaust of the racing engine. Guizzardi got out of gear again, and the men took the strain, not letting the car roll back. After an interval for breath the mechanic started again. The wheels bit, the car slowly mounted, and finally with a jolt the front wheels dropped over the first slabs, which made a sort of ledge. Not daring to stop, Guizzardi kept the pressure on, and the back wheels too climbed awkwardly over the ledge like a tortoise. The car stood on the bridge, and the radiator was refilled.

The passage over the slabs was made with the greatest effort at the slowest speed. Every block demanded an individual opera-tion to cross it, and the car stopped after each slab, sometimes resting only on two wheels, sometimes slumped apparently irre-vocably in a wide rut. But the crossing was made. Then came the descent, more cautious even than the crossing. Finally the car stood on the other side of the river, shaking as horses shiver with fatigue. The party mounted again, crossed marshy country overlaid with small humped bridges, and then came to the even longer marble bridge of the second loop of the Cha Ho. With more confidence this time Guizzardi set his machine at the slope, and within twenty minutes the party had at last written off the Cha Ho crossing.

The plain became more arid. Imperceptibly it rose. Now they were travelling among sterile foothills, and soon, through the haze of the continuous rain, they could see the iron curtain of the Kalgan mountains. As the Itala entered one bare village a swarm of men dashed on to the path and stopped them. It was the band of porters whom Borghese had hired, and their *comprador* informed the Prince that it was impossible for the car to go any farther under power. But Borghese told him he would keep on as long as he could exceed the speed of the porters and not cut his tyres to ribbons with the effort. They climbed up towards the Nankow Gorge, a narrow slit of light ahead of them in the distant mass of rock, like a saw-cut in ebony. Finally the road finished. They were a little over thirty miles from Peking, and it was still early afternoon. But there was no track beyond, except the bed of the torrent that when the rainy season was more advanced would crash down from Nankow. The Itala had to be taken up the river-bed, amid boulders, falls, pools, and stretches of wet sand, and the only possible traction was by the power of muscle.

Ettore got his tow-ropes out of the locker as they waited for the porters to come up. Two ropes were passed round the brackets holding the springs, and the porters grabbed them from each side and began to haul. The *comprador*, an old man, carried a whistle that indicated "Get set!" and a banner on which was written in Chinese characters "Obey your father's voice." The voice delivered a sort of capstan shanty, and the old man climbed like a ceremonial goat ahead of the party, whistling, singing, and waiting for his men to come in with the heavy chorus to which they heaved. The high walls of the gorge darkened the scene. There were six miles to go to complete the first stage. The car reared with difficulty over boulders, plunged convulsively as it surmounted them, rolled, checked, sank. Guizzardi stood in the car, bent over the driving-wheel, steering as finely as possible, flinching as the differential thumped on the rocks.

And so they came to Nankow. The exhausted Guizzardi, his back badly strained by merely standing at an angle for so long while he was hit by the shocks of the climb, did not know he was in the village, until he realized that the boulders had been dragged to the sides of the track, the middle being left pure mud, and the arch of a gate was closing on him. The boulders served as sidewalks to the one-street town of one-storey shacks, the street starting and ending with the essential defensive gate. There was an inn of sorts. Borghese's party took over the best rooms. Italian marines and French soldiers had already found quarters. They had been sent partly out of zealous comradeship on the part of the garrison commanders, and because the Ministers felt that an armed escort might be desirable for the first stages in case the porters were in the pay of the Grand Council to sabotage the motor-cars. The Italian squad reported to Borghese that his ox-carts holding the dismantled car body and the spare parts had already arrived. The time was 2.45 in the afternoon. Barzini, in some concern at having left his colleague du Taillis so early in the expedition, climbed the battlements of the village, which had a clear view over the plain. There was no sign of any vehicle approaching. At four o'clock a party was seen arriving from a completely different direction. The Italians ran out towards them. The group was a band of porters dragging the Contal tri-car, with Pons and Foucault puffing as they helped them.

"But where have you come from?" was the bewildered question. Pons's bright young face took on an expression of deep shame.

"From Nankow railway-station," he said. "We came from Peking by train."

At that moment, as Pons was making his explanations, Cormier, Collignon, and Godard were still fighting the Cha Ho bridges.

After a particularly long wait for Pons they had gone back on the road to find him motionless in the position in which Blériot was too often pitching his aircraft—nose down, tail up, and out of action. It seemed impossible for him to get enough weight on his driving-wheel to make progress. The drivers held a council of war. Pons was determined not to give up, but also embarrassed at detaining the others. They agreed that, since the exit from Peking was notoriously one of the worst stretches of the journey, the Contal should not be disqualified if it skipped that first stage. (It would not have been disqualified if it had been towed, but the porters had been sent on almost to Nankow.) But, since Prince Ching's Kalgan Railway was already operative as far as Nankow, Pons should turn round, drive back carefully to Peking—since his engine was absolutely sound—and take the afternoon train to Nankow.

How was he to get to the station? His geography had already been proved poor on the exit from Peking. Surely there was a very competent guide in the person of their 'shadow,' the minor mandarin who had apparently been instructed to follow them as they drove towards the Cha Ho. The man sat on his horse with wary disinterest, waiting for the next move. Goubault, the interpreter, went across to parley with him. If the forces split he would be able to follow only one party anyway, and to have Pons loose in Peking was obviously a greater national menace than the rest of them streaming away from it. The official was compliant. The motorists righted the Contal, and Pons turned it round and started back. "I'll see you this evening," he promised. But it was the four-wheelers that were not to keep the rendezvous.

Now at least they could give the engines their head. They swept along over the sandy route in impressive style. The triple roar of the caravan had a certain disquieting effect on various donkeys and ox-trains they came up with. And suddenly it had happened. The first of many carts they were to upset on their long *raid* was upset. As they sped majestically along a straight, flat road they suddenly reached a concealed dip, up which a chariot was being driven. It was a carriage drawn by two oxen, driven by a driver on the box, and with passengers unidentifiable within, as they sat behind the heavy dust-curtains which the Chinese used instead of glass. The oxen panicked and bolted. The carriage turned upside down. The driver finished underneath the vehicle, and the oxen, by some entanglement, finished on top of it.

The motorists braked and ran to the wreck. Not a sound came from it. The coachman was obviously alive, as could be seen from his swivelling eyes, darting from side to side like a captured bird's. As the Frenchmen examined him he permitted himself a few tiny cries, but did not move, as if he feared to discover the extent of his injuries. They pulled aside the curtain of the coach. A solitary passenger eyed them paralytically through his legs, but again would not move or speak, in spite of the agonized entreaties of Goubault. On the top of the pile the oxen impotently waved their hooves in the air. Inexperienced as the French were in the management of beasts, and since the beasts had first to be moved before the humans could be reached, they decided to rush to the nearest village for help.

But the nearest village was Cha Ho-tien, the community by the Cha Ho river. The inhabitants had enjoyed a wonderful show from the antics of Borghese and Guizzardi as they tried to cross the marble bridge. They had been standing for hours, waiting for the next performance by the foreign devils. Urgently Goubault explained to them the fearful accident up the road. They were not moved. They were waiting to see the cars cross the bridge. The Frenchmen decided that they could do no more. They turned their attention to the bridge.

It was a barricade, they decided. Beautifully carved with lions and dragons, but a marble wall, not a bridge. One would need to jump it. Resignedly they unpacked their jacks, pulleys, ropes, hammers, blocks, and tackle. With a prayer for the gods' forgiveness for desecrating an ancient monument they hammered an iron stake between two blocks of marble, crumbling the structure a little, but giving them a high and firm support for their pulley. They then fitted and greased a lifting tackle, and, inch by inch, heaved the Spyker bodily up the virtual parapet from the road to the bridge. It took two hours to get the Dutch car up. The experience they gained on it shortened the time·taken for the others. The rain fell all the time. The blocks of the bridge surface were now extremely slippery, and the cars had to be coaxed along them. Then they had to make the descent. And then they had to rig the tackle all over again as they came to the second bridge. When they had finished the sun was low, but they set out to make what speed they could. Inexplicably the Spyker's speed was very poor. Godard was signalling to the others with extravagant gestures of exasperation. Impulsively he stopped. "Some-thing is wrong," he announced. "I can't develop any power."

Bizac and Collignon bent over the Spyker like doctors. They listened to the engine, they adjusted the throttle, they tapped and felt and conjectured. Faulty ignition? Dirty carburettor? Change the plugs. Dismount the carburettor. Check the electrical circuit, adjust the valves, test the magneto. They did everything, and cursed as they remembered the great dinner that Major Laribe, who had also taken the train to Nankow, had promised them in their staging-post.

"There's only one thing left," said Collignon. "It must be the silencer." Like devils from hell he and Godard plunged under the car with a hammer and cold chisel, and began clouting the exhaust in controlled fury. Then, moving like robots, without a word, they got up. One went to the starting-handle. One took the gas and ignition levers. The engine started. It roared like a trom-bone. Mud and sand had clogged the exhaust, but hitting two healthy great holes in the pipe with the chisel had taken the pressure off the pistons. The Spyker bounded like a goat again as they hurtled over the ruts towards Nankow, with Collignon still tingling from the embrace with which Godard assured him that he had now forgiven him for the three-hour delay in Peking.

The man who had most to forgive was du Taillis. He was suffer-ing the spiritual and duodenal agonies of all journalists who cannot get their copy on to the wire. He had written his account of the send-off during his forced wait in the wet tea-garden. He had time, after heaving on the block and tackle with the others, to describe the first rigours of the journey as the car was slowly wheedled along the flags of the bridges. All that remained was to add the information that the Frenchmen had arrived in Nankow, and were on level terms with Borghese. And this he could not do—first, because it had not happened, and, second, because he was nowhere near a telegraph-station, since that was in Nankow. The night came inexorably down in almost visible stages, as if a devilish oculist were fitting darker and darker lenses over the eyes. Suddenly the last darkness fell, and they realized they could go no farther in this rough and unknown country. The friendly company of the French officers, the dinner prepared for them in advance, and that golden telegraph office, had all to be pushed from their minds. They had to camp.

They were all in a filthy temper, but just managed to cling on to the skirts of politeness. They were tired. They seemed to have no idea, in spite of Cormier's privations in Hungary and du Taillis's very varied experiences as a globe-trotter, how to put up a tent. Du Taillis had bought a new camp bed, but never re-hearsed its erection, and, responding to his irritation and fatigue, it collapsed with monotonous regularity. It was not a matter that troubled Godard, because he did not have a bed. However, they sensibly allocated duties. One laid out the tents; one rammed in the tent-pegs; one fixed the headlamps of the cars, which operated on acetylene gas produced from calcium carbide; and one lit the pressure stoves while his companions rummaged through the rations. By eleven o'clock they had devoured some pints of the Maggi range of concentrated soups, a few tins of sardines with Laribe's biscuit-bread, and a superb Milan sausage *"suprême réservé pour le Gobi,"* which had been presented by an Italian friend to Longoni, and which he had incautiously handed over to the general ration store for future consumption. Longoni had ridden out to Nankow on horseback, and was unfortunate enough to miss this delicacy.

In the middle of supper the fine rain which had fallen all day intensified into a heavy mountain-country downpour. They fled to their tents, which were already streaming with the small tor-rents of water pouring off the roadside. Du Taillis, having some inches of freeboard above the flood in his camp bed, sympatheti-cally watched as Godard, cursing gently, spread his blankets over tool-chests and packing-cases, and uneasily surrendered himself to sleep.

6 ◎ ◎ The Great Climb

The storm, which beat at the tents of the French and left angular pools in the backs of their cars exposed on the mountain slope, hardly disturbed the Italian party in the Nankow inn, though occasionally spouting water caught by the wind drummed against their paper windows. At dawn they rose, but waited for the rain to stop. Princess Anna Maria sat with her husband, who was now to leave her, for she was returning to Peking by the train. At seven it seemed clear that no break in the weather would come. The Prince bade his wife good-bye, gave the order for the start, and trudged heavily out of Nankow behind his gleaming vehicle. The porters had now hitched three beasts to the ropes to help them— a mule, a horse, and a small white donkey. They took the ropes. The old man with his dripping exhortation to obey the father's voice went first, like a beadle before a bishop. The chorus began, and the procession started, the car now flanked by the Italian sailors, who occasionally gave it a calculated shove. Ettore Guizzardi, standing at the wheel, as he was to do for four days more, developed a signal code with his hooter—one hoot, go— two hoots, stop. But either the damp or the constant use affected its tone, and the hooter soon grew hoarse.

The track followed an irregular, rising valley, through which ran a bounding torrent, sometimes level with the path, sometimes far below it. Down the skylines of the bare mountains there plunged the castellated battlements of fortified walls, secondary defences that sprang from the Great Wall of China, up and ahead, the watershed of the ramparts.

The march went on hour by hour, heaving, pausing, heaving, resting. They passed through square, fortified villages, and went round others, where the gates were too difficult to negotiate. Then the light began to be blocked from them as they came nearer and nearer to the face of the mountain, and for a moment there seemed no way through at all. But after a turn in the track they saw a thin slit in the rocks, and they were in the gorge itself. The cliff rose sheer above them, yet there were shrines and hanging temples in places that were apparently inaccessible, but had rough steps hewn out of the rock to reach them. The pillars were broken, the carved statues weather-worn, and the inscriptions faint. It was a place of old religion. Then the gorge widened, and the mountain range beyond displayed, silhouetted against the dull light from the west, an artificial, squared outline. They were within sight of the Great Wall.

Nearer peaks closed in again and shut the distant skyline away. The rain still fell—it had continued all day. Dragging the car cautiously along the edge of a deep ravine, they turned a bend and saw that the Wall was dead ahead of them. The ground was now a steep, forked cleft, so narrow that it cut into the outer walls of the Itala's tyres. But with a strenuous effort the whole party put their weight on the car, and heaved it on and through the gate of the Wall. They went on to the next village and gave up for the day, taking over a caravanserai—a broken-down inn, where camel caravans halted, in a square of rough ground surrounded by low stables and some inn rooms. Prince Scipio's brother left immediately the party arrived. He was to ride down the gorge back to Nankow and catch the evening train to Peking. In over eight hours the porters had towed the car twenty miles. The 'raiders' were now sixty miles from Peking.

Farther down the pass the same grim struggle had been repeated with the other four cars. The crews of the Spyker and the de Dions had woken shivering in the dark, their tents streaming, and all their belongings soaked. The garrison commander's 400 pounds of biscuit was a sodden, inedible mess in the back of the Spyker, and had to be thrown away. The motorists did not know where they were, but they heard from time to time the hoarse shriek of railway engines. The day lightened. They began to glimpse the high mountain above them, and then they could see the one pagoda among the curved roofs of Nankow, only about a mile away. In the dark of the previous night they had come farther with their engines than Borghese. There was a crack above them, and a cliff began to split in a landslide. The boulders fell, bounced, fell, and splintered, and the little rocks they broke up into came rolling to the feet of the Frenchmen. They swiftly began to pack their baggage. Goubault had gone off to Nankow as soon as the light revealed it, and now he could be seen returning, outdistanced by Major Laribe and his corporal Dalez, who were speeding towards them on horseback. Laribe promised them a hot breakfast in Nankow. They rolled up their soaking traps, threw them into the cars, and started the engines. Skidding and jolting, with the springs groaning under the strain of their load on this rough ground, they drove up the torrent, until the great mud canal of the Nankow High Street—brimming with a full night's rain—engulfed them, and their own porters took charge, and drew them into the courtyard of the inn.

They shared the excellent coffee which Laribe provided for them with Pons, who had waited for them as he promised. From nine in the morning until eleven they were busy initiating the porters into the routine of haulage. The Frenchmen were using larger teams of porters than Borghese, but they were more indolent, and the one interpreter, Goubault, had to explain a similar operation of tying on the ropes and settling haulage procedure to the four groups consecutively. Finally they set out. The Princess Anna Maria had stayed to see them off, and they warmly saluted her as she sheltered in a doorway in her dark Chinese gown, with the pantaloons tied at the ankle. She smiled, and turned inside.

The shanties started, and the party moved—a sizeable caravan, which compared creditably with the traffic coming down the pass, lines of donkeys, mules, and camels plodding in the rain as they brought down to Peking packs of hides from Mongolia and even goods from Russia. The slope was not steep at first, but awkwardly rocky. At times the path was invaded by the torrent, and they waded through the water, hitting their cars against rocks which rose up like reefs. The road steepened, and they began the long haul to gain about 2400 feet in altitude over a distance of twelve miles.

Prince Borghese had reported that the views were magnificent, but his reconnaissance had been in fine weather. They saw nothing, looked at nothing, save their boots and the mud, as they toiled at a task which was hard labour after some months of soft living. In the gorge of the hanging temples they glanced apathetically at the ancient relics, and turned their gaze back to their boots. At the steepest point of the route the track had been entirely obliterated by the works for the Kalgan Railway. They had the greatest difficulty in getting their cars through by striking out completely new paths for themselves. At the end of this stretch they came to a village. The headman welcomed them with courtesy, offered them tea, and begged them to stay. They had started four hours behind Borghese. They knew he must have passed the Wall. But they decided to halt for the night where they were welcome, and the expedition rested, straddled on either side of the Great Wall.

The next morning, Wednesday the 12th of June, the French were stirring early, but could find no trace of their porters. They had been far from satisfied with their efforts on the previous day, and had tried to add their own spurring to the somewhat lax supervision of the *compradores*. Godard's *comprador* was particularly infuriating. Rather than inspire his men from the front, like Borghese's, he led them from the rear. He did not march, but rode in a little cart. He held in his hand a little reed cage, in which two common sparrows cheeped, and as the day wore on he became more and more interested in his birds and less in his men, until Godard was furiously shaking him to get his porters working. The men had disappeared into the huts of the village as soon as they arrived on the previous night, and, spending some of their extorted gain on high living, ordered hearty suppers from their hosts, laughed and made merry far into the night, and then resorted to their opium. The result was that they were far too drowsy in the morning to be active, or even to get up without encouragement, and finally the Frenchmen sent the soldiers whom Laribe had lent them to rout them out of their beds.

Unwillingly the ropes were taken up, and the expedition moved on. When they came to the Great Wall a rest was ordered, and du Taillis with Longoni, who had joined the trek from Nankow, stopped to examine this wonder of the world, twenty-five centuries old and yet useless since Genghis Khan sent his invaders through it and over it.

Thick, comparatively squat compared with the towering defences of Peking, the wall marched along the mountain ridges, its brick-and-stone construction making it look like a yellow serpent against the darker rock. The writers took out their pads to sketch some phrases to describe it. Cormier and Godard whipped the convoy on and left them. The drivers had kept a wary eye on their porters. As soon as they sat down to rest the fans had come out of one trouser leg—which the Frenchmen had to tolerate—but the opium pipes came out of the other. When Godard rushed among them he was naturally unintelligible, and at this stage of the journey the Chinese were, in any case, genuinely surprised that he should take any objection to their habits. But when they did appreciate his object they realized that an obvious lack of comprehension on their part was their best support.

It was a point where the porters had to do more than pull. The rock path was so rough that the picks had to be got out to cut the tops of boulders away. Rough wedges had to be placed to give the car wheels a run up to the boulders, and often the entire machine had to be levered with their great crowbars to lift the wheels the last important inches. Then some intermediate, downward slopes began. The reports they had had were correct. The descents were so steep that every man had to be deployed to hold the cars back. For the drivers at their steering-wheels, with the brakes full on, these moments were the worst. The porters were being dragged off their feet on the ropes behind, and, when absolute precision was necessary to avoid hitting boulders with a shock that could easily break the springs or the delicate differential, the cars were genuinely out of control.

At the next village Major Laribe made his adieux and left on horseback, taking all but two of his soldiers. One of those who stayed behind was Corporal Dalez, almost as good a Chinese linguist as Goubault, who remained with them, and notably better at picking up a bargain by the wayside. It was Dalez who did the marketing, and du Taillis—biased on the subject of being cheated by foreigners—declared that the chickens he bought were twenty times cheaper than anyone else in the group could get them.

The terrain had changed. The ground was more sandy, though scattered with rocks. There was no obvious track at all, only a selection of ruts, which seemed the product of purely individual piloting. As if to match the desert aspect, the sun came out strongly at noon. The porters, who were not efficient in the sand stretches, sweated profusely, and fluttered the fans they still contrived to operate as they worked. Bizac shook his head and swore quietly as the uneasy march progressed, for the drunken way in which the cars were being pulled into sandbanks, or were diving as they rolled off a boulder into a rut, meant that the sand was invading the engines.

Longoni and du Taillis, who had borrowed a Mongol pony from one of the outriders to the party so that he could accompany his fellow-journalist, dallied a little as they told anecdotes of past assignments, then rode wide of the track as they tried to catch up. They knew that the party had decided to stay the night at Hwai-lai, a town of some size. It seemed a difficult target to miss, yet they did miss it, and rode in wide circles, with increasing despair as they contemplated a night spent without blankets on the rocky sand, with not even the comfort of the boiling Maggi soups, to which du Taillis was developing an addictive attachment. The day was dying when, from the top of a rise in the ground, a more significant hill asserted itself. Its outline, black against the orange sky of the sunset, revealed below the inhospitable ridge of its crest the square indentations of the familiar Chinese city wall and the curved lines of pagoda roofs jumbled with the blocked silhouettes of houses. Hwai-lai was ahead.

At first sight the town seemed as unrealistic as a backcloth in the Opéra-Comique, and the theatrical impression was heightened as they approached, to be welcomed by files of people hitting gongs, banging drums, and sounding bells and cymbals in the best tradition of a Paris chorus-line. As the journalists rode towards the gate they mounted the approach of a fine stone bridge, but had to retreat again when they found the principal arch missing in the middle. The way across the river was a narrow track of fascines, wrapped like big bundles of firewood and laid one on the other in the water, until the top was above the surface. Across this creaking, yielding causeway the cars had already been dragged. At the other side two ranks of Chinese soldiers were drawn up, dressed in loose blue overalls, with wide-brimmed straw hats strapped on their shoulders. The riders passed between the guard of honour and entered the formal gate of the town. The problem was now to find the inn. The escort of percussionists was delighted to guide them, and they streamed ahead, laughing and beckoning in the intervals of operating gongs and drums and cymbals, and making most realistic *honk-honks* in imitation of the car hooters, alternating with terrifying growls which were a passable imitation of the car engines. The procession ended in a courtyard of glutinous mud and worse, where indeed the car engines were running on test. Bizac had given them a rough clean-up, and started them to satisfy his disquiet after the passage through the sands.

This was the village inn. The yard was like a cesspit, trodden into a sticky sea by the hooves of the camels, horses, mules, and donkeys of the caravans which had already taken their refuge there for the night. In the buildings flanking the square the general odour endorsed the impression that the way of life of this community depended on livestock. It was overlaid by a strong smell of onions being cooked in various ways by the caravan crews in the communal kitchen. Du Taillis and Longoni inspected the range of bare stone rooms, seeking a bed for the night. They rejected the cells, which reeked too overpoweringly of opium recently smoked, and settled in a large room where Cormier was already installed. They threw their packs on the *kang*, or oblong brick bed, which they selected. The *kangs*, the only furniture in a Chinese inn, were high structures built like tombs in a mausoleum, hollowed below so that fires could be built inside them. The fires of wood and camel-dung were already smouldering. The bricks were warm, but the smoke was overpowering. Du Taillis rushed to throw open the window of framed paper. Cormier merely grunted. He had already tried this. Outside the window the inhabitants of Hwai-lai waited, fought to get their heads through to observe the travellers, shouted, pointed, commented and laughed, until after some minutes du Taillis shut them out

It seemed better to perish by suffocation rather than nervous collapse.

They moved moodily to the kitchen. Amid a high babble of sound the cooks of the caravan parties were busy with saucepans and urns. They were boiling soups, heating water for tea, and grilling strange pies stuffed with meat and herbs on red-hot plates standing over certain open fires. Courteously the cooks offered samples of their work to the travellers, but the food did not appeal to their taste. The Frenchmen contented themselves with taking water for their tea, and then set about cooking the chickens which Corporal Dalez had bought for them on the way. Dalez killed the birds. Longoni plucked them. Goubault singed and gutted them. Cormier and Collignon superintended their cooking. And the meal, supplemented by their tinned rations, was appreciatively eaten. The dog Pékine accepted the scraps.

The party retired to their chamber. There were nine *kangs* in the principal room, and the five men who had camp beds erected them over the tiled slabs. The rest piled car cushions, motoring capes, sheepskins, and blankets on to the roasting bricks, and tried to sleep. The noise of the livestock outside did not greatly disturb them. The activities of the livestock inside reduced them almost to mania. It seemed impossible that an apparently bare room could harbour so many bugs and fleas. The vermin emerged from the warm masonry to seek their prey. Nine bodies, stretched across the room, four feet from the floor, making a level which ought ideally to have been as calm as the surface of a lake as they relaxed in sleep, instead seethed like a crater of lava. They twitched, started, and sprang upward with little convulsive cries while a busy army gnawed its fill.

At the first dawn salute from the herds of pack-animals outside, the disconsolate 'raiders' rolled out of their beds, eyes rimmed thickly with lack of sleep. They shook off as many as possible of the creatures which had raided *them*, and beat a retreat into the open air, to find swarms of flies operating in such density as to create noticeable turbulence. They sent the soldiers to pitch out the porters, and started off again as early as possible. It seemed incredible that the porters, after a fair night's indulgence with opium, could bring out their pipes again on the march, even before breakfast, and take surreptitious pulls at them in the rest intervals which they were increasingly demanding. "We haven't even had breakfast yet!" stormed the disgusted Godard. He was up and down the line, snatching the pipes from their mouths, yelling, protesting, demanding justice from the *comprador*. The only result was to make the porters more wary, quicker to drop the pipes down the legs of their pants as this passionate devil approached. At 9.15 they did stop for breakfast in a village where a huge fire worked by a bellows promised a quick brew of tea. And, inevitably, there was sufficient cover in the surrounding houses for the porters to retreat for another, less hurried, draw at their pipes.

It was the morning of Thursday the 13th of June. Prince Borghese's party had been at work since before dawn—without the incitement of vermin the Prince was always on the road some two hours ahead of his rivals—and were fighting the most critical phase of the five-day battle for Kalgan.

The Italian sailors had turned back on the previous day, when they were in the high country between two mountain ranges. The chain which they had then left in the south was the buttress of the Great Wall, and they could still see the square towers of the spaced strong-points along every ridge of that horizon. Ahead of them lay the worst stretch, but for the moment, on the Wednesday morning, the car rolled on without too much difficulty, and there was time to salute the leaders of the last camel caravans of the season as they came down towards the capital, the camels often bleeding at the nose halter which tied them to the tail of the beast ahead. There was camel traffic in their direction too—generally the trains of unladen camels going back for the summer to the pastures of the Mongolian prairies, where their soft, sore hooves, torn by the rocks and mountains, could heal before another year of labour.

The towing-party was making a faster rate than the camel trains. But it, in its turn, was overtaken by the equivalent of the post-chaise traffic, the Government courier or the wealthy merchant going at the best possible speed to Kalgan or beyond. The faster vehicles were palankeens, or sedan chairs, carried by mules, and a troop of mules cantered behind to serve as remounts

If the passenger was an official he had an escort of servants according to his degree, and he attached to the outside of his palankeen the red case containing his hat of office, a tall straw cone. His importance might be guessed from the number of eyes on his peacock's feather, if it could be seen as he drew the dust-curtains to regard the notable, but apparently ludicrous, *chi-cho* as he passed. The Empress bestowed the decoration of the Pea-cock's Feather (One Eye), or with two or three eyes, with the same care for precedence observed by the British Sovereign, who stretched the Royal Victorian Order from Knight Grand Cross down to Member (Fifth Class).

They paused to lunch on cheese and corned beef outside Hwai-lai, and the population sauntered out of the gates to inspect them, carrying on the flattened palms of their hands, like waiters hold-ing trays, the cages of singing birds, which it was their custom to take for an afternoon walk. It was Borghese's easy reception of one of these citizens—who drained half a bottle of his wine, and, during the subsequent exhilaration, climbed on to the Itala, and tooted the horn until it sulked—which was responsible for the circus mood of the inhabitants who met du Taillis with gongs and cymbals on the following night.

After lunch they began the ascent of the Yean Jan range of mountains, the second in the three great terraces of mountain chains which they had to climb before their cars could run under their own power on the high tableland of Mongolia. The passes closed in, and the slope sharpened. The company of porters and crew braced themselves for the hotter skirmish, and with picks and spades, crowbars and levers, cut away boulders, built up ruts, and eased the car, groaning on its springs, over the worst obstacles.

They came out of the last of the day's defiles, and there, before them, lay a green plateau, a prairie by comparison with the steep and narrow track they had lately been forced into. Borghese's eyes lit up. It should be possible to drive the car. His animation was caught by the porters, who shook off the fatigue of the after-noon, unharnessed the horse and mule and donkey, detached the tow-ropes, and stood back like children awaiting a pantomime. Borghese untied the string that had kept the Italian flag furled through the ascent. Guizzardi started the engine. Borghese, Guizzardi, and Barzini were off at what seemed to them fantastic speed, though the ruts and pools and boulders never allowed them to get into higher than second gear. Drunk with pride and new-found power they lurched through villages, hooted madly as they saw ahead the fast palankeens that had passed them earlier, and laughed as the muleteers hurriedly dismounted to hold the heads of the beasts as they thundered by. The radiator began to steam. They stopped outside a village to refill it. The men of the community crowded round, and made a sort of conversation. They peered incessantly under the car. "Where is the horse?" they asked. They had brought water, and the beast had consumed it, but—where *was* the beast. Guizzardi took off the bonnet and showed them the engine. It meant nothing to them. They could not see the beast.

They drove in the evening to the quiet village of Shin Pao-wan, where the air was full of the song of birds. Cages hung by twos and threes at every door, all holding larks from the desert, and the people sat on their doorsteps and listened to the song. A *grande dame* of the locality, her face a thick porcelain paste of white and pink, and with scarlet lips, passed the invaders on a white mule, over whose flanks her rich silk dress fell in folds. She crossed a tiny bridge, took a last covert look at them, and was gone. The Imperial mail from Russia passed by, escorted by Russian cavalry, on the transit from Peking into Siberia. The mounted escort was able to give news of the progress of the rest of the motor-cars. Dinner was served. The Italians went early to their room in the inn to sleep. To-morrow they had to climb the third range, the most exacting stage of all.

Again they left before dawn, and in the dark they would not put the Itala to speed, but hitched back the tow-ropes for the porters, who had caught them up. Before them lay the massive Lian Ya-miao, the highest mountain in the area, and when they reached its face they found themselves trapped between the mountain and the turbulent Hun Ho river. A ford led through its yellow waters. Camels had the height and delicacy of tread to pass through it, but they would not risk the Itala. They were forced to take it on the narrow ledge running along the mountain. It was a dangerous, slow climb, with the car's wheels never more than inches from the precipice. The angle of the slope changed to a downward drop. The men had to fight the car, heaving it back from behind as its weight plunged it forward. At the extreme of tension Guizzardi stood at the controls, steering it to shave the mountainside, but groaning as the step twisted and splintered against the rock. When the men were exhausted they had to run for great stones with which to wedge the wheels while they rested.

The downward slope led to a stretch of black mud, into which the wheels sank a foot deep. The crew heaved on, shaking the mud from their boots and leggings each time they withdrew their feet. Ahead lay a paddy-field. There was no way round. Almost at the end of the flooded field the car stuck. It was immovable. Exploring with feet and hands, the porters announced that it was wedged in tree-roots. Guizzardi had to dismount a hatchet and cut straight down into the water, until he had severed the lengths of root, on either side of the wheel, which clawed on to the car. They continued, rested, ate, and took up the struggle again. The knife-edged corridor of the last and most terrible gorge was ahead.

The narrow path was now entirely composed of sharp, mobile boulders. They were ill-fitting, not beaten down into any solid way, but apparently left where the last fierce torrent had deposited them. The wheels caught between them, jammed against them, displaced them, and crushed them against the gearbox. The chassis was creaking as if the days of unnatural traction had strained it from its true shape. The responses of the porters to the shantyman came low and inarticulate, in a kind of drugged chorus. The gorge was now such a narrow V that one side of the car was continually climbing it, and the wheels were forced out of true by the weight of the vehicle. When the rock jutted out from the wall to bar the passage of the car completely the entire projection had to be cut away with picks. And then, suddenly, a strong wind touched the streaming faces of the sweating men, and they looked up and saw that there was broad blue sky ahead. The free air of the plains of Mongolia was blowing down on them, and they were within minutes of standing there, on the summit, letting it flow over their bodies like the sea. There was no need for more encouragement. With the machined co-ordination that the experience of the days had given them, the porters heaved, edged, hammered, and levered, until they ran almost lightly up the last diminishing slope and on to the Mongolian plain, as confident as a gun-crew at an artillery review.

There seemed to be not the peak of a single mountain ahead of them. They had outclimbed almost every crest, and they stood on a plateau 6000 feet high, appearing almost to offer a clear run into Europe. It was, in fact, a mirage, for the next hurdle was only twenty miles on. The surface was still too irregular for Borghese to risk the engine. If they could see no mountain, a high city wall was certainly jutting into the sky in the distance. It was the defences of Hsin Wa-fu, the administrative and military centre of the area. A detachment from the garrison was already galloping up to inspect them. They halted near, but did not speak, in contrast to the very friendly approach of all the Chinese they had encountered so far on the journey; and, after noting the number and style of the party with clear hostility, they rode off as if to report on an invasion force.

The Italian party moved towards the town, and found quarters in one of the inns. The porters, who were in a state of exaltation after completing so successfully their twelve-hour haul, lost no time in ensuring that some of the magic of the *chi-cho* rubbed off on themselves. They boasted to the crowds of townsfolk about the manner in which the car had run by itself on the previous day. Their tales were received not only with incredulity, but with derision. The bystanders' attitude of ridicule clearly penetrated to Ettore Guizzardi, whose pride had already been hurt by Borghese's order that they should enter even such an imposing town as Hsin Wa-fu at the end of the belittling tow-ropes. Unable to stand the loss of face, he suddenly moved to the front of the car, started it, mounted it, and sent it speeding round the courtyard of the caravanserai. The spectators not only believed at last: they feared. In a frenzy they streamed for the gates, leapt on to stable roofs, and out of the yard that way, and within seconds had completely fled the camp.

Before the evening meal Barzini, who had two newspapers to

serve, wrote his copy and walked to the telegraph-station. It was a round trip of six miles, and he had already completed thirty miles over the roughest country that day. In the telegraph office the two clerks on duty were recumbent on their *kangs*. The air was thick with the smoke of opium. The clerks were not hostile, but very high.

"I wish to send a telegram to Europe," began Barzini.

A clerk offered him a glass of tea. "We are in communication with Peking and Kalgan," he volunteered after long thought.

"It is the same line," said Barzini.

"For three hours a day we are in communication with Peking," explained the clerk, "and for three hours with Kalgan."

"Europe——" said Barzini.

"Peking," interrupted the clerk.

"And Kalgan," added his colleague.

Suddenly Barzini realized the impossibility of getting through to these happy minds in the short time he was to spend in the city. And if he could not communicate with *them* he would never reach Milan or London. He screwed up his dispatches, walked out of the office, and began the long trek back to the inn.

Another dawn start and an early haul brought them to the top of the last pass before Kalgan. The ropes were stowed. The crew mounted. The porters would not be needed for another twenty miles, after which they were to obey their father's voice on the final passage of all. The stowage of tackle and testing of the engine was done under the shade of some trees, in front of a graceful buddhist temple. An old blind monk in his saffron robe came out on to the steps on the arm of a brother, and listened, and nodded as the young monk explained the shape and apparent power of the chariot below, and—prompted by the proud porters, who felt they had a share in it—told of the far places the chariot was going to visit.

Borghese put the car in gear, and the Itala ploughed through sand and mud to Kalgan, the key to Mongolia. It was a strange, ancient, and prosperous frontier town of China's far west, which had shaken off early crudities, yet still retained the incompleteness of an outpost. Rough-hewn Kalgan had established itself over four centuries as the funnel through which the goods of China poured into Russia and the West. All the tea that had made the *samovar* the most important utensil in the Empire had passed through these unimpressive walls, until the cataclysmic upheaval in the tradition of trade caused seven years earlier by the opening of the Trans-Siberian Railway. The protection of trade made necessary a military command headquarters, and there were really two cities of Kalgan, the civil and the military, varying greatly in their style. They were four miles distant from each other, yet joined by mutual suburbs: this in itself, Barzini reflected, was difficult for his Western readers to accept; one assimilated the fact that the East was 'teeming' with its huge populations, yet one never prepared mental acceptance of the vast cities that must house them; and, if one finally acquiesced that Peking was probably 25 square miles in area, it was still difficult to apply a proportionate scale to unheard-of dots on the map on the fringe of Mongolia.

The Chinese commercial city was ill-kept. The streets between the warehouses were maintained with little consideration for public amenity. The garrison city was straight and square, easily commanded by artillery, neat with the whitewash passed over from its barracks and parade-grounds, and with a host of pretty houses, which proved that the military calling encouraged a certain elegance. Perhaps it came from the soldiers, perhaps from the quartermasters. The beau-monde of the West of 1907 (which was biased, but not unintelligent) believed that the Chinese produced businessmen of the utmost integrity and soldiers of low calibre, because men from the highest classes became merchants and men from the lowest classes became soldiers—the exact reverse being true of Japan. The soldiers of Kalgan were, in any case, Mongols, and not Chinese, and the suburbs between the cities was inhabited mainly by merchants who did not like to live where they worked. If the tea trade was dying, the prosperity of Kalgan was not yet doomed. A core of Europeans continued to live there because it was profitable, though they were outnumbered by the Europeans in the religious missions of all faiths, who had come back to Kalgan after fleeing from the Boxer massacres. There were some missionaries who combined commerce with the Gospel—notably a man who gave Borghese valuable intelligence of the route through Mongolia, based on his regular expeditions into the plains to spread mutual prosperity by judicious horse-trading and the Word of the Lord by distributing Bibles.

Soldiers, merchants, missionaries, and the rich Chinese agents all gave the Italians a warm welcome, as visitors to whom hospitality was due, new faces who livened their somewhat dull daily round, and pioneers who might yet blaze a new trail of commerce to revive their fortunes. An outstanding welcome was given to Prince Borghese by Dorliac, the local Russo-Chinese Bank manager. The party put up in the bank's offices, and turned its courtyard into an automobile pit.

In this courtyard the crew remounted the body of the Itala, discarded for the journey through the three mountain terraces, and Guizzardi decided to modify the exhaust. Anticipating the trip through the burning Gobi Desert, he believed that the heat from the engine should be dispersed as soon as possible. Since protests from the scanty population were unlikely to be effective he fitted open racing exhausts, welding two outlets direct on to the engine casing. While he did this Borghese made a number of diplomatic calls on the Civil Governor, the Tartar General, and representatives of the European community. In turn he received them in reciprocal hospitality.

The Itala reached Kalgan on Friday the 14th of June. On this day the French party was in the depth of the struggle with the third and last succession of gorges, having prepared itself for the conflict with a more peaceful night, deliberately spent away from the distractions of a Chinese inn, in a camp of their own pitching. In the morning the de Dions and the Spyker had been able to run under their own power, again never exceeding second gear. But the Contal tri-car had been unable to advance on its engine. The reason was its wheel-disposition, the very fact that it was a three-wheeler. The conventional cars could avoid the deep ruts made by generations of carts. On the narrow track they could still get their left-hand wheels on the bank between the ruts, and their right-hand wheels on rough ground. When the Contal shifted a half-width to one side the rear wheel still ran in one of the ruts, and there was not space to drive it completely on one side of the track. When the others reached the base of the gorge they waited for the Contal to arrive on its tow-ropes.

They came to the point where Borghese had declined to ford the Hun Ho, and had taken the destructive track along the face of the mountain. The decision of the Frenchmen was that none of their cars except the Contal was narrow enough to take the cliffside path, and therefore the river must be forded. Goubault and the French soldiers reconnoitred the river-bed on horseback, and reported that its bottom of fine gravel would not clamp unduly on the wheels. The horsemen then went back into the river to mark the shallowest spots, and, one by one, the cars hurled themselves into the stream at speed. Throwing up the yellow water in a high bow-wave, they made the crossing. But they found they had committed themselves to a succession of minor streams and marshes which lacked the clear gravel bed of the Hun Ho. They had to unship their tackle, and haul the cars by block and pulley through a number of tricky spots, taking far more time over the transit than the Itala had required; and in the end they still had to commit themselves to the final haul along cliff tracks crudely levelled between the rock-face and the preci-pice. The descents were, as Borghese and his crew had found, far more perilous than the upward hauls. Godard, in particular, nearly plunged to destruction when his porters lost control.

It was not until the next day, Saturday, that the party reached Hsin Wa-fu. Du Taillis and Godard made the long walk to the telegraph office that Barzini had already experienced with chagrin, but—such is the unpredictable aftermath of opium— not only got their telegrams away, but decided the officials were "charming." They slept that night twelve miles from Kalgan, very contented after a supper of fried potatoes *à la* Godard and stewed apricots *à la* du Taillis. The next morning they reached Kalgan.

For a long time they wandered quite lost among the tanneries and hide warehouses of the lower, commercial city, and momen-tarily they did not care that they were lost. They were enjoying a small triumph in the acclaim the populace gave them—the gods who were promenading in horseless chariots. The Civil Governor had already posted proclamations, bristling with large square seals, announcing that the visitors were friendly, the people should take care not to get in the way of their machines, and it was highly dangerous to touch them since serious consequences might follow; indeed, the serious consequences—apart from electric shock or the casualties from putting a car into reverse gear—were listed, and included the customary Chinese civil penalties, with the possibility of a visit to the execution ground. These warnings were sufficient to keep the crowd at bay for the first few minutes. But when Godard, with a touch of exhibitionism, smartly struck his horn bulb he went too far. A chariot that did not need horses—that the population had been prepared for. But a trumpet that did not need lips—how was this scientific marvel achieved? Disregarding any *ju-ju* about the untouchable *chi-cho*, the people of Kalgan hurled themselves on the Spyker, thumped and squeezed the horn, until the irascible Cormier ordered his fleet to turn and flee.

They found the Russo-Chinese Bank at last, with the Itala transformed in its courtyard. They accepted Dorliac's offer of garage space there, though there was no living accommodation remaining, and the Frenchmen had to put up at a poor hotel. But the immediate concern was to overhaul the machines. Cormier, Collignon, and Godard had conceded a two-day advantage to Borghese in Kalgan—which they would not have yielded if they had not waited for the Contal on the outskirts of Peking and in the power-runs between the gorges. They were due to leave at dawn on the morrow. There was no time to lose. Foucault and Bizac had a field day. They dismantled, greased, cleaned, tuned. Bizac removed the silencers of the de Dions, adding to the machine-gun rattle already created by the Itala under tests. Pons, making every effort to balance his tri-car towards the rear, sawed off his front mudguards.

Dorliac invited the entire party to a festive luncheon. Then the mechanics went back to their yard, and the drivers took a lesson in foreign exchange. The Mexican dollar, the common currency of Peking and the ports, would buy nothing in Mongolia. Throughout the provincial Empire the unit was the tael—a weight of pure silver; but it was an uncertain unit because the weight of the standard tael, and even its standard of purity, varied from province to province.

In Kalgan, which governed Mongolia, the tael was equivalent to 37 grammes of silver. It could be divided into 16 to make cattys or into 100 to make pieuls. The division was done quite simply—with a knife.

But although the expert might chop a bar of silver expertly into the right coinage as nonchalantly as a sailor cutting tobacco, the novice would need scales to weigh his off-cuts—and in any case all vendors regarded all purchasers as novices. The scales were, therefore, essential. Dorliac demonstrated them. A pan held by three silk threads operated an arm which marked the weight. The balance was easy enough to read, but cutting the silver seemed formidable. Cormier was the only one who had any confidence, and in the end most of the party gave him their dollars and accepted the taels he offered them, jauntily hacking them off a silver ingot with his pet Swiss Army jack-knife. Cormier was immediately appointed treasurer, and began his financial career by shaving off an infinitely small sliver of silver when Longoni bought a glass of milk. When both the woman and Cormier expressed satisfaction over the bargain there was a rush for the dealer's services. The most popular purchase was buckskin, which was offered very cheaply by the Mongols, and, apart from a strong goatish smell, seemed to give a guarantee of warm nights in the notorious cold of the desert and of Siberia after sundown. Cormier industriously hacked at his ingots, and halved and quartered his slices in order not to give too much money, putting all the little remnants into his pocket, where they accumulated, until he was nervous of bringing out his handkerchief.

The overhaul of the cars was completed. They were filled with petrol and oil. Dorliac gave the party a farewell dinner. It was not as gay as the luncheon. The travellers were tired and preoccupied. But Dorliac, a true Russian, did not spare the toasts. And at the end of the dinner they rose all together to touch glasses and drink to the success of the trip. Reveille was at three in the morning. They were to be off at four.

Under the influence of Prince Borghese the expedition left the Russo-Chinese Bank at Kalgan punctually at four. But they could not leave the city. The gates were locked fast, as they had been through centuries of nights, and a sentry had to be wakened before they could emerge. The tireless Italian had reconnoitred the country by horse on the day before the French reached Kalgan. He reported rough, rising country for fifteen miles, over which the cars should be able to move fairly efficiently, and then the last, and perhaps the most gruelling, mountain climb of all before the positive plateau of the Mongolian plain was reached. For this stretch the porters would again be necessary, and they had been sent off the previous night.

The remaining French soldiers had stayed behind in Kalgan, two men only accompanied the motorists to the final preliminary staging-point. One was the Chinese major-domo of the Italian Legation in Peking, who had travelled with Borghese as interpreter since the departure from the capital, and was now a fourth passenger on the Itala, to his intense discomfort. The other was the French attaché Goubault, who had interpreted for Cormier's party. He kept up with the caravan on his horse.

The route lay up a steep valley, as yet untouched by the rays of the sun. The Itala managed to hold twenty miles an hour at the beginning, but gradually slowed. The Spyker, fully loaded as it had always been—the Itala had had its body remounted, but had not yet taken on its spare fuel or its baggage—was forced to come down to first gear, and to stop every quarter of an hour to let the engine cool. The de Dion-Boutons followed, but the Contal was soon out of sight. Borghese came first to the foot of the gorge.

The porters had not yet arrived. But from a temple half-way up the cliff a frail old man emerged, with a teapot and cups and a great dish of hard-boiled eggs, with portions of dry pastry. The Civil Governor of Kalgan was paying his last respects, and, through an *aide*, offered breakfast at the Mongolian frontier. The crews of the first four cars made an excellent meal, and Borghese called for his porters and set off on the last haul. The Frenchmen delayed inordinately, waiting for Pons. Finally the tri-car appeared. It was being pushed by Pons and Foucault. Again the third wheel could not disengage from the ruts, and the engine would not drive. Nothing was said to the unhappy crew. But to the others the prospect of the Contal's driving into Paris seemed remote.

Of all the hauls they had made with their porters this last climb seemed the worst. They had constantly to use levers as well as their ropes. They declared that it would have been a hard task even for goats, but, at the cost of exhaustion, they finally did it with cars. In two hours they reached the top. At last they saw the true tableland—a limitless plain of green. They started their engines, and ran on for another few miles for the rendezvous with Borghese's carts, which carried, as well as his spare parts and heavy luggage, the portable cans of petrol which they had all remitted from Kalgan. They reached the rendezvous. Now Borghese began finally to strip for action.

It was Monday the 17th of June. The time was noon. In the seven days since leaving Peking the raiders had completed roughly 200 miles. There were some 9000 miles to go. The next thousand miles were probably the most hazardous. This was the crossing of Mongolia. They had been unable to plant any stores of spare parts in the area, and if they broke down no help could be expected from anyone but the members of the party—certainly there were no mechanics in Mongolia. All they had been able to prepare, and this was at heavy cost, was the petrol dumps which the camel caravan had laid down at the telegraph relay-stations in the desert.

Borghese put ten days' provision of food in his car. He filled his spare tanks, giving him fuel for 600 miles of normal travel, and brought his potential up even more by packing in some of the

45-litre (10-gallon) cans of petrol that had been brought to the spot from Kalgan. He fixed a battery of spare tyres on the back of the car, and piled more behind the front seats. It was already obvious that, for the first stages at least, the perfectly adequate back seat between the wing tanks would be occupied by stores, not crew. The third man would, in fact, have to sit on the floor-boards of the car, by the feet of the navigator, with his own feet, or one of them—all there was room for—on the carriage step. Fortunately, the step was still existent on that side. The other had been torn off in the gorges.

Having allowed for stores and crew, Borghese could then allocate the extremely small space remaining for luxuries, like warmth, shelter, and comfort. There was a litter, on the grass around the car, of furs, beds, waterproofs, map-cases, and the odd camping gadget that every one acquires before a long journey, "because it may be useful." Most of this would have to be abandoned. The first to be rejected were the beds.

Instead Guizzardi was rigging a large canvas hood over the car, supported on substantial iron stanchions, which fitted into holes and grooves already prepared. The hood was intended to give cover from sun and weather by day and a complete shelter for the car and the crew at night, when it was dismounted, and put up again in a different, ingenious way. With this basic protection it was possible for Borghese to abandon the camp beds with a light heart. But the hood was to last for only a day.

The whooping crowd of porters had caught up now with the stationary cars. They had already been paid off, and they need not have come. But this was an adventure in which they had had some hand, and they were not so keen to spend their money that they rejected the natural urge to witness the climax of their work. In addition there was a large amount of loot to be collected. The huge mound of impedimenta round the Itala could certainly not be loaded, and perhaps the other cars would be forced to jettison stores. But the porters had also been joined by Chinese soldiers and some caravan drivers, who had temporarily halted their beasts, and rushed over to see what was happening. The jostling crowd was pressing in a little too closely on the pile of possessions. Guizzardi, with peasant caution, seized one of the stanchions of the hood, and drew a magic circle in the ground round the car and its crew. Nobody dared to pass it. Across the circle the loot was now handed out—heavy spare springs (the loss of which was later regretted), two of the four steel-plate tracks, which Borghese decided were too heavy to take any farther, the fine camp beds, mattresses, tins of jam, even spare petrol.

The other four drivers had no decisions of this nature to make since they had left Peking loaded as they meant to continue. Godard had certain difficulties, but only because of the plight of Pons. Pons was desperately trying to take the weight off the front of his Contal, yet the front was the only area where any baggage or stores could be carried. Godard already had the scanty bedding and personal luggage of the tri-car crew. He took on board the Spyker now the heavy tool-kit and set of spare parts which Pons was carrying, all Pons's food and petrol stocks, and his spare tyres. It meant that the Spyker must, for Pons's sake, keep very close to the Contal. The extra cargo also crippled the neat stacking of Godard and du Taillis's gear. They were forced to lash the extra luggage down with cord hitched to any suitable projection.

Accepting the spare tyres was critical. They were not heavy, but bulky. To accept them Godard had first to unload and abandon his precious crate of Mumm's champagne. Then he had to leave behind some of his petrol. He did the best he could. He lashed one ten-gallon can on his right-hand running-board, wedged another in the middle of the tyres which already crowded the other running-board, set a can in du Taillis's place to go between his knees, and with his passenger's help pushed another into the hard-packed space behind the seats. There was still one can left.

Should he take the petrol and tell Pons to take back some of his gear on to the Contal? Godard thought quickly. Then, with a great goalkeeper's side-vault, he sprang up, and gave an enormous kick at the last can, which was perched on the end of the front mudguard as he had considered its fate. The can fell down, and burst open. Ten gallons of petrol—perhaps 120 miles of desert travel—leaked into the short, dry grass. Du Taillis shook his head. "You have made a mistake," he said. "You should not have wasted your reserves. Who knows what can happen to us?"

Godard said nothing, but with a very slight nod indicated the pathetic parcels of Pons's baggage littering the neatly disposed Spyker, and then the face of the Contal driver. He was already looking all in. He and Foucault had pushed the awkward machine many miles that day without aid. The young man's face was drawn and grey. His cheeks were sunken, and his eyes were swollen with fatigue. Du Taillis could not find it in his heart to continue reproaching Godard.

Godard shrugged his shoulders, smiled, and picked up his dog Pékine. Then, quite lightly, he uttered his most serious miscalculation. "I should think if we can't reach Udde, surely our friends won't refuse us a few litres of petrol."

Udde was a telegraph-station, and for Godard the next fuel point, roughly 370 miles away. On their schedule the party hoped to reach it in two and a half days' time. There were two routes from Kalgan to Urga, the holy city of the Buddhist lamas in the north-west tracts of Mongolia. One, the Mandarins' Road, was the most commonly used. It was the track for the ox-drawn carts, and had a number of relay points and rough caravanserais along its length. The geographical placing of these points stretched the route into a broad curve, but the extra length was compensated by the comparative frequency of travellers along it, who afforded the prospect of some assistance in distress, even as messengers. The party had, however, rejected this route. They chose the camel track, which passed no habitations or sources of food along its length—indeed, very few wells—but because it struck almost straight across the desert was 100 miles shorter. It was calculated that its surface, not being broken up by the cart-wheels of the Mandarins' Road, would be better for the cars, and apparently essential for the Contal. And navigation across it had become a simple matter since, six years earlier, the telegraph line to Russia had been laid along it. The telegraph-posts had merely to be followed or, if the surface forbade it, at least kept in sight.

The general route being followed to Europe was a haul to the north-west for about 1500 miles, taking them sixteen degrees higher in latitude, and then a course roughly due west through Tomsk, Omsk, Nijni-Novgorod, and Moscow. In view of the change of latitude Borghese decided that his party must retain the fur cloaks they had bought, though he was at present broiling in khaki drill and a solar topee. The furs were eased under the ropes containing the high, ungainly load at the back of the Itala. Guizzardi, supreme with an engine or a chassis, had the single inefficiency of being an incompetent packer, and none of his party could improve on his work. Borghese checked that the rest of the party were ready. The porters chorused a farewell. Barzini gave Goubault a brief dispatch—"We are crossing the Mongolian frontier . . ." scribbled in his notebook—and begged the Frenchman to have it telegraphed from Kalgan. The engines started. The party advanced. Goubault watched them, and galloped south. It was three o'clock in the afternoon.

They went down the valley and on to the plain. The going was still rough. Ettore Guizzardi was sitting on the floorboards of the Itala at Barzini's feet, taking some of the strain on the carriage step. Immediately he began to groan—not at his own discomfort, but at the terrible punishment the car was taking. Clearly it was far too heavily loaded. At every bump the back springs, which had started almost flat, yielded, and brought the weight of the chassis down on the differential. "We are breaking up!" he cried. It was only a question of which would go first, the springs or the differential casing. They could never repair the casing, and they had left their spare springs in Kalgan. Prince Borghese at the wheel, pale, but resolutely in control, answered curtly. "Nothing will happen immediately. But the car will not stand this for long. We shall have to decrease the load at the first opportunity." "Now?" pleaded Guizzardi. "To-night," declared the Prince, and drove stolidly on.

The cars began to gain speed as the surface improved. The mountain country was falling behind. Du Taillis, in the Spyker, with the high petrol-can between his knees, allowed himself to relax and reflect that now, at last, they were really on the way. And he began to shape a few phrases for his first dispatch. The wind was catching his face. For the first time in a month the air seemed pure and keen. The dust of Peking was only a memory, along with the claustrophobic enclosure of the mountains and the suffocating rain in the gorges. In the exhilaration of the moment the Spyker and the Itala occasionally raced each other. First

Godard would lead, and then Borghese, both more seriously interested in their comparative performance than they pretended. Then they would stop and wait for the de Dions, and at least wait to hear the sound of the Contal behind.

They ran on for forty miles, and then camped for the night. They stopped near a cluster of houses, in a small cultivated area where they knew they could find water. The women working in the fields saw the strange machines stop, and ran away in terror, limping on their deformed feet into the plantation. The men surrounded them, watching in silence as the Itala crew dismantled their car hood, and converted it into a spacious tent, supported by the Itala, and including the car in its shelter. Again the Contal was late. It was still being pitched on to its nose, and the exhausted crew had had to push it for several stretches of bad country. It was clear that the enemy of the three-wheeler was not only ruts, but sand. There were hundreds of miles of sand ahead. When the Contal finally arrived the Frenchmen formed a laager, the four cars on the outside of a circle and the tents of the crews in the middle. The lay-out of the Italian tent compelled a certain privacy for Borghese. But the cooking was done jointly, and the journalists were appointed chefs. Du Taillis, the soup king, shredded an ample supply of cakes of Maggi—preserved soup was not then tinned, but produced in cubes like Oxo—and Barzini began the preparation of an Italian speciality. It was at this stage that the Itala crew discovered that, through improvidence, absent-mindedness, or misplaced generosity to the porters at the last stop, they had lightened the car so drastically that they had no cooking apparatus. The French were operating on efficient petrol pressure-stoves, and Barzini had no stove at all. Rejecting the offer of camel-dung from the large crowd who were now watching curiously, Barzini did the best he could to heat his speciality with a soldering lamp. But his contribution to the banquet tasted evilly of oil.

The mass of villagers had been joined by a striking young Mongolian, who had ridden up with two retainers. They dismounted near the laager, spread carpets, crumbled a pack of camel-dung, and made a pot of tea. Then the leader approached the party. He was a fine young man, dressed in purple silk, with a yellow silk hat. He began to talk in an obviously friendly manner. Borghese and Barzini could both get along in Chinese, but had not added the Mongolian language to their studies. The unflappable Borghese, however, produced a Mongolian phrasebook, which he had not jettisoned yet, and understood that their guest was a chief, that they would probably pass his village on the morrow, and that he would be delighted if they would drop in for tea.

The sun set. The light was held on the vast plain, but in the advancing gloom of the south-east little could be seen. The Mongolians had evidently heard something, however, for they rose and looked out over the dark plain. A horseman was approaching. He was a Chinese soldier sent from Kalgan, and he carried mail that had arrived there that morning addressed to members of the expedition. The soldier hardly stayed for thanks, but remounted, wheeled into the night, and set off on the sixty miles to Kalgan.

They opened their letters from home, and held the pages up to the west for the last of the twilight to catch them. Here, in Mongolia, to be taken in mind to Paris, Rome, Milan, Provence, on the very eve of such an uncertain adventure, moved them profoundly. They sat on in silence after the light was gone, remembering the past and trying to hear again the sound of the words in their letters, but forgetting them, and all except Barzini too shy to strike a match and read them again. Most of them had wives; Godard had never committed himself for long, though there were travelling girls in one or two fairs, now perhaps plodding through France, who owed him for some delight, and might have dropped him a line. But they could not write—the sluts!

The glow of their cigarettes was all that they could see of one another now. Idly at first they began to talk of when they would get home.

"It is 12,000 kilometres at the minimum," said Bizac. "We are in June. Unless we get trapped by the winter in Siberia we shall arrive in time to celebrate the New Year with our friends."

"Don't exaggerate," interrupted Cormier. "Before the start I calculated daily averages of one hundred kilometres. I expected plenty of snags, though I admit I did not allow sufficiently for the triple barrier of the mountains up to Kalgan. But we can make up for that, and I still stick to 120 days. We shall get to Paris for the opening of Parliament in mid-October."

"We shall get there when we get there," said Collignon blandly. "The only thing that worries me is whether my cigarettes come through with the rations. *Des cigarettes de la régie*—French State-monopoly cigarettes," he emphasized. "They are the only ones for a good smoke."

Du Taillis had already committed himself in *Le Matin*—though he had never confessed that it was he who wrote it—to a journey lasting between two and three months. He hesitated, and then decided to take the plunge. "What are you talking about!" he exclaimed. "On the 1st of September I shall be bathing in the sea from the sands of Olonne or Royan."

They looked towards Borghese, but he did not commit himself. They knew that he had never paid high tribute to the organizing calculations of the Paris committee. If he thought he could do it in less time—well, he had planned conscientiously enough.

They lapsed into silence. They had dined. They were at peace. They sensed a relaxation of tension, and felt the beginnings of comradeship. They had the same aim. They faced the same risks. They each had comparable courage. The moon rose in the clear sky. The descending cold crept into their bodies, and an occasional shiver as they breathed made them realize how deeply it had taken possession of them. But still they did not stir. They felt that they wanted to prolong for ever this moment of peace and nearness of spirit. It was the first time they had ever been alone in one another's company, and eaten together and sat silent afterwards. Borghese, Godard, Cormier, Collignon, Pons, Barzini, Guizzardi, du Taillis, Longoni, Bizac, Foucault. They were never to be all together again.

8 ◎ ◎ Acceleration

At three in the morning of the next day, Tuesday the 18th of June—Waterloo Day—Pons and Foucault were sent off first on the Contal. It seemed hard that the crew which was the most exhausted should take the field first, but the tri-car had been forced to a standstill many times on the previous day, causing undeniable delay to the others. To give it a start should mean that the expedition would lose less time, and the other crews would be in a position to lend a hand when they came up, if assistance was necessary. An hour later the Spyker and the two de Dions started together. The Itala remained, not because the Prince was not now burning to start, but because the crew were having great trouble in fixing the luggage. Borghese had jettisoned the remaining two steel tracks, the stanchions intended to hold the hood over the car during the day, several crowbars and other heavy tools, and five days' provisions. The hood was now bundled as a tent for the night, but it was difficult for the Italians to keep their various packages lashed together as they rose above the lines of the reserve tanks. It was almost five o'clock when the Itala started, its large flag glowing in the level rays of the rising sun.

The Frenchmen, as motorists and sportsmen, had agreed that it was unreasonable to restrict the high-powered Itala to the comparatively slow speed of the convoy. This might mean that when there was a demand for all-out aid the Italian crew would be missing. But it was felt that, if it were necessary, the Itala was the best machine to be called back to give assistance, since it could cruise at fifty miles an hour or more. They did not want to condemn a car built for such high speed to the fatiguing operation of chugging along with the ten-horsepowers, and they did see the

ogical function of a fast car being used for scouting and organizing purposes—a rôle which admittedly demanded a co-operative
crew. It was felt that an understanding that Borghese could be a
lone wolf, yet would still co-operate with the convoy, reconciled
all the interests at stake.

Godard and du Taillis, enjoying the responsive drive of the
Spyker engine, pushed confidently forward, never more than a
mile or so from the de Dions. Camel track or no, the path was still
heavily rutted, and the car's springs were dangerously flattened
with the extra weight of the Contal's equipment. Indubitably the
most comfortable passenger was the dog on the writer's knee.
They depended on sound, rather than sight, to check the where-
abouts of the others, for the vegetation of the Mongolian plain
was of the type that springs fast and high after heavy rains, and
on either side of the track it was often taller than the car. Some
fifteen miles from the start the three medium-horsepower cars
came up with the Contal. Godard leaned out and called as they
passed.

"Eh, bien, ça va?"

"Ça va!"

The Spyker plunged down. Although the general line of the
country was that of a plateau, there were a number of deep,
sunken ravines, with a very fast approach and a short but difficult
rise. The stream running through the particular cut they were
negotiating was dangerously muddy at the bottom, and as they
emerged from fording it and ground painfully uphill they agreed
that it was not a crossing to be made at anything but fast speed,
for fear of getting bogged in the mud. It occurred to Godard that
Pons might fall into difficulties here, so they stopped at the top
of the rise, watching the de Dions bumping up towards them, and
prepared to see the tri-car through.

After some time they heard the characteristic noise of Pons's
one-cylinder engine. Then he came into sight, and started descending the valley. Godard shouted—which was useless—and
made urgent signs to clap on speed, which Pons evidently understood. The Contal disappeared into the ravine. There was a
minute of uncertainty. And then his engine was heard roaring
towards them, and he pulled up in the middle of them.

"Ça va, Pons?"

"Mais oui, fort bien."

Godard seemed to be concerned for Pons as for a favourite son. They put the cars in gear again and went on. For about two hours the four of them kept company. The ground was difficult but not enough to irk them by unduly restricting their speed, and at just over twelve miles an hour they began to enjoy the sensation of driving in convoy. Then Godard responded shamelessly to the invitation of a level straight, and put his foot down.

Du Taillis said mildly, "But this is how it should be. It would be good if we could drive into Paris like this, one following the other."

"I don't doubt it," growled Godard darkly. "But you can't ask too much. You don't make an omelette without breaking eggs, and, in any case, you want to be sure that no one has the idea of burning up the others."

"Burning up? What do you mean?"

"Ah, it's a pity you're not an old shuvver like me. You know, I've done the Pyrenees Circuit, the Taurus, Paris–Berlin——"

"Burning up?" repeated du Taillis, interrupting the recital of the Godard dossier.

"Getting past another driver, and not caring a damn so long as you get there first. Now I'll bet——"

"Oh, I've got it."

"Now I'll bet a hundred to one that this Borghese has only one idea in his head, and that's to burn up the rest of us."

At this moment Borghese came up on the track alongside them. They had to admire the performance. The Itala soared along the short grass with infinite grace, as if it were gliding. The Prince drove casually, hardly seeming to pay attention to the road, but pointing out to Barzini at his side various features of the landscape. As he passed the Spyker he slowed to exchange a few words alongside them, and then cut an extravagantly graceful curve through the long grass, and, nonchalantly placing the car on the track again, went on lightly and effortlessly ahead.

The words which du Taillis heard Borghese say are these: "I have just passed Pons. He is very close behind you. He says everything is going according to plan (*tout marche à souhait*)."

Godard watched the disappearing tail of the Itala rather sourly as Cormier pushed alongside and asked what Borghese had said. Godard repeated the message, and added, "There he goes. There's a chap who is only looking for the chance to burn us up."

Cormier, in spite of his professed allegiance to light cars, was also somewhat nettled at the sight of the Itala disappearing with such grace. But all he said was, "That chap ought to be careful. If this is the way he starts it won't be long before he's got a clapped-out Itala on his hands."

That is how du Taillis remembered the incident. Barzini, however, who was driving with Borghese, had an entirely different recollection. As he reported it, the Contal was stopped when they passed it. Pons and Foucault seemed to be examining the engine. Borghese slowed down to offer help, but Pons said it was not necessary. Borghese guessed that they were waiting for the engine to cool, put on speed, and went ahead. *Half an hour* later they overtook the other cars, and greeted them. There was no mention of the Contal being just behind or of everything going according to plan.

Whatever the truth of the matter, Pons was out of the race.

The two de Dions and the Spyker went on together, making no attempt to keep up with the Itala. Cormier took the lead, and he, in his turn, put on a burst of speed, with the temptation of a gentle downward slope ahead. The others kept up with him, making little attempt at navigation. Du Taillis had a map on his lap, in the shade of which Pékine gratefully slept. It was a small-scale map, and the crossroads marked on it ought not to be very far away. Still, it was difficult to judge, and there was always the distant guide-line of the telegraph-posts . . . .

There were no telegraph-posts.

Moreover, there were no tracks showing that the Itala had passed this way.

Du Taillis shouted to Godard, who raced alongside Cormier, and, with three magnificent skids never bettered in the Circuit des Pyrenées, indicated that they should stop.

"The telegraph-posts have disappeared," yelled du Taillis. "Borghese was steering by them."

Cormier refused to concede that his navigation was at fault.

"In this sort of country there's only one road. There just happen to be a few alternatives that all lead to the same place."

All roads might lead to Rome. But this course was leading to Vladivostok. They concluded this when, after another ten minutes' drive, there was no sign of the posts or of Borghese's tracks. Cormier finally agreed to turn square left on the present line, which meant a passage through the head-high grass, in the hope that they would find the posts. No one had a compass. And no one made a serious attempt to read the sun.

The three cars pushed into the high vegetation, and came into ground that was more like dune-country, with sparse, spiky grass, and hares running ahead of them as the cars flushed them out. Then they ran into marshes. Finally they came to a marked track, and the traces of the Itala's anti-skid tyres were clear. So was the line of the telegraph, almost straight ahead. They turned right, and continued their journey along rough and rising ground that forced them into bottom gear. They found a place to get water for their radiators, and then they thought of Pons.

Would the Contal have followed their tracks? Or, since it would not have been diverted by speed or company, would it have stuck to the line of the telegraph, which also carried the Itala's tracks?

They waited for an hour. They found a height from which to survey the plain, and, in turn, kept their Goertz trihedral binoculars on the path by which Pons ought to arrive. They listened, and heard nothing. And then they reasoned out what must have happened.

Pons was almost at their heels. Borghese had said so. The point where they had diverged from the true path was only four miles after Borghese had passed them. Pons would have come up to the fork very soon after them. He must have seen that the tracks diverged, taken his own bearings, and continued correctly on the left-hand track. He would have passed this point two hours ago. No wonder they could see no sign of him. He must be twenty or twenty-five miles farther on the way to their next staging-point.

Pons at that moment was many miles behind, on the track where Borghese had left him. Everything was not going accord-

ng to plan. *There was nothing wrong with his engine. He had
simply run out of petrol. To be accurate, he had half a litre left in
his tank.*

*It was mid-morning. There was no cause for alarm. He had
been keeping up with the convoy, and they would soon stop to
wait for him. They might even ask Prince Borghese to race back
to assist him. It was all a part of the understanding.*

*It was high noon. Surely it was time they had turned back for
him now.*

*It was evening, and the two men were dying of thirst. "Oh, yes,
Foucault, dying. The body has certain reserves, but we were
living beyond our reserves when we started. Granted, there may
be some animal life in us when they find us, but what if our minds
have gone first? We must find water, Foucault. We must leave the
machine and find water, and we must go while it is still light; so
that we are back by the machine when they find us."*

Pons and Foucault walked off into the plain.

Prince Borghese swept on to the north after passing the Spyker
and the de Dions, and he too took the track to the right at the
fork. But he quickly noticed that the line of posts was disappearing to the left, turned and came back to the crossroads, and took
the correct track.

The high vegetation had petered out, and they were running
through a green desert of thin turf, broken by outcrops of flat
rocks. On this pasture many herds of wild Mongol ponies were
grazing, and the arrival of the car seemed to have the same effect
on each herd. At the sound of the engine they would raise their
heads, sniff, and sight the car. Then they would turn, by some
herd reaction, and charge in a solid mass to within a few yards
of the car. At that point they would stop, as if petrified, then turn
and run along the path of the car. But the car outdistanced them
every time. Borghese was driving it at up to forty miles an hour.
But a look-out was watching for him. Ahead of them they saw a
comparatively high, framed erection, rather like a fire-brigade
observation point. It stood in the middle of a collection of *yurtas*,
the ancient dwellings of the nomad Mongols which resemble an
igloo covered with felted wadding—the *yurta* and the igloo may

have the same prototype. As soon as they were observed by the look-out a crowd dashed into the track to stop them, and they recognized the silk-clad Mongol headman who had visited them the previous night. They took tea with him, and dishes of mare's milk and cheese, and were about to end their social call when they heard a voice ask, "*Sprechen Sie Deutsch?*" Prince Borghese answered in German, and began a technical conversation about the Itala car with a young Mongolian. "But where did you learn German?" asked Borghese. "In Berlin," the young man answered. He had spent two years in Berlin, at an international exhibition, to which he had been transported merely to be a Mongolian living in a *yurta*, in the heart of a Berlin hall. At the end of his contract, having learned German in order to talk to the visitors, he returned home to his own plains and his mobile *yurta*.

By noon the Italians had come to the end of the grassland, and the soil was hard red earth, much more irregular in surface than the level plain and harder on the speeding car. And suddenly the engine failed. They were out of petrol from the main tank. They had, therefore, used 83 litres (18 gallons) of petrol, which, by their calculation, should have taken them 130 miles. It was also their calculation that well within 130 miles they should have reached their staging-point, the telegraph-station of Pong-Kiong. While Guizzardi transferred petrol to the main tank and Borghese tightened the ropes lashing their gear the Prince discovered that part of their luggage had dropped off the car. It was Borghese's personal valise. It was an irksome loss to a man of such spruce polish, who had to reconcile himself to going without a shave until he reached the civilization of Siberia.

Borghese decided not to start square searches for the Pong-Kiong relay point, but to go straight ahead. If he had under-estimated the distance he would soon find the post. If he had passed the station, perhaps because it was at a distance from the trunk line and connected by a spur, they had food and fuel to reach the next point and beyond, and they could camp in the desert. But within an hour they had sighted the small compound enclosing a well, where the operator and his small daughter lived alone with three linesmen, 200 miles from a town.

Mister Luck, the telegraph operator had, like all his professional

colleagues, some command of English, which was the international language of China. After a light lunch Barzini wrote his
copy straight on to the telegraph forms which Luck provided, and,
out of interest, went with him to the transmitting-room to watch
the message go out. Luck did not seem very sure of the routine.
After consulting all the regulations, and apparently having difficulty in filling in the official preamble to the telegram, he very
deliberately wrote "No. 1" in the appropriate space on the form.

"Your first to-day?" asked Barzini conversationally.

"No, sir. My first."

"Your first this year?"

"No, sir. The first from Pong-Kiong."

The station had been established six years, and this was the first
message that had originated from it. Luck's usual daily task was
to receive telegrams from Udde, the next station west, and to
relay them to Kalgan—or vice versa—because the signals would
have been too faint for the farther station to receive if there were
no intermediate station to pick them up and send them on. The
traffic Luck handled was of the highest importance. Messages in
diplomatic code or mercantile orders affecting delivery from the
Pacific to the Atlantic would pass through him. He had relayed
the exchanges concerning Chinese Government permission for the
present *raid*, passing between Paris and Peking. Now he was
sending a message, date-lined Pong-Kiong, which would crackle
by way of Peking, Shanghai, Singapore, Aden, Malta, and Gibraltar, and be on the desks of news editors in Fleet Street and
Milan well in time to be set for next morning's newspaper.

Meanwhile "our special correspondent" applied himself to
making a lamb stew in a large pan held over the flame of a soldering lamp.

Five hours after the arrival of the Itala, the Spyker and the two
de Dions drove into the compound. Jean du Taillis jumped down
from the Dutch car, displaying a grey hold-all and asking,
"Whose is this?" Some Mongol horsemen had come across it
after the Itala had passed, and stopped the Spyker many hours
afterwards to request the driver to deliver it.

Godard's first question was, "Where is the Contal?"—though a
glance round the yard, where Guizzardi alone was greasing his

car, had been enough to tell him that the optimism of the French drivers had been false. Pons had not preceded them to Pong Kiong.

Mister Luck, delighted to have company, converted the telegraph office into a dining-room for his guests. But supper was a gloomy meal, not improved by the fact that Barzini's stewed lamb was uneatable. The party was continually listening, hoping to hear the high splutter of the tri-car while there was still light in the sky. Cormier checked with Borghese the last contact with Pons. Borghese repeated that Pons had said that all was well and did not need anything. There was little open conversation. Occasionally the French spoke half-sentences among themselves. They were waiting for an offer by Borghese to use his speed and go back next morning to find the missing crew. At the pace he had set that day he could go and be back by nightfall.

The offer did not come. Borghese went to bed. At ten o'clock the French crews were still talking. Du Taillis, as organizer, was firm about the duty of all the contestants. According to the agreement which all had made, it was absolutely necessary to halt the *raid*, work out together a methodical search-routine, and pick up Pons before going any farther. Du Taillis had no direct authority over the drivers, and he did not put this 'ruling' point-blank to Borghese. He stressed it with the remaining drivers, and, after ten at night, the blunt Cormier went in and woke Borghese, and presented their conception of his duty and his promise.

Borghese's answer was, "I am leaving here for Udde at three in the morning."

Cormier tried to stress the plight of Pons and Foucault. Borghese said they were still in the inhabited zone and Pons would have no difficulty in getting food and, if necessary, manual help.

"But Pons has only Russian money on him. I have been carrying all the silver. He has no Mongol money."

"Then leave him some here," said Borghese.

"I haven't enough."

"You certainly have ten taels. Leave that. I will lend you another ten myself, and that will make twenty. It is more than he will need. The telegraph operator will hold it for him."

1. Guizzardi stood all day, bent over the wheel, flinching as the differential thumped over the rocks.

2. The Itala passes the last Mongolian camel-caravans of the season.

3. Borghese replaces his day canopy, seen above, with a tent for the night. The canopy was abandoned next morning.

4. The Governor's escort chases the Itala at Urga.

Borghese, under strain, steadies himself with spade, and a porter kicks the Itala's wheel raight.

No alternative but to take the Trans-Siberian Railway: the Itala at Lake Baikal, crewed by policeman, whose red flag is extended to stop approaching trains.

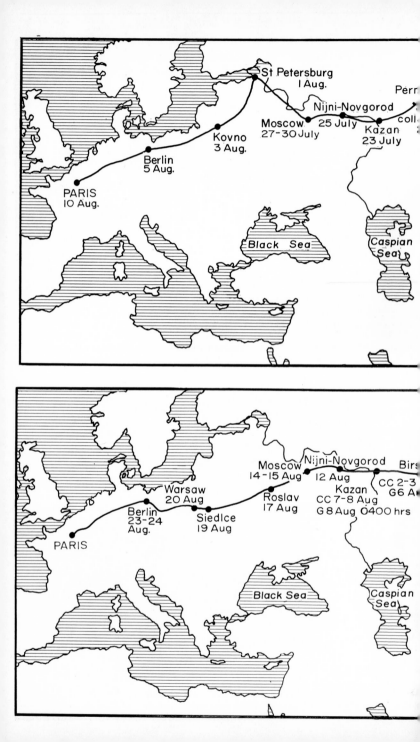

Top map:

St Petersburg
1 Aug.

Perm
[coll...]

Nijni-Novgorod
25 July

Moscow
27-30 July

Kazan
23 July

Kovno
3 Aug.

Berlin
5 Aug.

PARIS
10 Aug.

Black Sea

Caspian
Sea

Bottom map:

Moscow
14-15 Aug

Nijni-Novgorod
12 Aug

Birs

Warsaw
20 Aug

Roslav
17 Aug

Kazan
CC 7-8 Aug
G 8 Aug 0400 hrs

CC 2-3
G 6 A

Berlin
23-24
Aug.

Siedlce
19 Aug

PARIS

Black Sea

Caspian
Sea

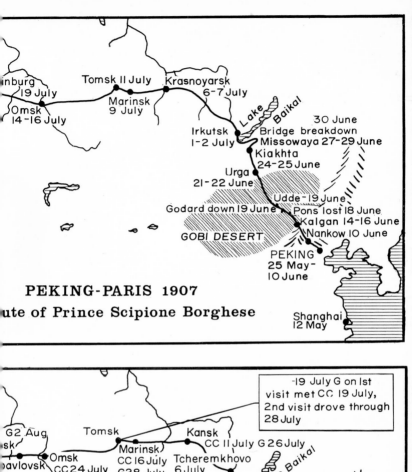

PEKING-PARIS 1907

ute of Prince Scipione Borghese

Map labels (top, Borghese route):

- inburg 19 July
- Omsk 14–16 July
- Tomsk 11 July
- Marinsk 9 July
- Krasnoyarsk 6–7 July
- Lake Baikal
- Irkutsk 1–2 July
- 30 June Bridge breakdown
- Missowaya 27–29 June
- Kiakhta 24–25 June
- Urga 21–22 June
- Udde –19 June
- Godard down 19 June
- Pons lost 18 June
- Kalgan 14–16 June
- Nankow 10 June
- GOBI DESERT
- PEKING 25 May– 10 June
- Shanghai 12 May

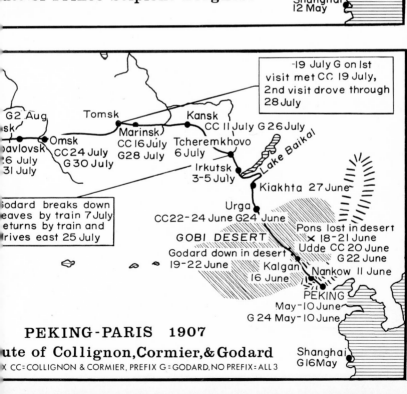

PEKING-PARIS 1907

ute of Collignon, Cormier, & Godard

X CC=COLLIGNON & CORMIER, PREFIX G=GODARD, NO PREFIX=ALL 3

Map labels (bottom, Collignon, Cormier & Godard route):

- –19 July G on 1st visit met CC 19 July, 2nd visit drove through 28 July
- G 2 Aug
- sk
- bavlovsk CC 24 July G 30 July 26 July 31 July
- Omsk
- Tomsk
- Marinsk CC 16 July G 28 July
- Kansk CC 11 July G 26 July
- Tcheremkhovo 6 July
- Lake Baikal
- Irkutsk 3–5 July
- Kiakhta 27 June
- Urga CC 22–24 June G 24 June
- Pons lost in desert X 18–21 June
- Udde CC 20 June G 22 June
- Godard breaks down leaves by train 7 July returns by train and drives east 25 July
- GOBI DESERT
- Godard down in desert 19–22 June
- Kalgan 16 June
- Nankow 11 June
- PEKING May–10 June G 24 May–10 June
- Shanghai G 16 May

7. Reversal of fortune: the Itala in difficulty near Lake Baikal.

8. With rope and hatchet the Siberian plate-layers rig a derrick before rebuilding th
bridge behind the Itala.

9.   Charles Godard   Jacobus Spijker

10. The postcard Godard sent Spijker after his magneto was repaired. It is date-stamped Tomsk and reads: Tomsk, Siberia, 20 July, 1907. Godard, Pekin-Paris. This is the state of my Spyker after a tough crossing of the Gobi, the Walls of China, rocks swamps, Lake Baikal. On the back he wrote: "I can assure you that if I had been helped, and if I had had the petrol, Borghese would not have been the leader, although his car is 60 horse-power.

11. A verst-pole on the Siberian trakt. Without speedometers, the only way the c crews could judge speed was by counting the verst-poles against a stop-watch.

12. Borghese enters Paris: the 10th of August, 1907.

Cormier came out of Borghese's room and reported the conversation. Longoni did not understand why his compatriot would not come out to hold a conference with them. Cormier, still concerned about Pons, could not conceal an additional, professional uneasiness about the Prince's movements.

"He's leaving to-morrow," he told the other drivers.

"He means to burn us up," said Godard.

Du Taillis perceived where their thoughts were taking them. If Borghese took up the *raid* it would be asking a great deal of the others to stay. The comradeship had disappeared in a day. The *raid* was already developing into a race. The professional drivers had much at stake. They had a responsibility to their commercial backers as well as a personal interest in the prestige of victory. If Borghese, with his authority, said that Pons was sure to fall into good hands, it would be easier by the morning for the rest to believe it. Borghese was a scholar, a gentleman, and an experienced explorer, and he knew more about Asia than anyone there. Borghese was leaving. That was certain. Du Taillis knew already in his heart that the others, even Godard, would follow. And where the 'raiders' went *Le Matin* must go too: du Taillis also had a commercial responsibility. The most constructive thing he could do in the circumstances—and here he had the ready help of Godard—was to set the most detailed plans in operation for a search for Pons and Foucault to be begun in the morning by Mongolian horsemen, whom he would pay. Fortunately, the operator Mister Luck was a responsible man, with the personality and initiative to direct this operation.

But *why*? Why would Borghese not go back? Was one day so important to him, when he had waited longer at Kalgan, admittedly under closer observation from Peking? Had he now summed up the varied capacity of the opposition? Was the low performance of the Contal irksome to him? Was he glad to get rid of Pons? "There is *some* reason," said du Taillis, "some excuse or perhaps a more acceptable reason that I don't know, which makes it important that the Itala should continue its course from first light to-morrow."

Jean du Taillis did not know the contents of a second Press telegram which Barzini had already dispatched that night, before

Prince Borghese went to bed. It appeared in the *Daily Telegraph* next morning, below the first message, and it read:

PONG-KIONG, *Tuesday (later)*

The Contal tri-car has found it impossible to proceed any farther. The competitors are therefore reduced to four: MM Cormier and Collignon on the de Dion Boutons, M. Godard on the Spyker, and Prince Scipione Borghese on the Itala. It is hoped that we shall now be able to accelerate our pace.

◎ ◎ The Skeletons in the Gobi

Nobody thought that Pons and Foucault were dead. Without food or shelter in that plateau of extreme daytime heat and night-time cold they must be extremely distressed. But if they could be found that day they should be all right. A serious difficulty was that if they were picked up they had neither money nor language. Du Taillis wrote a letter in French telling Pons exactly what had happened, which was the correct route at the fork, and detailing in the most sympathetic terms the decision of the other drivers to go on. He instructed Mister Luck, in English, to send horsemen —whom he had to recruit from any nomad encampments in the surrounding area by sending out one of his linemen—to look for the Contal crew, and to take them the letter, with silver to buy provisions, and to conduct them on to Pong-Kiong. Once they arrived, Mister Luck, who also had no language in which to communicate with them, was to entertain them and send them on their way to Udde. Contact could be maintained with Luck by the rest of the party through the telegraph line. The horsemen would naturally have to be paid.

It was Godard who remembered the vital necessity—petrol. Pons would need fuel to get to Pong-Kiong and more to get to Udde. The petrol situation in Pong-Kiong was bad. Godard himself, eking out his money, had reserved no petrol in Pong-Kiong, calculating that he would take enough on board at Kalgan and the stop beyond it to reach Udde, where they had all reserved large supplies. What petrol had arrived in Pong-Kiong by camel caravan had been well below the requisition. The seams of the tanks were faulty—as Godard had demonstrated with one kick

outside Kalgan—and there had been serious evaporation. Som
of the tanks in the compound had been only half full. They ha
been legitimately claimed by the drivers who had ordered them
though it is true that all the cars except the Spyker carried larg
reserves. Godard had arrived at the telegraph-station with thre
45-litre tanks aboard, and these had leaked on the journey.

Godard now took, on his own responsibility, the most quixoti
decision of the *raid*. Part of his petrol stock was Pons's by right
That he must have. But Pons would also expect to fill up again a
Pong-Kiong. Barzini, reflecting Borghese, might have declare
that Pons was out of the race, but du Taillis and Godard wer
making it as practicable as possible that he should continue. Th
other drivers had taken all the available petrol, arguing that the
had ordered it, and if the total supply had leaked it was a cas
of first come first served. But if Pons was still in the race he woul
need petrol at Pong-Kiong to enable him to get to the ampl
stores at Udde.

Without elaborate explanations to du Taillis, Godard foun
some sound tanks among those which had now been emptied b
the other drivers. He poured into them the contents of his thre
partially full tanks. He was able to fill two adequately, and had
pint or two left for himself. He placed this residue quietly in th
Spyker, where du Taillis must at first sight take it for a full tank
He gave Mister Luck one 45-litre tank with instructions that th
horsemen must carry it to Pons as they searched for him. He tol
Luck to keep the other, and give it to Pons when he arrived.

He now knew definitely that he had not the fuel to get to Udde
Therefore he would have to borrow it from the other drivers. The
could well afford it, but that did not mean that they would neces
sarily give it. Having a clear idea of their characters, and also o
their driving habits, he concluded that he would have to approac
them in different ways. Prince Borghese, the lone wolf, would b
off as soon as possible, and not be seen for the rest of the day
Negotiations would have to be started immediately. He drew th
Italian aside, and asked for the favour of a can of petrol, to b
repaid out of Godard's stocks at Udde. Borghese, who the pre
vious noon had been ready to go on to Udde with the reserves h
already had in the car, replied that he was very short, but h

vould do what he could, and instructed Guizzardi to siphon out
a certain amount from one of his tanks. The loan amounted to
about a dozen litres. Godard realized that it was entirely inadequate for the journey, but conveyed his charmed thanks and set
his mind to the problem of cracking the even harder nut of the
le Dion team.

The journey to Udde was a straight dash across the Gobi
Desert. The calculated distance was 170 miles. This stage had
been the bogey of the trip since the first day the Paris committee
met. This was the section for which the crew had light-heartedly
rained by exposing themselves to the khamsin sandstorms in
Suez. Perhaps they had exaggerated its menace. But it was not the
tage over which Godard would willingly have gambled his life.
There was also the consideration, which was not idly shrugged
off by Godard, that he was gambling with the life of du Taillis.

There was one task which du Taillis had to be asked to do
without unduly alarming him. Godard could not write English,
and did not know the formula of sending telegrams. He asked du
Taillis to telegraph to Udde requesting the head of the station
here to send out, as a precaution, a man on horseback with two
cans of petrol to meet the Spyker as it came in across the Gobi.
Under the best conditions, Godard reflected, the span of extreme
danger might be cut by thirty miles. Du Taillis sent the message
without comment.

Prince Borghese rose early, put his silver into the pool of taels
which Cormier was collecting for Pons, nodded curtly as du
Taillis told him of the mounted search that was being organized,
heard Godard's confidential request for petrol, and gave Guizzardi
his instructions. He strode to his car. Tall, stern, with his shaven
face and lean neck deeply weathered by his outdoor life, he
looked, in his drill tunic and breeches, cavalry boots and leggings,
like a general before battle. And the effect was not diminished
when he put on his topee. The cars left Pong-Kiong together. The
tala immediately took the lead. The rougher ground yielded
temporarily to a stretch of prairie, and Borghese edged the revs
up, until he judged he was doing sixty miles an hour. At that
speed they raced small herds of antelope and gazelle, and were,
in turn, challenged from a distance by occasional groups of

mounted Mongolians, who soon realized that the contest wa
beyond their power. Borghese, satisfied, eased the engine to
speed that Barzini could better appreciate. It was Barzini's tur
to take the floorboards.

The Italians had time in hand to be tourists. They stopped t
examine the construction of the occasional well which the
passed. They took photographs. When they saw a strange whit
building ahead and to one side of them they immediately turne
towards it, their archæological references at the ready. It was
low, complex, massive edifice, with the sort of primitive Byzantin
line suggesting that it really went deep into the earth and showe
only the domes and roof levels of an underground cathedral. I
was an ancient Buddhist monastery. From the red ornamente
roof-line of its lime-washed temple a battery of gutters projecte
like oars from a galley to drain the rain far from the walls. A ver
old man came out of the temple. The Italians went towards hin
and greeted him, but he made no acknowledgment. They pointe
cameras at him, and he gazed mildly at them. When they drov
away he was still in contemplation of a world into which the
did not enter.

The wind had blown strongly all day, and now it was whippin
sand into their eyes. The sun was high as they came to the edg
of the desert. The word *gobi* in Mongolian means dish. The Gob
Desert is the basin of an ancient sea. They entered the sand sea a
if by a slipway, plunging steeply down a slope of one hundre
feet to the great tossed bed of soil and sand and rock scorched b
the intensified heat of the concave of the Gobi. This was the lan
where no one passed by day. The skeletons of oxen and camel
and mules were nudging white relics of disaster. After many mile
they found a well, but as they dashed the water over their head
they found that the skin of their faces was already broken an
bleeding. Guizzardi's hands, pitted with the small, oil-black cut
which his job made a commonplace, had swollen and burst in th
sun, so that the flesh slit below the cuts.

They got back into the car. There was no conversation, no ca
culated quip, only endurance to be offered. After a long, leve
stretch they plunged again. They had come into a lower basin
This was the most feared part of the Gobi, an expanse of fort

miles, which the caravans knew they must cross in a single night, or if the high sun came up on them, all but the strong would die. The well at which the caravan drivers watered their beasts and filled their skins before that hazardous crossing was marked by a sort of petrified forest—a concentration of shrines to God, made of high piles of stones. Every passer added a stone and said a prayer for survival. The shrines were grimly crowned with the skulls of horses or oxen, and they fluttered with ribbons of little flags and paper labels with prayers written on them. For the movement of wind on flags and prayer-labels had the same significance to Buddhists as the flicker of altar candle-flames had in the west. On the bed of the lower sea the bones of beasts lay intermittently in thick profusion, where a sandstorm had blown up and driven the caravan to a halt for the following sun to pick off its victims.

The Italians were now suffering severely. The pith helmets of Borghese and Guizzardi gave them some protection, but Barzini had scorned to buy one. With his panama hat, the brim bent back by the wind of the car's speed, and his raw red face, he looked like a postcard caricature of a promenade masher. They regretted the decision to jettison the stanchions, which would have given them the protection of the car's hood through this exacting day. At two in the afternoon they were met by a man on foot, leading a camel laden with two 45-litre cans of petrol. He stopped them, and gave them a telegram. It was addressed to du Taillis, and they gave it back to him. With words from the Mongolian phrase-book they told him that he must go on—on to the south to deliver his load to the Spyker. They checked the time, and found that they had to go on driving for three hours more over the rapidly worsening terrain before they reached the relay-station of Udde. The Mongolian must have been on his trek since dawn, and it seemed likely that he would have much farther to go. Well, it was Godard's business, and Borghese washed his hands of it. The Italian party went on in the silence which their arduous journey and their individual thoughts mutually dictated, and at last they sighted the lonely telegraph-station of Udde. There they were welcomed by the affable operator-in-charge, Mister Johnson.

Goddard had seemed to du Taillis to be in low spirits from the

very start of the day. He revved his engine briefly, then turned
to du Taillis, and screwed up his face in a grimace. "Ah, this i
no way to justify the nickname you have given me. Let's put a
good face on things. Tartarin du Gobi! It's very fine, I'm sure
though I'm not very clear who this Tartarin is. Well, I'd better
live up to the name."

He shrugged his shoulders, and jerked his face towards the dus
cloud raised by the receding Itala.

"We must do our very best not to get lost to-day. To have Pon
and Foucault left behind is quite enough for one trip."

And he shoved in the gear lever, and set the Spyker at the long
climb out of Pong-Kiong, which he had to take in second.

After little more than a mile Godard suddenly stopped
"Where's Pékine?" he said sharply.

They realized that they had left the dog behind. "It's no dis
tance. We'll go back for her," said du Taillis.

Godard broke out into a protest that seemed artificial in it
force. "*Jamais de la vie*. Not on your life. I'll never have it said
that I sacrificed the success of this race for a bitch. I'll never ask
my old Spyker to do a yard more than is necessary to reach Paris.
He paused, and added quietly, "It's a hell of a shame. But it's just
too bad."

It was then that du Taillis began to size up the situation. The
petrol problem was so bad that Godard would not even drive the
four extra kilometres to pick up Pékine.

"Never mind," said Godard apologetically. "Pons will pick
her up."

Pons had been standing by his silent machine since dawn, hi
eyes fixed on the horizon for the first sight of his companions
Then he made a decision. "We'll use our last drop of juice, and
go to meet them," he told Foucault. They started the engine, and
drove up the track. Within a quarter of an hour the engine
coughed out.

It was five o'clock in the morning. "We'll walk," said Pons. The
two men started walking. Pons reckoned their pace at six kilo
metres an hour.

It was eleven o'clock. They had walked over twenty miles. The

…ad passed no villages, seen no nomads, and could hear no sound
of motors. Their thirst was clawing at their bodies. They explored
the ground for water. They found one puddle in the centre of
drying mud, thick with insects. They fell down, and put their
mouths to it and drained the puddle, and spat out the insects.

"We will walk back," said Pons. They turned back on the way
they had come. It was not so easy walking now, and they took
eight hours to reach the Contal. They had seen nobody.

It was seven o'clock in the evening. They were very ill. They
threw themselves on the ground and slept there, retching.

After the decision to abandon Pékine Godard drove fast. He
was determined to keep ahead of the de Dions. They passed the
prairie, ran on to the sand, slithered down the wall of the Gobi
basin and past the skulls on the Mongol shrines. They were running very well. They could count on having done 80 kilometres.
There were 200 to go.

The engine of the Spyker misfired, then failed.

"No juice," said Godard.

Du Taillis swore.

Godard spoke fast and conspiratorially. "I've still got five or
six litres in the tank behind, but I've got to make Cormier think
I'm completely dry. If I can get ten litres from each of them, with
what I've got we can still do another hundred kilometres if the
ground is the same as it has been so far. That will put us only a
hundred kilometres from Udde. We can always ask for another
loan, and, in any case, we shan't be so far up the creek."

The de Dions were driving up to them now. "Ready?"
whispered Godard. He threw up his arms in despair, and
yelled, "Out of petrol! Absolutely out. Our tanks are completely
dry."

Cormier and Collignon looked at each other with what seemed
deep astonishment. They too were poker players. They got down
and elaborately examined their tanks, peering into them, dipping
them, and shaking their heads.

"I've already used thirty litres just to do eighty kilometres," said
Cormier.

"The bloody liar," whispered Godard to du Taillis. "I haven't used much more than twenty myself." The Spyker was fifteen horsepower, the de Dions ten horsepower.

"I had to go down into first for a lot of those sandy spots," said Cormier defensively. "Anyway, the petrol is evaporating. I don't wonder, in this heat. Hey, du Taillis, what's the temperature?"

Du Taillis put the thermometer he carried into the shade by the side of the Spyker.

"Well, what's the temperature?"

The thermometer read 47° C, over 116° F. Du Taillis could not believe it, but he had to report it.

"There you are!" said Cormier with rough triumph, and proceeded to get in his proposal first. "Look here, Godard. We have a hundred and eighty kilometres to go." (Godard made it 200.) "Collignon and I have each got a hundred litres left. We'll give you five or six litres each, and that will give you a chance to get to a well. We shall pinpoint the well, and then we'll know where to send you the juice from Udde."

Godard, having decided that this was not the last fight, gracefully accepted the offer. Cormier and Collignon gave him some petrol from their spare tanks. Godard estimated it at about eight litres altogether.

"You go first," said the de Dion drivers.

"The swine!" muttered Godard to du Taillis. "They've each got a built-in forty-litre reserve tank under the seat. Next time I'll let them know that *I* know. What they have given us is useless. It means only fifty kilometres. We shall be less than half-way to Udde."

"Well, we must go as far as we can," said du Taillis.

Godard drove fast. He had to keep in front, not only to take the advantage of a slight lead to pour in his six-litre reserve. They had plunged into the lower basin now, where the skeletons of the beasts were thickest. As they drove they talked in brief sentences. Godard seemed depressed about his chances of getting much more petrol from the others. Du Taillis could not understand this.

"But they're sportsmen."

"Once they're off the grid," said Godard, "they're wolves."

It was an hour and a quarter since they had borrowed the petrol. The Spyker stopped. Godard jumped down, and cast an anguished look into his tanks. "Dry as a bone," he said.

Du Taillis scanned the surface of the desert for some sign of water. There was no vegetation at all, beyond some spikes of spear grass.

"What rations have we got?" asked Godard.

"Some ship's biscuit, a cold chicken, and two litres of water," said du Taillis, and then he burst out furiously, "Look, they can't do this to us. At least they haven't got their knives out for me. I'm not in the game, and I don't mind going on my knees. I shall plead with Cormier to give us a few litres to get at least half-way from here to Udde. We've asked Udde to send some one out with petrol for us, and if we can get on a bit farther it will only be a matter of a few hours before that horseman reaches us. And what about rations? Cormier can't refuse us a little water and biscuit and one or two tins of something."

"Now's your chance," said Godard tersely.

The de Dions were coming up in close order, with Cormier in the lead. Du Taillis moved across to be able to speak to Cormier as soon as he stopped. But he did not stop. As he passed them he called out confidently, as if everything had been settled, "There's nothing you want, is there? I'll get your juice sent to you as soon as I arrive in Udde."

Collignon had suddenly found that he had to concentrate intensely on the sandy surface. He did not look up, and he did not say anything. The de Dions accelerated, and were gone.

Even Godard was so dazed with the expertise of Cormier's rejection that he had nothing to say. Du Taillis, almost weeping with rage, was unable to speak. They watched the dust from the de Dions, until the northern horizon was clear again. Suddenly they realized that they had been motionless in the sun for many minutes. They felt desiccated. Godard took off his sun helmet to readjust it, and then became practical. "We must pitch the tent," he said. "We need the shade."

They lay inside the tent when it was up, exhausted with emotion. They had tied up the brailings, but the wind which brushed over their bodies had no element of coolness. Du Taillis looked at the thermometer again. It read 45° C—only two degrees below the figure he had incredulously given to Cormier.

"I want to know everything we have to eat and drink—everything," said Godard. They catalogued the cold chicken, some blocks of concentrated soup, a little chocolate, which was uneatable, and the two litres of water. They cursed as they remembered the 24 bottles of Mumm's best bubbly, abandoned only a few hours ago.

"Let us leave the chicken until to-morrow, when we shall be hungrier. The chocolate will be edible at dawn if the nights are as cold as I imagine. We shall have soup for supper—if only we can get some water." He sat up, and crawled out of the tent. "I'm going to look for a well," he said. "Don't worry. I shall never get the car out of sight."

Godard tried to make a methodical search within the area of a circle for two kilometres around the car. He found nothing. Over two hours later he stumbled back to the tent, exhausted and despairing.

"We cannot have soup for supper," announced du Taillis. "We have a petrol stove, but no petrol. We can chew the cubes of concentrate, but it may make us very thirsty."

"I shall not have anything," said Godard, in the depths of depression. "I can't eat, and I won't drink. I wonder if Cormier has reached Udde yet. What's the time?"

It was seven o'clock. Cormier had got out of the Gobi bowl, but had found a succession of hills in the country leading to Udde, which were more than the de Dions could manage with ease, and at seven o'clock he had decided to camp. He was fifty kilometres from Udde. Like du Taillis and Godard, the de Dion crews had eaten nothing that day. They therefore did justice to the meal of meat and vegetables prepared for them by Longoni. Cormier noted in his log that the camp was in a charming situation; they had a good meal, and passed an excellent night, disturbed only once or twice by the bell on the tail-end camel of a passing caravan.

No caravan passed the Spyker. Godard had thrown himself down early to sleep. Du Taillis closed his eyes, but found no escape, and stared upward into the dark for most of the night. Godard stirred, and began to talk fast. He was still asleep. Du Taillis thought he must be delirious. "We cannot wait for the petrol," he insisted. "We must start walking. We'll push the car in front of us. We'll get it along somehow."

At last du Taillis slept, distressed and exhausted, like Pons and Foucault, lying very still by their machine, 200 miles to the south. Cormier, Longoni, Collignon, and Bizac passed their excellent night below Udde. The Italians slept within the telegraph-station. Of all the 'raiders' they were the first to rise, and they were able to receive news of the de Dion encampment from the leader of the camel caravan which had passed them in the course of its long night's journey, and come into Udde before dawn. Borghese left word with Mister Johnston that he would reach the next telegraph-station, Tuerin, that night, and go on to Urga, the capital of Mongolia, on the morrow. At Urga he would wait two days to see if the others could join him. Urga was nearly 500 miles north-west of the position of the Spyker at that moment. He hurried his crew into the Itala, and set off while there were still stars shining in the west. They all found the air very cold, and were grateful for the furs they wrapped around them.

The night air—it had dropped to 4° C, or 39° F—had solidified the chocolate Félix Potin, which du Taillis had pronounced a glutinous mess the night before, and the Spyker crew took some for breakfast with a small allowance of their scanty water. Without spoken agreement Godard and du Taillis stood in turn by the car, facing north, to report movement on the horizon as soon as possible. The watch continued for five hours, and the sun was climbing higher, until it became intolerable. At ten in the morning Godard gave a croaking shout. Some one was approaching—from the south. There was a figure on a camel. They ran towards it. The rider was a Mongol woman—Godard still had the objectivity to remark that she was incredibly ugly. The woman was not unfriendly, though apparently not of the highest intelligence. She offered a skin containing a few drops of muddy water, which the men eagerly drank. Godard made urgent signs to her, speaking encouragingly in French. She seemed to have no comprehension, so he became his own ostler. He got out the tow-rope from the back of the Spyker, hooked it to the front spring, and harnessed it to the camel. The woman watched, fascinated Godard beat the camel with his hands, and, though whimpering the beast consented to move forward, dragging the car. Godard took his place at the wheel. For one moment he was the old Godard of the *Océanien* and the Hotel de Pékin. "Tartarin du Gobi!" he roared with a flourish. "Gee up!" The camel plodded painfully along. The soft sand built up against the wheels. Within forty yards the Spyker was immovable. The woman waited patiently while the men dug with their hands. The camel moved on. The car dug in. The woman waited. Finally she moodily untied the harness, threw the rope on the ground, and went on to the north without a word.

The sun came up stronger. Du Taillis had hastily packed the tent as Godard took the wheel, and it was thrown into the back of the car. They were too dispirited to pitch it again. "The chicken," said Godard. Du Taillis unwrapped it. It was nothing but a writhing mass of maggots. They threw it away. They poured themselves a tiny ration of water, and made it last an hour, taking little sips at long intervals. They sat slumped in the car seats all through the day. As the light faded they began to move about, walking solitarily around the car, and stumbling over the animal skeletons which cracked and crunched under their feet. They were both now in the grip of fever. The moon rose, and the air cooled, and they were too far sunk in apathy to raise their tent. They pitched on to the ground, and lay half conscious, aware only of a great sadness. For ten hours they lay there, quite incapable of movement. Then they heard the unmistakable tinkle of bells. Prostrate, they raised their heads from their arms, and saw a caravan approaching. Dozens of huge camels were coming towards them, and twelve Mongolians were plodding at their side. The caravan came on, straight towards the car. The Frenchmen were shaking and laughing, but they could not get up. "Thank you, thank you," they whispered. The camels passed them. The Mongolians looked down on them, and did not stop. Du Taillis and Godard heard themselves screaming. "Help—please—please —please!" The Mongolians made no response. They looked down on them as though they were already dead. The caravan passed. They heard its bells long after they had ceased to look at it.

And suddenly Godard gave a great cry of anguish, but it was not for himself. "Pons!" he shrieked. "Pons—Pons—Pons—Pons!"

Pons was cursing them all—Borghese, Cormier, du Taillis, Godard. It was thirty-six hours since he and Foucault had crashed to the ground by their machine after walking forty miles to seek rescue. When they woke they had one obsession in their ringing heads. They must see people. If it meant being butchered, as the Chinese officials in Peking had warned them, they must find people. They walked square off the track, knowing that their companions had abandoned them, trusting themselves to any passing caravan. The immense plain, shimmering in the sun, only emphasized their isolation. They seemed the only men in the world. Stumbling on, they saw the low huts of a nomad encampment. They did not immediately run towards it, but turned back to get their machine. It was almost a part of them, it seemed their one means to get to Paris, and they must bring it to the camp while they recovered their strength. They found the Contal, and began to drag it. The ruts which had defeated them every day since they left Peking overcame them again. They heaved and struggled, but could not disengage it. They exhausted the remainder of their puny strength, and then fell down in the dirt beside the comic contraption that had consistently humiliated them. And that is where the nomads found them. They carried the limp bodies to their huts, and tended them, and when they were well delivered them to a troop of cavalry sent out by the Kalgan General to search for them. Pons and Foucault travelled slowly to Peking, and the Contal was left rusting on the plain. Bitterly attacking all their old companions, they never ceased to proclaim that they had been betrayed.

Betrayal was a conception in the minds of Godard and du Taillis when they were calm enough to discuss their situation. It was two clear days since they had wired to Udde for petrol, and almost as long since, on the agreed schedule, Cormier should have arrived at Udde. But now, having accepted the fact that there was no one to rely on but themselves, Godard was strangely cheerful. He would go and find help himself, he declared. Du

Taillis stared at him. He was gaunt and weak, but the fever seemed to have left him. "You stay by the car. I shall go prospecting," said Godard.

There was no point in objecting. Du Taillis split a soup-cake—their water was entirely gone now—and sat against the car while Godard went off. The time passed dully. Later—how much later? It was two hours, du Taillis afterwards checked—there was a shout, and du Taillis looked up to see what looked, in his daze, to be a mounted pageant of *The Vagabond King*. Godard, whooping like a principal tenor, was approaching, seated on the croup of a magnificent horse controlled by a superb rider. Behind him trotted a smart troop of irregular cavalry, dressed in turbans of velvet and cloth of gold, with long red silk ribbons fluttering from them. Each man carried a carbine across his chest, and in a belt gleaming with silver buckles was fixed a long dagger. Godard had been a successful prospector. He had gone out and found himself a troop of the warlike Kunghuz tribesmen.

The tribesmen hobbled their horses, and squatted round while Godard and their chief negotiated a complicated bargain. The main clause, which had to be agreed without any intelligible language, was that a horseman should ride day and night to the telegraph-station at Udde to requisition petrol. He was to take a letter, written by du Taillis in English, explaining their position and the urgent need of help. Once this had been apparently understood—but *was* it understood, du Taillis wondered—the far more intricate business of fixing the price for the deal had to be completed. First Godard produced some currency scales from the car, but had to explain that he had no taels to weigh in them. Then he conveyed that the chief *would* receive taels even before delivery of the petrol, and that the silver would be obtained from the telegraph-station at Udde. For this, the most delicate link in the transaction, du Taillis's letter enclosed banknotes, which he begged would be changed into silver. Then they had to agree the number of taels. For this they needed an abacus. Godard delicately took from the chief's neck a string of coral beads. Then he began counting the beads slowly, pausing after every few beads to see if the chief would agree that the number of beads indicated corresponded to the number of taels to be paid. Obviously nothing could be agreed without conventional haggling. Consequently the chief spent a long time shaking his head and signalling to Godard to continue counting the beads. And there had to be occasions when Godard would shake his head and slide his fingers back to a lower number. After an interminable time a bargain was struck. Godard sealed it by presenting the chief with his gold watch-chain.

The chief rose. His men mounted, and they all rode away. But Godard still seemed impatient. He had insisted on a subordinate clause to the treaty. And it was complied with. One hour later fresh horsemen rode up, leading two camels, which were harnessed to the Spyker, whacked into movement, and abandoned by the tribesmen as soon as the car was under way. Somehow, using only sign-language, Godard had got agreement to this interim traction until the petrol arrived. He sat at the wheel, smiling again at last, and du Taillis could only watch him with weak affection as he preened himself.

The camels were harnessed at one o'clock in the afternoon, some forty-four hours after the breakdown. The motorists did not know how far Udde was or when their aid would be brought. They could only go on, slowly moving. They drove all through the night, sitting in the seats of the car. They drove all through the following morning. They had not eaten or drunk for twenty-four hours. The sun was high again. Du Taillis, still a journalist with an eye for copy, noted that the temperature went one degree higher than ever to 48° C. They were blistered by the sun. There were wide, vertical cracks in their lips, which tortured them as the blown sand ground into them. The camels faltered, and the crew got down and dragged them along. Surely the tribesmen had not understood, or had been satisfied with Godard's gold chain, or had ridden off with the petrol and taels. Now du Taillis saw the double logic of Godard's demand for the camels. They were retrievable pledges, rather than traction.

The camels swerved off the track, and no effort that the men could make would shift their stolid march. They had sniffed a well, and they made for it. The men rushed ahead of the beasts, and found a square hole full of fetid mud. They squeezed the mud in their hands, and drank the liquid as it fell. Du Taillis fumbled in his pocket for his last tablet of Chocolat Potin. It had melted to an insipid paste, and he tore it apart like glue to share it with Godard.

They dragged the camels on. The chocolate had only increased their thirst. They dropped the camels' leads, and the beasts stopped. Du Taillis and Godard had suddenly been struck by the same thought. They scrambled on their backs under the car, turned the radiator tap, and sucked alternately at the outlet pipe. The last drain of liquid in the radiator gave them each two mouthfuls of oily water. But they declared it was exquisite.

They crawled back to the side of the car and climbed into the seats. They had been exposed now for three days, and they had not slept for a day and a half. They were completely inert. Vaguely they heard loud cries, and watched two horsemen expertly unshackle the camels and lead them off. And with a start they awoke to reality again. Were they being robbed of their last pledge? They blinked into the blinding sunlight, and saw, far away it seemed, a violet shadow approaching. The shadow grew larger, split into detail. It was the troop of wild horsemen, galloping towards them, shouting and laughing, riding with their right arms pushed out straight before them, the fist closed, the thumb up, in the gesture for "All's well," which the horsemen of the desert used long before there were racing motorists.

The deep, uncomplicated joy of the Kunghuz that they had succeeded in their mission infected the Frenchmen, who had been almost unconscious with fatigue. They uncapped the petrol-tank, poured in the petrol, whose rarity they had never so well appreciated, signed to the troopers to bring skins so that the radiator could be filled. The chief laughed as he showed them the taels he had been given at the telegraph-station, and Godard laughed, and told him he was a hard bargainer. "One swing of the handle," as Godard used to boast. It took more than one, though the Frenchmen had not the strength for many. The car started. The cavalry cheered. And they trotted along beside the Spyker in a glitter of silk and silver for a number of kilometres, until, with a shout and a wave, they wheeled their superb horses away into the desert.

"We can reach Udde in three hours," said Godard, settling in his seat as though he had just stopped for tea. His eyes hardened, and he took the Spyker through the sand in exhilaration at the delight of power and, perhaps, at the thought of vengeance. But the surge died, and he was beginning to drive shabbily when a man came running from a hut ahead, obviously meaning to cut them off. As they slowed he continued running and his arm came out with the thumb up for friendship. In his left hand he held a tall copper vessel. It was an enormous teapot, full of boiling-hot perfumed tea.

They stopped the car and took the tea. They drank it in great scalding draughts. It seemed to burn the dry scales of exhaustion from their mouths and gullets and give them fresh flesh again, and they could feel the effect of it filtering into their limbs as if they had injected a drug. The sweat formed on their chests and backs like springs of water. It fell off their filthy foreheads like rain. "I never believed it," said du Taillis with a grin. "These colonial types have always said that no iced drink can pull you round like a hot one, and now I know they were right."

"What shall we give him?" said Godard.

The man was smiling and chuckling at their enjoyment. Godard pulled out the scales, and he backed away. But when Godard wagged his finger to say that he had no money their host came forward again. They pulled out the little gifts they could offer, and tried to make the man take one—an electro-plated knife and fork, a penknife, even an empty petrol-can. He smiled and indicated No. At last he plucked up confidence. He pointed to Godard's head. The Frenchman could not understand. He touched Godard's pith helmet—a ridiculous object, bleached grey by the Gobi sun. Godard took it off, and gave it to him. In sheer pleasure the man went down on his knees to thank them, put on the helmet, and went away, turning round and smiling every few steps. For the first time for days du Taillis laughed. It was his great jungle roar again. The sound was an echo of the thunderclaps in the saloons of the *Océanien*, but the sight was not the same. The lips that were once so theatrically scarlet were thick and grey and striped with brown blood. The reefs of once-white teeth were yellow with sand and scum. But the laugh was true, and it was to the sound of the laugh that the two men entered Udde.

Mister Johnson, of the Chinese Imperial Telegraph Service, in charge of the Udde relay-station, had not deliberately failed Godard. On the morning of Wednesday the 19th of June he received du Taillis's wire from Pong-Kiong requesting ninety litres of petrol to be sent fifty kilometres south of Udde by horse-courier. He had dispatched a man on a camel, whom Borghese had met in the afternoon, and whom the de Dion party met next morning. For Bizac had awoken the crews in their camp at four o'clock with naval efficiency, and they were soon off. Within ten kilometres they came across a tent, from which the messenger emerged, and again tried to present his message for du Taillis. Cormier and Longoni tried to make him understand that he must go much farther. With no linguistic link at all they found it diffi-cult to convince themelves that he really understood how far he must go, but finally they left him, with elaborate signs to press on.

They came to the square desert compound of Udde at eight o'clock. Mister Johnson, who after years of quiet was as active in hospitality as the stationmaster at Victoria in Coronation week, welcomed them sincerely, explained that Borghese had already left at three that morning, and asked after the Spyker. When he heard that his courier had reached the spot originally requested, but that the breakdown had occurred much farther south, he declared that the camel would never reach Godard in time; a man on horseback must be sent out with more petrol. The price would be high. He would try to keep it down to ten taels. Cormier, the treasurer, gave Mister Johnson this money, and actually saw a Mongolian ride off on horseback with the petrol, though he did not arrive in the deep bowl of the Gobi where the Spyker was stranded.

Cormier asked Mister Johnson to telegraph to Pong-Kiong for news of Pons. There was no news. Cormier, very worried, then telegraphed Dorliac at the Russo-Chinese Bank at Kalgan, telling him that Pons was missing, asking him to do everything possible, and to reply to Cormier at Tuerin, the next station up the tele-graph line. Cormier then put his own story over for *l'Auto*.

Cormier decided to push on to Tuerin, and after that to Urga, where he would wait for the Spyker. This was as clear a breach of the agreement for mutual aid as Borghese's decision to abandon Pons, which Cormier had stoutly fought. Cormier reported that he would get to Urga before he stopped for Godard because he did not want to exhaust his food reserves. Borghese reported that he would wait two days at Urga, as, he emphasized, he had done at Kalgan.

It was a feature of the Peking–Paris *raid* that, before the days of radio, its competitors were in touch almost constantly with the newspaper desks of the world. In Mongolia the telegraph-stations were far apart, and messages could be delayed. Once the motorists were near the line of the Trans-Siberian Railway they could get messages away almost at will. Therefore, although the terrain was as tough as the hardiest explorer could expect, outside the jungle, the daily chronicle could be dispatched in the most sophisticated manner, and the writers would know that newspaper-readers all over the world would be studying it at breakfast-time next morn-ing. From the point of view of the contestants, there was one drawback to this. Every day's exploits had to be made tidy. Every action had to appear civilized. Nothing must go through that the readers could query. The effective result was that a cover-story had to be prepared for every action, however justifiable.

The cover-stories were, in fact, passing over wires that were in sight of du Taillis and Godard as they bandied thoughts of be-trayal in the desert. Cormier's was being tapped out as he left Udde at one o'clock on the Thursday, taking the sandy track to the north. Borghese had worn furs in the morning. Cormier and Collignon were under tropical heat at noon. But the wells were more frequent, and they were able to stop and draw really cold water to chill the cool tea which they carried with them for refreshment.

Towards evening they found a well so excellent that Cormier said they would camp there, and Longoni declared he would have a bath. The desert wells were square openings in the earth. framed in wood, quite shallow, and built with a separate wooden feeding-trough for animals. Besides the pack-animals, camels, horses, donkeys, and mules, flocks of sheep and goats were frequently driven along the caravan path. Except in the worst stretch of the Gobi Desert the wells were spaced about twenty-five kilometres, sixteen miles, apart. At the well where the de Dion party camped there were no other guests for the night, and Longoni took his bath without giving offence to Mongolian preconceptions of salubrity or, for that matter, modesty. But *le petit italien* still felt it necessary at 7 P.M. to wear his sun-helmet.

The cuisine of the de Dion party was improving daily, and this evening, at about the time when Godard and du Taillis were staggering drunkenly over the brittle skeletons of dead beasts, the crews consumed *potage printanier, hachis de bœuf de conserve, purée de pommes de terre, compôte des poires.* Cormier confided to the Imperial Telegraph that it was "succulent—it lacked for nothing." After dinner Bizac had gone to fill two canvas buckets from the well 200 yards away when there was a shout. He came doubling back to the camp-fire with his buckets empty. "I'm not going to the well," he announced. "There is a bear going the same way."

Cormier's passion was shooting. He had brought his Winchester with him on the trip. He jumped up to get it, and walked warily towards the well. The bear seemed the right shape in the twilight, but a little too polite for a bear. Cautiously Cormier advanced, until he distinguished the intruder as a huge shaggy wild dog which had come off the desert for a drink, but was waiting until the visitors had finished at the well, with a sort of "After you, sir."

The next day, after a fairly fast trip across plain desert, they came to the striking community of Tuerin, an ancient monastic settlement of the Buddhist lamas, set near a huge cliff, which rises out of the desert in as imposing a shape as the Rock of Gibraltar. The monks in their blood-red robes signalled to the Frenchmen the route to the solitary telegraph-station, away from the lamasery, and Cormier was able to telegraph Dorliac and Mister Johnson. He got no news of either Pons or Godard, but heard that soldiers from Kalgan were out searching for the Contal crew. Borghese had left Tuerin at three that morning. He was now a full day in advance of Cormier and Collignon.

The few Westerners who ever came to Tuerin usually commented on the striking architecture and unforgettable setting of the monastery by the mountain. Cormier's recollection of the place was that good-quality rice and exquisite fresh milk were obtainable there, which, added to the *potage julienne* and *bœuf à la mode*, was converted to an excellent *riz au lait* in Longoni's skilful hands. At the time of its consumption du Taillis and Godard were jolting through the dark, sitting in the silent car, behind the slow camels.

On the Saturday the de Dions left at 5.30, and made slow progress on the rocky ground of the mountain country. But the rough terrain yielded to a plain again, and they had a burst of speed. Then Cormier sighted antelopes. Nothing could restrain him from hunting them. Collignon, Bizac, and Longoni waited almost three hours while he tried to stalk a beast for the pot. Eagles and vultures flew overhead, and the skeletons around the cars showed that the birds of prey were well catered for. Cormier came back in a bad temper. He could not get near a beast. They drove on. The vegetation was changing, and they were putting up partridge, duck, teal, plover, and even heron. Cormier itched for a pot-shot at the game, but he had only ball cartridge handy.

The country changed again. The hills were rising. But as they came down a very rocky valley into a stretch of scree they saw pine-trees on the tops of the hills ahead. There was green grass in the fields, and cows were feeding. A stream in the nick of a valley ran pure, clear water. They had finished with the desert, and quite soon they would leave Mongolia. Between two mountains, furry-edged with pine, they could now see its capital town, Urga. The distance of fifteen kilometres, ten miles, took two hours to drive because of its loose scree paths and six rivers—all connecting with the great river Tola—which it was necessary to ford. The de Dion crews drove into the first built-up area to present

themselves, but discovered that it was the Chinese city, and were
directed to the Russian. There, in the Russo-Chinese Bank, after
a warm welcome in the purest French from Madame Stepanoff,
the wife of the director, Cormier sought out Borghese, and told
him of the Spyker's breakdown, adding that he had that moment
received a telegram announcing the car's arrival at Udde and the
assurance of the crew that they would get through to Urga in two
days. "The Spyker crew have asked us to wait for them here, and
I have come to ask you to do this. Collignon and I will certainly
not move until they join us."

The Prince replied that he could not lose so much time. On the
stage out of Urga he would have to ford the river Iro—as, indeed,
they all would. He had had information that day that as a result
of early rains the level of the Iro was now four feet high, which
was a serious height for a motor-car. Bad weather was expected,
and he did not intend to allow the Iro to block him. He would
leave next morning at four o'clock, but he would wait for the
others at Irkutsk, which he intended to reach in nine days'
time.

Prince Borghese had left Udde at dawn on Thursday the 20th
of June, leaving word with Mister Johnson that he would wait for
the others in Urga for two days, which he was now cutting to
one. He had learnt from the caravan leader that the de Dions
were camped within forty miles of the station. The first part of
the next stage was low hill-country, with occasional steep ascents
on loose stones and some soft sand-patches which tested the
engine. But, for the most part, Borghese was able to drive at great
speed. Indeed, he remarked that the motor-car had never had
such freedom since its invention, running across this unpopulated,
uncultivated country, with—even if it had no roads—certainly
no speed restrictions. The grass came back to the soil, very thinly
spread at first, and for the first time since they had stopped in the
Chinese villages below Kalgan they heard the song of birds. They
stopped to enjoy it. High in the sky were thousands of larks, making
a very sweet, piercing song. They were the progeny of the birds
who had been already trapped and sold to the eastern villagers
for their music.

For forty flat miles they crossed the thin green plain, putting up the water-birds but being ignored by stiff-standing flamingos. Then a stony desert began again.

Ahead of them, still fifty miles away, they saw the great face of the rock that marked Tuerin. The land in between was difficult and broken. It was another great basin, but not smooth like the Gobi. It was a succession of crests and declines, the irregular bed of some vanished sea. The heat and fierce light tired the travellers, and the sudden reappearance of the great rock, now only ten miles away, was a mental relief, if only for its solid density. It was a mountain fault, ripped away to show horizontal layers of savage reefs, over the jagged edges of which they now began to climb. They were grinding up the mountain track when over the hill-top there appeared four great golden globes, shining in the sun and apparently suspended in the air—the massive domes of the Buddhist temples of a starkly ascetic community. "It is impossible to describe," Barzini reported in the *Daily Telegraph*,

> the impression of profound surprise when from amid the rocks we saw the sun shining on high golden globes, crowning some superb Lamaist temples, built in the severe style of Tibetan architecture. Then, round the temples, was scattered a little town of white houses, with pagoda-like roofs. It was the holy city of Tuerin, a lama settlement, whose walls have never been crossed by the foot of a woman.

It was true that the town was exclusively male, except for the innumerable dogs who bred undisturbed by mental reservations about carnal desire; it was also true that near by was a settlement exclusively female, where the cries and laughter of children, which were so markedly absent in Tuerin, were, by contrast, obtrusive. The red-cassocked monks surrounded the car, and the dogs gave the same attention to the wheels as they do in European cities. The Itala crew were directed to the telegraph-station, remote from the holy city. Here they calculated that they had completed their first 1000 kilometres from Peking, and weighed out enough silver to buy a lamb for a celebration supper. Next morning they set off for Urga, in sudden high spirits at the realization that their north-west passage was bringing them back to the temperate zone, where there were signs of life and cultivation, and even the caravans could travel in the day. They were all gay. The Prince, at the wheel, sang *La Petite Tonkinoise*, and raised his speed to fifty-five miles an hour as he raced a herd of antelope.

The three cities of Urga—Chinese, Mongolian, and Russian— lay in a triangle some miles from one another, locked at night behind high, palisaded walls. Three other strong-points were also prominent in the stony plain. The Russian Consulate was a fortified villa, defended by trenches, barbed wire, and artillery, and gar- risoned by Cossacks. The fort of the Tartar General was not far away, battlemented and loopholed, with the silhouettes of sentries showing above its ramparts. The Grand Lama of Urga, the living god in whom Buddha was reputed to reside with only slightly less intensity than in the Dalai Lama of Lhasa in Tibet, dwelt in a white monastic palace, which did not exclude his wife and concubines, and was sited so that it was comparatively easy for access by the Russian Consul, within whose sphere of influence the dignitary then lay.

The crew of the Itala were directed to the Russian city, and found their way to the Russo-Chinese Bank. They were enthusi- astically greeted by the local manager, Stepanoff, and led to rooms reserved for them, passing through a great hall, decorated with the flags of the contestants, in which a long table was already laid for a banquet. Borghese asked Stepanoff to request the official Peking–Paris Raid Committee to delay any formal reception until there were more competitors to share it. But the Russians, who had been preparing for the event for many weeks, seemed to be anxious to hold a banquet every night during the period that the motorists were passing through. The Italians had arrived early in the day, and during the afternoon they received official visits from the Chinese Governor and the Tartar General. The Governor arrived at speed in the middle of a squadron of cavalry, his palan- keen's four poles resting unshackled on the saddle-bows of four Mongolian troopers, who had to keep exact station at the gallop if the palankeen was not to roll in the dust. The Tartar General put shrewd questions about the use of the motor-car in war, asserting that a force of ten armoured vehicles could take Mon- golia in four days. The Prince assured him that such a regiment was not envisaged—a statement which Lord Haldane at the British War Office could not conscientiously have endorsed.

Borghese announced that he would stay for a day in order to meet Cormier, who was now expected. The great table was used for an 'unofficial' banquet that night, and on the next day Borghese diplomatically returned calls. The Chinese Governor requested the extreme favour of a ride in the Itala. The Prince was delighted to agree, since the Governor was the official arm of the Wai Wu Pu. In a rich silk gown, with his peacock feathers of rank projecting from his round velvet hat, the Governor entered the car.

The Itala started with a suddenness that shocked the Governor's escort. Their horses were still tethered to the rails of the Residence. With a secret smile Borghese accelerated, the Governor's pigtail shot out horizontally behind, and the Itala streaked in a cloud of dust across the plain to the Russian city. The escort roared a rallying cry and dashed in pursuit, cloaks flying, scabbards rattling. The Governor arrived, an easy first, at the doors of the Russo-Chinese Bank. His empty palankeen came flying up on its four horses, and the Governor was borne back to his Residence in more conventional, though apparently no more comfortable, style.

The two de Dions had already arrived, and Madame Stepanoff began to exhibit symptoms of deep despair as she realized that when the Spyker came there would not be enough beds for all in the expedition. But Borghese solved this dilemma by announcing his departure next morning, though Stepanoff begged him to stay. The Prince was firm, and it was therefore planned that the banquet arranged for that night should be an official function. In the middle of the preparations messengers arrived from the Chinese Governor, obviously a better-intentioned person than Prince Ching. He had observed as he descended, somewhat windswept, from the Itala that other 'raiders' had arrived, and wished to send presents to the drivers. The presents were a pair of fat lambs, pure white except for their black heads, with two pitchers of wine. The whole consignment was clearly intended for the banquet that night, but Madame Stepanoff's three young daughters annexed the lambs to play with, and grew so fond of them in such a short time that the lambs were saved from the slaughter and adopted as household pets.

At nine the company met for dinner, under the flags of Russia, France, Holland, Italy, and China. In all there were some thirty guests. Silver sheaves of candles lit the room, which had the mellow panelling and decor of an apartment in Moscow. The furniture was in the heavy and ornate style of the West. The crystal and the cutlery, the food, the conversation—and, inevitably, the speeches—seemed to place the function within the frontiers of home, though they were still in the Chinese Empire. Russian officers, consular officials, professional men, and their ladies, delighting in the chance to don full dress for the occasion, courted the sunburnt travellers and toasted them with the linguistic aptitude of the international upper class of the day. The 'raiders' were back in champagne country.

It was the night of Saturday the 22nd of June, and Godard and du Taillis had driven jovially into Udde. Mister Johnson, who had had responsibility for them for four days, was delighted to see them, and to make up in some way for the unfortunate fact that two of his three consignments of petrol had gone astray. The treasures of his small larder—one chicken and two tins of condensed milk—were presented to them. Du Taillis accepted gratefully, and asked if the food could be cooked. Mister Johnson came from Shanghai—in fact, he was training his relief now so that he could go back there to be married—and he had a sense of European style. He had made up beds for the Frenchmen in a form that in no way resembled a brick *kang*, and he had put out bowls of water, soap, and towels. Du Taillis merely wet his face as a first toilet, for he was burning to send his copy. While he was writing his telegram he asked Mister Johnson to get in touch with Pong-Kiong and Tuerin to give news of his rescue, and request Tuerin to pass it to Urga—the information came to the Itala and de Dion crews before the banquet. At the same time Udde requested news of Pons. The transmitter was in du Taillis's bedroom —it was considered the best room—and the apparatus rattled back a message on the blue paper ribbon addressed to du Taillis from Mister Luck at Pong-Kiong.

The message, composed in Mister Luck's version of English, read:

> Du Taillis. *Udde*
> Your another automobile was broken on the way. Therefore they would not be able to walk. What shall you do.
>
> Luck

Du Taillis was alone writing in his room when his telegram came through. It was not exactly clear. But du Taillis concluded that if Pons and Foucault were not able to walk at least they could be presumed to be breathing. But obviously they could not go on with the *raid*. He tore the slip from the machine and ran out into the courtyard of the compound, where Mister Johnson was superintending the cooking of the chicken. He asked him to request Pong-Kiong for full details, and to advise Pons and Foucault to get back to Kalgan by horse. Du Taillis then wrote a telegram to Dorliac at the bank at Kalgan, asking him to send out forces to pick up the casualties. And he went back to complete his copy for *Le Matin*. While these messages were passing Godard, after four days in the blue, was sweating away underneath the Spyker, greasing it with ample supplies they had found in Udde.

They sat down to Mister Johnson's *poule au riz*, inferior to Longoni's production, which Cormier had so highly praised the night before, since the milk was condensed, not fresh—inferior, certainly, to the banquet which was then being prepared in the bank in Urga. But neither Godard nor du Taillis could do justice to Mister Johnson's cooking. Du Taillis's stomach after his 3-day ordeal was in a fearful state—he had contracted dysentery, which never left him for the rest of the *raid*. Godard was in high fever. They merely picked at their food. But they were determined that they had no time to be ill. They put in a call for five o'clock next morning, went to their beds, and collapsed on them fully dressed. And all through the night, by du Taillis's ear, the chatter of the telegraph passed the traffic of two hemispheres—politics, commerce, and a modicum of good news.

They were weak but lively as they jumped into the Spyker next morning. The rising sun had never seemed so glorious. They were each of them clinging to an identical private resolution. It was to cut out Tuerin as a staging-point, flash through it, and go on—to attempt the through run from Udde to Urga. The main strain would be on Godard. But when they mutually confessed their intention du Taillis knew that Godard was game.

They climbed, found the plain, dashed through the partridges and past slow files of camels, making obscene signs at the caravan leaders in memory of their crude rejection in the desert. They had no food at all, only a stock of cold tea that they had brought from Udde. They drank a small flask every two hours, not stopping the car even for this. After twelve hours non-stop they came to the mountains of Tuerin, which looked to them like the jagged peaks of Dante's Hell. At the summit they saw, like a vision from elfland, in the rays of the declining sun, the curved pagoda-roofs of the strange city of Tuerin. For the third time that week the monks and young seminarists of the monastery ran towards the strange chariot that seemed to be passing them regularly. The Frenchmen stopped only to refill their water-tanks from a thin, cool stream, and sped away from the holy city. They were half-way to Urga. The way was firm, and for the first time since Peking they knew the true inebriation of speed. Godard had his ignition advanced to the top and his foot on the floor, and they soared over Asia like a shooting star.

The long twilight closed, and full darkness came down. The moon was shrouded, but in its dull light they kept on. Suddenly Godard pulled up fast. What seemed an immense chasm was gaping in front of their wheels.

"We're off the track," said Godard. "There are no telegraph-posts. We ought to go left."

"No, right," said du Taillis; "we crossed the line of posts a quarter of an hour ago."

They wandered haphazardly in the dark, seeking the track. At last they came across the poles, but still there was no road. They followed the line, bumping over the debris of old camps left by gangs who first set the line up, and finally distinguished a more beaten path.

"We'll have a glass of water," said Godard, "and then go on."

They had been relying on the moon, which was near the full.

But it dipped behind hazy clouds. Du Taillis got down and lit the acetylene headlights. It was about midnight.

It was one o'clock, two, three. They were falling about with sleep, and the car was bumping badly.

"It will be first light in an hour."

"We'll be able to see what we're doing. We shall go much more quickly then."

"All right. Stop. For one hour, not more. We won't get out of the car. We'll just flop out on the seats."

They wearily pulled over them the blankets from behind their seats, and slept. The cold woke them up within the hour. It was half-past four.

On again. They had come to the edge of a ravine. The track divided, one way going over the mountains, the other down a timbered valley whose slopes were planted with cedar. It was the end of the desert. Urga must be near.

They skidded down slopes which brought them alongside the river Tola. They saw the shape of Urga within the ring of mountains. The sun was beginning to pierce the valley, and in the cities ahead they saw it glint on yellow roofs, the green tiles of pagodas, and the unexpectedly thrilling line of the bell-tower of an Orthodox church boxed in by white Russian houses.

If they had been more alert, they knew, they would have been more nervous of the fords across the branches of the Tola, which they had to risk without the encouragement of seeing other traffic cross them. But they set the Spyker at the turbulent streams, and came through, and flashed across the plain and through the palisades of the Chinese city on the stroke of five o'clock.

Du Taillis had one objective—the telegraph office, towards which the posts still led. The operators were asleep, But he beat on the door until they opened. "*Le Matin*, Paris via Udde, Gobi, Monday, 6 A.M.," he scribbled. "We have completed in one stretch the stage from Udde to Urga, where we have just arrived to-day, Monday, at 5 A.M., having done 617 kilometres in 23 hours. Du Taillis."

385 miles in 24 hours stood as an individual record by the Spyker for the rest of the Paris *raid*. In Godard's condition, after his ordeal in the desert, it was an outstanding performance,

particularly in view of the entire absence of made roads.[1] But for prolonged endurance even this was to be made insignificant by the later feats of Godard, the "old shuvver."

[1] Within a week, on the 29th of June, 1907, the Australian cyclist Selwyn Francis Edge, then thirty-nine years old and turning his attention to cars, put up a longstanding 24-hour record on the race-track. In a 60-h.p., six-cylinder Napier he drove for 24 hours round Brooklands and covered 1581 miles, at an average speed of nearly 66 m.p.h. Fifty-seven years later the 24-hour record was raised at Le Mans to 2911 miles, at an average speed of over 121 m.p.h., by Jean Guichet and Nino Vaccarello in a 3.2-litre Ferrari. The difference was that Guichet and Vaccarello were co-drivers, operating alternately, whereas Edge drove alone and without relief—in fact, after a glass of beer he drove home to Cobham at the end of his run.

11 ◎ ◎ No Sale

It was Monday morning. The de Dion crews had spent an easy Sunday, not getting up till nine—letting Borghese go off on his own at five after the banquet—and actually having *café au lait* served in their rooms at breakfast-time. Collignon and Cormier went off in the car to explore the exit from Urga and take a look at the towns—they were astonished to see Mongolian women riding horses astride. Cormier sent telegrams. He was delighted to find a French State courier using the faster overland route to Paris, to whom he entrusted his diary and twelve rolls of film, with a number of private letters. They dined simply in the evening, and went to bed early.

On the Monday Bizac, as usual, was up early, and heard the beat of the Spyker engine as it approached the Russo-Chinese Bank at 8 A.M. He opened the gate, pointed out the garage that was reserved for the car, and ran to wake the others. But they too had heard the engine and were dashing from their beds. They came down and met Godard and du Taillis in the yard.

It was a wary reunion. But the Spyker crew set the mood. Du Taillis was determined to demand no explanation from Cormier. He had already heard from Bizac of the departure of Borghese for Kiakhta—as he expressed it, "with no more care for us than for Pons"—and he had resolved that, at least while they were in the company of the kindly and hospitable Russians, the French should present a united front.

Godard seemed to bear no ill will at all. The ploy over the petrol was just a part of the drivers' game. Cormier had meant no more by his refusal—at the sheer technique of which Godard still chuckled with admiration—than the raising of the ante, even if, with his reserves, he could have afforded to give. The near-tragic consequences were not intended. It had all been something of a chapter of accidents.

Godard, in any case, was in no condition for a fight except on a matter of life and death. He was all in. He had collapsed on a heap of wood in the yard. He could not stir, and hardly spoke, beyond a faint welcome flourish *à la* Tartarin. It was inconceivable that he should yield so utterly to exhaustion that he could not give the figures of his run.

Du Taillis, who had suffered less physical strain, responded to the friendly faces and the balm of the Russian welcome by bounding back into brief vitality. It was he who chaffed Madame Stepanoff, who had been awakened by the noise, and came bustling down. In a minute he had her shouting with laughter and declaring that they were just a couple of brigands—dirty, raw, and as dishevelled as if they had slept a week in a ditch. If Monsieur Cormier were not there to vouch for them she would have run to her room and barred herself in.

While Madame Stepanoff hurried off to order breakfast for them Godard and du Taillis drank bottles of beer and exchanged curt gossip with the others. Du Taillis had fresh news of Pons, received in a dawn telegram at Udde. Pons was already declaring that if he must abandon his tri-car he would still cross Mongolia by horse or camel, come through Urga and Kiakhta, reach the Trans-Siberian Railway, and get to Paris by the route, if not the machine, that he had planned. Cormier commented that he could not expect them to wait for him, and they were all due to leave Urga next morning.

In the kitchen Madame Stepanoff was crying with pity for the exhausted newcomers. But she sent in a good breakfast, with more iced beer, and had the servants warm the boilers for a real Russian bath.

Godard and du Taillis went to bed for a few hours. Du Taillis got up soon and wrote a long dispatch for *Le Matin*. He was weak with dysentery and seemed to have the symptoms of malaria. But they both came down to a lively family lunch, with some fifteen members of the irrepressible *raid* committee in attendance.

At luncheon Madame Stepanoff proposed an excursion. "We'll all go to see the living god," she said.

"Living god?" echoed du Taillis, and the status of the Grand Lama was explained to him.

"It's quite useless, my dear," cut in Stepanoff. "He wouldn't receive Borghese. And the Prince was really pressing. He pulled all the diplomatic strings."

"Nonsense," said Madame Stepanoff. "The Grand Lama wouldn't see Prince Borghese because the Prince took the Chinese Governor out in his motor-car. He thought he should have been invited first." Madame Stepanoff gave a lively account of the adventure of the Chinese Governor while the guests sipped a liqueur.

At that moment a servant entered to announce that emissaries from the Grand Lama had called. The living god would condescend to see the motorists.

"What did I say?" said Madame Stepanoff. "We'll all go in the cars."

The three Stepanoff children were bundled into the Spyker, having to be detached from their pet lambs, which it was not thought tactful to take. The party drove across the plain to the Grand Lama's palace.

There was a long wait outside the palace. The Russian interpreter talked earnestly with a courtier-monk. It seemed that one of the reasons for the Grand Lama's invitation was that he had once been given a motor-car by a foreign deputation, but from the day it arrived it had never been persuaded to go. Perhaps the raiders' would care to overhaul it.

"Not interested," said Cormier bluntly. "We haven't come to see a car. We want to talk to the living god. Tell him that if he doesn't come out in person we'll go away without looking at anything."

Another half-hour passed.

There was a flurry on the palace steps. Courtiers were coming out backwards, with every sign of respect. The Grand Lama made an ostentatious entry with his wife, passed the bells and great drums, which were used at solemn ceremonies, and came down the courtyard.

"God, this god is ugly," muttered Bizac.

After inspecting the cars the living god commanded that they should be started. Cormier then invited him to sit in his de Dion. The Grand Lama declined, but instructed one of his courtiers to get in, and laughed as he was driven round the courtyard.

Finally the message was passed to Cormier, "Can you examine the car of the Grand Lama and tell him why it does not go?"

Ten Mongolians pushed a box on wheels into the courtyard. It looked like a motor-car. It had wheels the right shape and even a dashboard. But it would never go. The Frenchmen recognized it as a dummy from an American shop-window. Cormier told the Grand Lama through his interpreter that it could never be made to go.

"What is your advice?" he was asked.

"The best thing I could tell you to do is to buy another," said Cormier briskly. "Now, why don't you take a run in my little de Dion. Just to get the feel of it. It's a wonderful little machine, ten horsepower, very strongly built, economical, will go anywhere and I can let you have it for . . ." He faltered as he tried to translate francs into taels.

"It's a snip," he concluded. "Price quoted ex-works, of course. But delivery as soon as you like."

The Grand Lama smiled distantly.

"No sale," said Cormier, and he got back heavily into his car.

When the crew of the Itala slipped out of Urga at dawn on Sunday the 23rd of June they knew that they had left the sands of the desert behind them for good. There were still 300 miles to traverse before they were out of Mongolia and across the Siberian frontier, but, in spite of warnings they had received from the Russians in Urga, they believed that their car had passed the most testing stretch of the *raid*. By 5.15 A.M. they were bogged deeper than the clearance of the back axle, and were prepared to walk back to Urga to apologize to the travellers whose tales they had taken so lightly.

There was no road or obvious track. They were prepared for that. There was no comforting line of telegraph-posts, for the Imperial Chinese system ran west for many hundreds of miles through Mongolia, and not north-west to Siberia. Borghese drove cautiously up a gentle valley, bright with a grass that was suspiciously green. But, in spite of his slow speed, he could take no corrective action when the car suddenly stopped dead, sank rapidly to one side, as if its left wheels were falling on a hydraulic jack, and embedded itself in a swamp, with the back wheels still racing. "Cut the engine!" yelled Guizzardi, who had been pitched out of the car and could see the driving-wheels digging their grave. Borghese switched off and jumped out to inspect the damage. The rear axle was below the surface on the left, and the car was held up only by the rear petrol-tanks. The left rear wheel was bending under the weight so seriously that it was creaking audibly. Guizzardi tore out his crowbars from the back of the car and tried to force the rear up, but the iron merely sank into the mud. "We want planks," he shouted. "We'll take the floorboards," said Borghese. They ripped out planks from the floor of the car and set them in the mud to act as a base to take the weight of the levering. But the planks split and broke, and were pushed into the mud.

They had a long-handled spade, of the type used by Italian roadmen. They began to dig an incline from the front to the track of the back wheels, hoping to make a slope by which the car could climb out on its engine. But as they removed the top surface the car sank deeper.

They realized that one of them must go back to Urga to bring back a team of men with stout planks and horses.

While they wrestled with the shame of this humiliating prospect, and cursed the fact that they had abandoned their steel runners after Kalgan, they suddenly saw a line of Mongolian ox-carts breasting the slope of a hill ahead. And the carts were laden with pine-trunks.

They ran towards the caravan, rattled a bag of Russian money under the noses of the men, and dashed back towards the Itala, each with a pole on his shoulders. The Mongolians followed with more trunks. They laid a pole down in the mud against the back wheels, thwartwise. They shoved other poles under the car, levering on the horizontal pole, and by heaving on the long trunks raised the car with ease, inches at a time. As the back came up they stacked stones under the wheel. Then they worked on the front. At last the car stood level, propped on stones. They got out their tow-ropes, hooked them to the rear springs, and tried to drag the car backward. But with comparatively short ropes they could not apply enough strength to move the machine. "The oxen!" ordered Borghese. The caravan leaders were made to understand. They hitched three oxen to the back of the car, added their own weight on the ropes, and finally moved the Itala out of the morass. The operation had taken over three hours.

"Tell me the way to Kiakhta," said Borghese in Russian as he distributed the salvage fees.

One of the Mongolians understood, and could speak the language a little. "There are two ways," he said. "One passes over the mountain, and the other keeps to the plain."

"Which is the best?" asked the Prince.

"You are on the best here."

"Kindly show me the worst," said Borghese, and he was directed to the mountain route.

They climbed into the ring of mountains enclosing Urga. And then they had to descend. A steep slope peppered with boulders led down to a ravine, on the brink of which the track continued. The car began the descent, but was blocked by two of these boulders jammed against the front wheels. Borghese and Barzini got down to tug them away, but could not shift them. "I'll do it with the engine," said Guizzardi. He revved the engine and eased the Itala over. The car immediately dropped forward with the sharpness of the incline and shot down the hillside. The foot-brake, heavily greased, failed to hold it. Borghese was clinging to the car, fighting at first to hold it, and then being swept down with it into the ravine. Ettore was as tense as a gladiator. Suddenly he heaved on the wheel, wrenched the car into a right-hand slip and up over a pile of stones, pulled back the handbrake, which was the more powerful of the two, and slithered to a stop.

Barzini arrived panting. All he had been able to do was to chase the car down the hill shouting "Stop!" and dodging the tools and baggage which had been cascading from the back as the car hit boulders, bounced, and bucked—and more of their luggage-lashing parted. They collected their pieces, tied them in again, and set off. Borghese decided to try an original route to Kiakhta. The plains were swamps. The mountains were chutes. He would try a circuit round the mountains, keeping as far as possible to foothills.

As a result he put the car into a quicksand.

Without warning the Itala sank under them. They jumped out immediately. As their feet hit the surface it yielded a little, and then sprang back like a trampoline. They looked at the ground, and were horrified to see that it was heaving. They were in a vast pocket of liquid mud, whose top surface had dried in the sun, but had only a tensile strength comparable to the skin on a cup of *café au lait*. They swiftly tried to measure the depth of water underneath with their long spade. It slipped through the surface and into the liquid without resistance as far as they could push it.

The car sank steadily. The axles were immersed. The carriage step was under the surface. As the chassis paused on the mud crust before a final plunge the crew furiously tried to lighten it, struggling in the firmer glue of the surface, but terrified all the time that their boots would break through to the liquid.

They cut away the cords of the spare tyres ranged on the back of the car. They threw out all the baggage, and even unbolted the tool-chest. The descent of the Itala seemed to be halted for the moment. "We must *think*," said Borghese. And then the 'English officer' made a profoundly English suggestion. "Let's have a cup of tea," he said. They made the tea in a saucepan, to which Barzini dutifully applied his soldering lamp.

They talked, and agreed that now, at last, one of them must go back to Urga. It might take many days. There was no hope of a passing caravan to rescue them this time.

There was, indeed, no caravan. They were on no caravan route. But the luck that even the best general needs again favoured Borghese. Some distance below the foothills there appeared a line of carts, drawn by horses, with the high wooden horseshoe arch of the Russian tradition guiding the harness over the horses' necks. Barzini raced straight towards them, bounding into unseen patches of quicksand, but always extricating himself. It was a tribe of Buriats on the march, moving to new ground like gipsies. After a short parley their chief agreed to examine the sunken car. But, having fixed the high price of fifty roubles for his help, he did not call in his men. Instead they stood a hundred yards off, making no effort, merely watching and waiting.

Waiting for what? The chance to attack them by night, now that they knew the travellers had roubles? If this was their intention they delayed too long. As vultures sight a fallen beast, other eyes had focused from the surrounding country on the halted trek of the Buriats and the two waiting camps. A number of Mongolians rode across the plain from points where perhaps some *yurtas* were concealed in brushland. As their horses converged on the quicksand area they made a sizeable troop. They dexterously picked their way through the ground and surrounded the Italians.

With no preliminary bargaining the Mongols started working

at the car, but soon saw that without tools the outlook for recovery was poor. Borghese tried to indicate that they needed poles. He was apparently understood, and some of the men hurried off on their horses, and returned at the gallop, having tied the ends of long planks to their saddles, dragging the free ends on the ground. Under the sullen eyes of the Buriats the operation of levering up the car was again started. This time Guizzardi even unbolted the body so that only a stripped chassis remained to be lifted. After three hours they had raised the Itala. But again they could not drag it back by their own strength. Oxen! More mime from the Italians. Further departure by the Mongolian horsemen. From somewhere they drove up a whole herd of oxen, but the shortness of the tow-ropes allowed only four to be harnessed. And the haulage of the beasts could not be co-ordinated. They tugged, but never in unison. It was impossible to get concerted action from them.

Impossible? Ettore had caused enough terror through Mongolia with his engine and its trumpeting racing exhaust, and at last the shock-wave of the Itala's forty-horsepower snarl could be put to practical effect. He ran to the front and started the engine. The beasts bowed their heads together, until their great horns swept the ground, and tore at the soil to get into flight. Ettore ran round, got into the driving-seat, and revved the engine with a great lunge. The car seemed to spring upward with the reaction of the oxen. It was sucked out of its station as Ettore, propelled almost horizontally over the bonnet, cut the engine.

The oxen were unharnessed. The Italians bolted back the car body and once more reloaded their luggage. Borghese paid the Mongolians and got them to guide him out of the quicksand area. Without their local knowledge he would have driven from one morass to another. But Borghese followed the winding path of the horsemen and emerged on the solid plain, leaving the silent Buriats continuing their own march. The night had fallen, and the car's headlamps were not working, but Borghese continued by moonlight for some time, until they camped by a small stream and crawled exhausted into their tent. They had been in action for seventeen hours that day. They had no idea how much true progress towards Kiakhta they had made.

They cursed when they awoke, for they saw that they were in marsh country again. One of the Italians walked ahead of the car whenever the ground seemed treacherous. They were constantly stopping and sheering away to find a safer path. Every stream they came to was first forded on foot. Finally the great river that was gathering together all the water from this swamp basin appeared before them. It was the rushing river Iro, 300 yards broad, and menacingly swift.

Without a word Ettore Guizzardi waded into the water. The sun was warm, and the bathe was no hardship, but he stumbled and swerved as a rock moved under him, and the current caught him. Long before he was half-way across, the water was up to his waist, and he came back.

"It is too deep to ford," he said. "The water would stop the engine, and we should be caught broadside by the stream."

Barzini had what seemed to him a brilliant idea. "We must take it over on a raft," he suggested. "Where can we find a raft?" His eye wandered to a hut in a small plantation near by. "There's the raft! We must buy the hut, knock it down, and build a raft from the planks."

A number of Mongolians could be seen hurrying from the hut, as if they had somehow overheard the suggestion, and wished to get out before the place was bowled over by a white man's hurricane. They came towards them, and Borghese made some sort of conversation with them. One Mongolian term which he knew very well by now was the word for oxen. He suggested oxen. The Mongolians did not seem surprised, and at the sight of the Prince's money went off to fetch some.

Ettore prepared to modify the car for its river journey. He dismounted the magneto, heavily greased the engine, and bound it round with oily rags. He unbolted the lower casing of the engine to give a better clearance over the river-bed. Then, with the magneto, also wrapped in oily rags, safely in his bosom, under his thick woollen vest, he sat at the driving-wheel. The oxen were harnessed to the car. Dozens of Mongolians, who had now appeared to share in the fun, leapt on to horses or astride the oxen, or plunged into the river leading the oxen, and with great shouts the crossing was started. Prince Borghese led the way on a stately horse, like Napoleon crossing the Berezina, and a few admiring Mongolian women, also astride horses, followed him closely. The oxen shuddered and wavered as the force of the mid-stream current hit them. The car was jolting roughly on the gravel bed of the Iro, and the water was rushing high over the remnants of the floorboards. The cattle-leaders pushed their goads into the flanks of the beasts, and with a new effort the deepest point was passed. With great shouts and bellows and the tossing of horns the Itala was drawn smoothly out of the river and up the stony bank, leaving its own gushing stream of water to flow back into the Iro.

The crossing took two hours and a half, with an extra hour to remount the magneto and engine casing and get the car moving again. The land now was firmer, and Borghese managed a fair speed for some twenty-five miles. They passed through a pine-wood that seemed inexpressibly Russian, and they had the urge to speed on, for the frontier surely could not be far. But the forest gave place to plain, and the plain reverted from grass to sand. The sky was darkening rapidly, and in the middle of the plain they heard the first gust of a hurricane. The storm leapt towards them over the sand, lifting the loose surface into a high pillar of dust. It was on them. They were blind, in the centre of it. But Borghese, at the wheel, would not even stop the car. Bending low, almost flat in their seats, they pushed their way through the vortex and on through the diminishing force of the storm. But when the hurricane had passed they still had to fight for Kiakhta. A stretch of sand dunes lay ahead, offering nothing of the limitlessness of the desert, but much of its hopelessness. The depth into which they sank was never exceeded in their passage through the Gobi. They had to dig at the soft sand ahead of the car to reach a harder bed for their tyres. One stretch of half a mile took an hour to cover. At the end of the dunes they had to climb a steep hill. And from the top they saw Kiakhta.

The first thing they noticed was factory chimneys, and even that made them homesick for the West. But there were houses and church spires—a town with a shape they understood—hard up against the last town in China, the frontier station of Maima-chen. A narrow strip of space marked No Man's Land, with a tall pillar on the actual line of the frontier. On one side of the open space, the side which the Itala approached, there was the quintessence of China—a squat settlement, infinitely colourful, with its silk banners and painted dragons and an irrepressibly friendly people. The last Chinese they spoke to emphasized this warmth. He was a young man who stopped them to ask in English if they would accept his hospitality as they had with his colleagues. He was the telegraph operator, and in his private house they washed four layers of mud from their faces—black from the bogs, yellow and white from the rivers, and brown from the paste of hurricane dust and sweat. Then, clean, dined, and wined, they went on to the frontier.

A soldier, square, smart, and gruff, stopped them. His military cap was flat. His uniform tunic was white. He carried a cross-belt and sword. His boot heels smacked together as he saluted them. He stood on the step of the car and directed them into the Russian Empire—to the office of the Chief of Police. The Chief received them gravely. There was official business to be done. He handed each of the motorists a bundle of documents. The first was a special permit authorizing them to carry two pistols each.

Again there was a Russo-Chinese Bank to receive them. The manager in Kiakhta was Monsieur Sinitzin. His house was as lively, and as luxuriously served, as Maxim's in Paris on a spring evening—but this was a Maxim's in the Russian style, less gilded, more timbered, and much less rigorously organized. Barefooted servants with flowing kerchiefs and costumes that seemed designed for the stage passed and repassed under the voluble exhortations of Madame Sinitzin, who was sometimes in the most elegant gown, sometimes dashing in from the kitchens with her hair tied up like a pudding and a great soup-ladle in her hand. The house seemed full of guests, bearded men in long silk blouses and shining calf-high boots. They were all reputed to be millionaires, though more impoverished than they had been. For Kiakhta had made its fortune from the tea caravans. The tea changed hands here, being brought in from China and sold to the merchants of Kiakhta, who had their order-books filled to send it wholesale all over the Empire and beyond. Until seven years before, fifty million pounds of tea had been packed here every year. The Trans-Siberian Railway had wiped the entrepôt clean, but the arrival of Borghese along the old camel route excited keen interest. He had moved from Kalgan to Kiakhta in seven days, a fortnight faster than the camel schedules. Could motor-cars be introduced to recapture the tea from the railway? These were the discussions at the convivial Sinitzin dinners, which did not start until midnight and snowballed on through ten courses, sandwiching sides of meat and braces of geese between the caviare and the bortsch at one end and the fresh fruit from Italy at the other.

It was on this scale that Madame Sinitzin prepared a hamper for Prince Borghese when he left Kiakhta two days later. Chickens by the half-dozen and roast quarters of lamb were being packed in the hamper, with wine and beer and brandy, when Borghese courteously refused them on the ground of their weight and bulk. He could be prevailed on to accept only two chickens and some wine in order to avoid offence.

The rain had been falling for twenty-four hours. The Italians had been listening earnestly to warnings of the bogs and steep earth slopes of Siberia, which they were inclined to accept after their experiences on the way to Kiakhta. The weather outlook depressed them. But far more seriously than this they were worried about their petrol and oil supplies. The Nobel Company had telegraphed to Borghese in Peking confirming that they were assuming responsibility for his fuel supplies through Siberia and Russia. The first stocks, they had claimed, would be found in Kiakhta, and with them would be an exact schedule of the stocks which would have been delivered to all the other stages on the route, with a note of the distances between the stages. When they arrived at Kiakhta they had found this schedule—but there was no fuel in store in the town. Borghese sent urgent telegrams to St Petersburg trying to hasten delivery, but got no satisfaction. Late on the Tuesday before their dawn departure Sinitzin remembered that a Russian friend of his, one of the merchants in the town, had bought a small motor-car some time before, but it had broken down, and there was no one to repair it. With the car he had bought a large supply of petrol, and it might just be possible that he had some left. Borghese called on the merchant, and was shown the drum in which the petrol had been. There was an adequate supply left in the bottom, and Guizzardi tapped it to restock the Itala. They were well supplied for the next stage, but were quite uncertain about the future. If the stocks had not come through to Kiakhta there was no reason to suppose that they had reached the other fuel points.

In low spirits the Italians drove out of Kiakhta in the dripping dawn. At the deserted crossroads of the main town a policeman was on duty—a Western touch—and he gave them a smart salute, which cheered them. A troop of drowsy Cossacks rode slowly back to barracks from night guard in the countryside, swathed against the weather in heavy grey greatcoats, with their bayonets glinting dully over their heads on their long slung rifles. The motorists grew more lively as they met or passed the swelling volume of traffic on the road from Verkhne-Udinsk—little wheeled swing-boats called tarantasses and the heavier telega carts. Occasionally in a town a policeman, his medals and ribbons brilliant against his white tunic, would salute them and direct them. They passed through a succession of villages, all grouped on the one main street, all with houses built in the rough-hewn timber of Siberian architecture, all with their tall church in its churchyard at one end of the street. Then the road curved in towards the broad, white-watered Selenga river, which they would have to cross by ferry. A friendly, bearded countryman hailed the crew of a raft which had just carried a telega to the other side. It returned. It was a broad but frail-looking pontoon manned by a crew of four, two men pulling each long oar. It hardly had room to receive the Itala. The crew moored the boat to the bank, and Ettore cautiously drove down on to it. When the front wheels of the two-ton car were on board the raft dipped and bucked outward, and the moorings began to give. Quickly the crew fastened fresh hawsers. Ettore very slowly drove forward, advancing the weight so that the lee side of the raft gradually came up, and finally the car was aboard. The raft sat low in the water.

The men pulled out into the stream, and the peasant manned a tiller. When they were mid-stream they heard a high, echoing siren, and round a bend in the river chugged a stern-wheel paddle-steamer. Its very appearance gave the motorists a feeling of warmth and familiarity, and they waved energetically back to the passengers, who ran to the rails to see them. The boat passed—the first steamer they had seen since the *Admiral von Tirpitz*—and, rocking in the waves of its wake, they came ashore at Novi-Selengisk.

They began to pass through a fertile plain which now, for the first time in Russian history, was being settled and cultivated by peasant immigration from the West. This had been made possible only by the new railway. Inevitably the sound of the Itala produced terror in the horses and cattle which were grazing in the fields or being used for draught work. Borghese at first, shocked with his effect on the beasts, stopped his car as he saw a cart approaching, and yelled, "Hold your horses! Hold your horses!" But in the end the crew became hardened to their havoc. Women working in the fields fled at the approach of the explosive exhaust. But the men remained, standing with their hands on their hoes; and with great politeness, but infinite pathos, as the car passed they took off their hats and bowed, so that their fair, shoulder-length hair fell about their eyes.

The Italians were coming up to the embarkation point for Verkhne-Udinsk—they had to recross the Selenga to reach it—when from far away they heard a whistle they all recognized. They were halted, measuring the width of one of a hundred little wooden bridges they were crossing in that water-logged plain. Ettore, an old railwayman, gave a shout and pointed. Far across the Selenga the high engine and black-and-yellow cars of the Trans-Siberian Express glided through the timbered hills as soundlessly as in a dream, only the angle of its smoke-stream indicating its speed. The sight seemed such a link with home that they all responded. They cheered the train, unheard.

They crossed a ferry far more elaborate than the last and came to the white city of Verkhne-Udinsk. Again they sought out petrol supplies, and again no stock had been left for them. In desperation they drove to the store of the principal grocer. He let them have his entire stock of fifty litres, eleven gallons, remarking that the citizens would have to go dirty for a little while. The only use for petrol there was for household dry-cleaning.

Borghese took rooms in the stuffy inn which served the town. The car was tucked in the courtyard, and Ettore went through his daily routine of checking and greasing. At this staging-point he made his first tyre renewal. None of Pirelli's spares, which they carried like a concertina buffer on the back, had yet been needed, but Guizzardi changed one outer cover at Verkhne-Udinsk. The party went to bed, liberally sprinkling their couches with anti-vermin powder. But no preparation they carried could repel Russian fleas. They twitched all night, listening to the bugle-calls of the garrison and the stamp of soldiers continually changing guard. For in Siberia the army had to occupy every bank and public building. In the morning, when they crossed another arm of the confluence of rivers about the city, there were sentries at the ferry-point.

And still it was raining. They burned their petrol away as they skidded or slithered crabwise along choppy black seas of mud. At the slightest slope two of the crew had to dismount and cut branches and bushes for the wheels to grip on. Their legs were caked to elephant width with the black slime. The wheels sprayed the mud all over them. They had given up cleaning their faces, except to wipe craters for eyes and nostrils. And they were so unused to the cold that it felt as if the mud had frozen on their faces. They had come into the country served by the railway. As soon as the line had been laid, all upkeep on the roads seemed to have been abandoned. In terrain where bridges were essential the neglect of the road bridges meant that the way would soon be impassable. Within the day they came to the point of impasse.

They were running through a forest which led down to a valley where the roar of a river was clearly audible. Suddenly they heard voices calling them, and saw railway workers running towards them. "Stop—stop! The bridge is down." By the time they had stopped they could see the gap in the timber. "Is there a ford?" asked Borghese. They were directed upstream, but when they came to the ford they could see that the river was too rough and high for their engine. After a wait of some minutes men came to them from their work in the forest, and agreed to go to fetch horses, at a price of one rouble per horse. The requisitioning took an hour, and then the motorists saw a group of long-haired *mujiks* riding horses along the farther bank. They set their horses into the river, and came across. There were six of them. First they carried the luggage, which the motorists had unpacked, across the river on the horses' backs. Guizzardi was again busy shrouding the engine in grease and tightly tied rags. The riders came back, and harnessed the horses to the Itala. Riding like postilions, with one man even astride the bonnet of the car, they whipped their horses into the river and heaved the car to the other side. The luggage was stacked again. Another few yards of the journey to Paris was completed, in a time of three hours.

They were now approaching Lake Baikal, an inland sea as large as the area of Belgium. It lay like a broad wedge across their path, presenting a front of water as long as the distance from Moscow to St Petersburg, and they had to get round it or over it. The Paris committee had always maintained that the journey round its verge was, under the road conditions obtaining, virtually impossible, and that it was perfectly legitimate for the 'raiders' to cross it by ferry.

But their information was incomplete, and their assessment of Borghese's determination inadequate. The ferry-port of Missowaya had fallen into almost complete disuse since the recent development of the railway—though the town was still an important winter marshalling-yard for the sledges which carried goods and people across the sea when it was frozen. But, whatever the state of the port, Prince Borghese, when he arrived at Missowaya, was quite firm that he would get through to Irkutsk on the wheels of the Itala. The party would go round the lake.

Missowaya was a depressing police-ridden town peopled by political exiles. But the Italians found some comfort in it. At least their fuel supply system had heaved itself into operation. The mayor of Missowaya, to whom the prince had a letter of introduction from Sinitzin at Kiakhta, proudly revealed that he held the party's stocks of petrol, oil, and grease. The crew gratefully restocked the car. But the mayor was most pessimistic about the party's chances of reaching Irkutsk by land.

However, they set off, on Friday the 28th of June, on a clear, cold morning, which was at least blessed by the absence of rain. But the track round the lake simply did not exist. Overgrown with grass and blocked by fallen trees which sent them on detours through the marshy woodland, the abandoned road led past post-houses which had fallen into ruins—the stables which had held their relay horses half-demolished and wholly looted. The bridges had not been deliberately despoiled, but the parapets of most had gone under the weight of winter snow. And as they gingerly crossed the unprotected surfaces they knew that sooner or later there must be crossings where the main planks themselves would have rotted and never been repaired.

The expected stoppage came within a few hours. They had passed over one bridge, which sagged ominously even when they walked on it first to test it. They decided to set the car over it at a fair speed in order to take the weight off individual planks as soon as possible. They started the Itala, and went on to the bridge. When all the Itala's weight was over the river the crew heard a sharp double crack, like two quick rifle-shots, and the car lurched a little at the rear. Guizzardi, who generally took the wheel at the bridges, did not alter his acceleration at all, and the car did not settle, but plunged on over the planks. They looked back, and saw a hole in the bridge where two of the planks had snapped, allowing some sections to fall into the river. "Well, that solves any query about turning back," commented Borghese.

The next bridge spanned the Mishika, a major river. They gave one glance at the gap two-thirds of the way across, and knew that there was no chance of getting over it. They backed, until they found a path leading down to the bank. In front of a little cottage a woodcutter was lacing on his boots. "*Do svidania*," he said.

"*Do svidania*. Can you direct us to the ford?"

"There is no ford here, little father. The Mishika is above a man's height. There is a boat."

He pointed out a sort of coracle, shaped out of a tree-trunk. It seemed that one boat would be necessary for each wheel.

"How do you get the cattle across?"

"They swim." He looked downstream, and they could see horses swimming diagonally against the swift current.

"How would you get this car across the river?"

The woodman thought for a minute as he laced his boots. "Well, the bridge could be mended," he suggested.

"Is that possible? Are there men who could do it?"

"We can all make bridges, and there is plenty of timber."

"How long would it take?"

"Get six men, and it will take a week."

Barzini was the most enthusiastic. He could already read his headlines: "Italian motorists building bridges in Siberia." He declaimed it to his companions. But Borghese shook his head drily.

"We have already been told of three more major bridges which are down, not counting the small ones and the others we are likely to break. We have not contracted to reconstruct the communications of the Russian Empire. No, we are going back. But we shall still round Lake Baikàl by land."

He squeezed Barzini's arm affectionately. "You'll get an even better headline," he promised.

Two days later they crossed the Mishika—by bridge. It was a great iron bridge, much longer than the one they could not pass before, because they made the crossing nearer the lake, where the river was far wider. The bridge connected cliffs sixty feet high over the turbulent river, and as they passed they leaned over to watch the yellow water rushing below. And they laughed with the continuous, helpless laughter of schoolboys.

They had not built a bridge. They merely borrowed the use of it, and about a hundred more, from the Trans-Siberian Railway. They were lurching along the railway sleepers, one side of the car within the railway track, the other nearer the edge of the sleepers than they would ideally have chosen—for on most of the bridges there was no parapet. Their motion was a peculiar, slow gallop, disconcerting enough to the crew and tending to induce seasickness in their passenger. For they carried an extra man. He was a policeman, and he brandished a large red flag. It was a very necessary part of their equipment. The policeman used it to stop the trains.

The brainwave had come to Borghese as they were parleying with the woodcutter, but it took two days to put it into practice. They left the woodman and made their way to the local railway-station, where they put some preliminary inquiries. Then they returned to Missowaya. To do this they had to find their former road-track again and mend the bridge they had broken in passing. They were back in the house of the mayor by the afternoon, and they immediately sent a telegram to the Governor-General of Siberia asking permission to pass along the railroad. Borghese was determined that he should start at the top when requesting permission, but he was still uncertain whether the matter would not be referred to St Petersburg. Within twenty-four hours they got an affirmative reply, and the next morning they were off again. They took, as extra equipment, two planks to run the Itala up on to the railway embankment—and a timetable.

The timetable was necessary because they had to work out what stages of the single-track line they could use between the passing of trains, and where they could find sidings to lay by while the trains passed. They went by 'road' to a small station beyond Missowaya, where they picked up their policeman. They found a spot where the railway ran alongside the track and was only six feet higher. They built a slipway with old sleepers and their two planks and drove the car up on to the railroad. Then they began their strange journey along the line which led to Moscow.

The speed which produced the least destructive rhythm to the car was a monotonous lollop of ten miles an hour, and they proceeded at this pace until 9.15 A.M., when it was time to clear the line for the eight o'clock train from Missowaya to pass through. They came to a siding where they could draw off the main line, and, not wishing to waste time, took the advice of the railwayman there and went back on to the road, intending to rejoin the railway at a level-crossing some miles up the line after the train had passed.

The muddy tract through the woods was almost pleasant after the jolting on the railroad. They were now quite used to this kind of country and the rickety bridges by which the route passed over streams. But the policeman, sophisticated after a few years of railway service, was far more apprehensive. And when they came to one bridge, which looked no more rotten than the others, and they halted to make their usual survey he took one glance at the torrent, ten feet deep, which surged below them, and quickly jumped off the car.

Prince Borghese walked back from the centre of the bridge

where he had made his inspection, got back into the car, and settled in his seat.

"Right," he said to Guizzardi.

Ettore drove the car forward slowly. The bridge swayed somewhat, which was not pleasant since there was no parapet, but their rule was never to halt in the middle. The car went on.

The planks under the back wheel gave way completely. The jerk as the car fell backward made Ettore stall the engine. The back of the car fell downward, until the chassis took the weight of the car on some sound planks at about the middle of the chassis girders. With the car revolving on this fulcrum the front wheels came up, until the chassis was completely vertical. The Itala then fell bodily through the hole it had made in the bridge. A beam of the bridge caught the car by the front springs and it was held— its tail in the torrent and only its great brass headlamps projecting above the level of the bridge. The sound of splintering wood, which had continued while the car fell, suddenly stopped. Then the car swung farther in its rotation as the heavy engine pulled the front back and down.

Borghese, in the front seat, had raised his hands as the car took its last vertical plunge, and caught on to a beam of the bridge. But the car continued to sink quickly, so that his body was squeezed between the beam and the dashboard, with all the weight of the engine bearing down on him. In one moment of panic strength he actually lifted the descending car, which had not finally settled, by raising his shoulders purely with the strength of his handgrip, and in the split second of strain he heaved himself out of the trap and fell into the back of the car and on into the torrent, with nothing worse than cracked ribs.

Ettore, whose movements were restricted by the steering-wheel, went down with his ship, and finished upside down with his feet in the steering-wheel, hanging over the torrent. He then gripped the back of the car, let his feet fall, and with the momentum swung forward to the ground at the side of the stream.

Barzini was in the back seat between the spare tanks. As the car fell the luggage caught the bridge planks first. The ropes holding it had little resistance and broke, and the luggage showered downward past Barzini's head. As the engine swung over his head the hot oil from the sump poured down over his face and body. He hung there trapped and suffocating. Then Ettore, who had recovered first, snatched him like a catcher on the flying trapeze and swung him to where he stood, in a few inches of water, at the side of the torrent.

As for the policeman, he was sprinting back towards the shunting siding to get stretchers from the first-aid hut and bearers for the bodies.

Borghese and Barzini were bruised and disabled. But the Prince was already examining the car with Ettore to assess the damage. Petrol was oozing from the upper seams of the tanks which were not so well sealed as the bottoms. Tools like the shovel and pickaxe were broken, and the planks they had brought for access to the railway were matchwood. There were dents and broken straps, but the only damage that seemed serious was that a crank supporting the differential was bent. It would have been a much more destructive crash if they had not carried their concertina bellows of spare tyres vertically on the back of the car. They had taken the shock like the springs of a pogo-stick.

The policeman came running back with a gang of twenty platelayers who had been working on the line. After a lengthy expression of wonder and relief at the comparative safety of the car crew he gave the linemen their orders and inaugurated an amazing feat of salvage.

The gang of tough Siberians were incomparable in the use of the hatchet—and they all carried one. Their only other tool was an inexhaustible supply of rope. The car had swung back to its directly vertical position, and they first moored it there. They got two lines round its chassis behind the engine, and made them fast to trees on the bank, with an obtuse angle between the two lines. They then chopped down all of the bridge surrounding the fallen car. Working from both sides of the river with their ropes they heaved the back of the car up and let the front sink down until the machine was level, but standing in the torrent. The next phase was a complete rebuilding of the portion of the bridge which still stood—on the side of the river from which the car had been driven. The structure swarmed with red-smocked, high-booted men, their long fair hair streaming as they swung their axes on the supports and relaid the planks. In a very short time they had built a sloping plank road from the back wheels of the car to the original approach of the bridge, and when it was done they simply hauled the Itala backward on to the road again. Within three hours of the accident Ettore was swinging the starting-handle.

The engine did not fire. Oil had flowed to the top of the cylinders while the car had been suspended, and Ettore cleaned the ignition points, for which he had to detach the flanges holding the makes-and-breaks of the low-tension ignition system in the upper parts of the cylinders. Then he went round to the front again. At the second swing the car started. But, having satisfied himself that it would go, Ettore insisted on a complete overhaul of the engine, which took nearly two hours more. At two in the afternoon the luggage was all replaced and the Itala was ready for action again.

They went back to the railway. By now the crew had been increased to six by the addition of two of the most enthusiastic of the railway workers, who stood on the frame at the back of the car, steadying themselves on the luggage lashing, as if they were the footmen who ride behind state coaches. As they came near the port of Tankhoy, which they had decided must be their stop for the night, they were urgently signalled by a level-crossing keeper. "Get off the line," he yelled. "There's a train coming. It has already left Tankhoy."

They had survived emergencies enough for one day, and it seemed superfluous that they should now get stuck on the railroad. But as the wheels turned to surmount the rails they dug in at the front, in the track between the sleepers. The Siberian linemen got down at once to push. The angle was impossible. The car would have to be lifted.

The whistle of the approaching train could already be heard. The linemen ran to a pile of old sleepers, and hacked some into wedges to make an inclined bridge over the iron rail. They shoved other sleepers under the car, and began to lever it. Every one was out of the car except Barzini, who was too badly bruised to be of any physical use. The train was now in sight. "Jump!" shouted Prince Borghese. But Barzini's muscles at that moment would not even allow his legs to stretch. He sat there paralysed as the train approached. "Then *heave!*" roared Borghese, and with a last great ram on the lever the car was edged over the rail and off the track.

The train passed. It was a clanking freighter. As Barzini said, it was not the class of train that should run them down. Borghese drove the car back on to the railroad again, and in this manner they rode in to Tankhoy. In the station buffet—which, they were beginning to find, provided the best refreshments *en route* in Russia—Borghese ordered champagne. And there Borghese learned that there would be no more narrow escapes from collision with trains, for the Itala had now been officially scheduled as a special train, and would be worked into the service to Irkutsk along with the local trains and the Trans-Siberian Express. The temptation was great. But the forty-mile journey along the tracks had not improved the structural reliability of the Itala—nor, of course, had the incident at the bridge. Borghese decided to cut swiftly across the neck of the inland sea by travelling with the Itala for twenty-five miles aboard the ice-breaker *Baikal*.

Between three and five o'clock the next afternoon they completed the lake crossing and began the drive to Irkutsk, hoping to ride the sixty miles before dark. The rain had returned. The mud renewed its old enmity. And long after sunset, when the lights of Irkutsk could be seen across the steppe, the car finally bogged down.

They were rescued by a party which had come out from the city by carriage. In the dark the Italians found themselves shaking hands with a man of whom they knew nothing, except that he had a warm voice, and had guided them out of the morass on to a serviceable road. Then he introduced himself—Radionoff, member of the All-Russian Peking–Paris Committee. No further explanations were necessary.

Radionoff piloted them to his enormous house, standing in spacious grounds, in the city of Irkutsk. "A bath is ready for you," he announced. "And dinner will soon be served."

At midnight, a few minutes before dinner was ready, a number of Radionoff's friends arrived informally for the meal which was usually available at that hour. They smothered the Italians with friendship, technical enthusiasm—and curiosity. Have you been attacked yet? You should never have tried that last stretch in the dark. Are you any good with a pistol? Have you come across the convicts yet?

Apart from the melancholy political exiles who formed a large part of the population of Missowaya, the Italians had had no contact with any category of criminals. But there was a serious problem of civil security throughout Trans-Baikalia. During the war with Japan the Pacific prison-island of Sakhalin was defended by Russian convicts, who were later brought into Siberia. Many were released for their gallant records in the fighting. Others escaped. Once they were free some of them formed gangs which raided prisons to release other convicts, and mounted attacks on banks for their money. It was for this reason that civilians were armed, and the motorists had permits for two pistols.

Dinner at the Radionoffs went on into the dawn—which comes early in the summer-time in Siberia. The party broke up, having made arrangements to take their guests on a one-day spree in Irkutsk after breakfast. The holiday lasted till the following dawn. When the visitors, exhausted by their rest, drove off to the west at eleven o'clock that morning they found that they were taking Radionoff with them. He had never travelled by car before, and could not miss the opportunity.

The Italians rarely ate a large lunch on a full day, and, after the junketing in Irkutsk and the late start, Barzini and Guizzardi knew that Borghese would never favour a stop on this particular stage. Radionoff seemed to have summed up the Prince's temperament before he embarked, for he had climbed on to the car clutching a large luncheon pack. And soon after the journey started his hand would be dangling in front of the faces of the crew with a sandwich, a pie, or a portion of chicken on offer.

They passed an area where an alternative track for the Trans-Siberian Railway was being constructed to absorb more traffic. Hundreds of men were working on an embankment where the rails would be laid. Barzini thought affectionately of the tousle-headed linemen who had rescued the Itala and travelled on its step. He looked keenly at these workers as they drove past. With a curiously touching gesture the men stood up straight from their levelling and digging as the car passed, and each took off his cap and bowed. The long hair that Barzini was looking for was not there. The men all carried a degrading brand. Exactly half of their heads were shaven. Chains shackled their feet. These were convicts.

Radionoff passed out more pies.

The Stepanoffs gave another dinner-party on the night of the visit to the Grand Lama. Usually Godard would have responded to the occasion with his liveliest tricks of sociability. But he had had only two hours' sleep since his all-night run from Udde. He excused himself comparatively early, and went to bed to try to build some reserves for the urgent task of catching Borghese—now forty-eight hours ahead.

Bizac roused them all in the morning. Du Taillis was aching cruelly with the symptoms of fever, but he dutifully stirred. The cars headed for the pine-covered hills which marked the way to Kiakhta. The de Dion-Bouton drivers had reconnoitred the exit from Urga previously, and did not think they needed a guide. But now that the three cars were travelling in convoy again the drivers agreed that they should take it in turn to be the pilot. For the first stage it was Cormier who led the way.

But he could not get up the first testing hill. The road into the mountains quickly settled to a slope of one in three, and the incline proved too much for both de Dions. They were very heavily laden. Each carried 600 kilograms, some twelve hundred-weight, of gear. Apart from food stocks and the minimum of clothing necessary to protect the crews from cold and rain, the little two-cylinder machines carried tyres, spare parts and tool-kits, petrol, oil, and the hardware of bedding and cooking needs, along with quite an armament of defence weapons. Cormier, the hunter, carried two guns, a Winchester and a Hammerless, two revolvers, and a heavy load of ammunition, both ball and shot.

Everything had to come off if the de Dions, in particular, were to get up the steep and slippery hills. They unloaded the cars at the bottom of each difficult slope, walked alongside the cars to push them as they slithered from side to side with the skids of the spinning driving-wheels, and then had to make three journeys up and down for each ascent to get their belongings back on to the car. Even then they often had to consider a repeat operation at the top, for the downward slopes seemed to hint at greater danger. But by putting the cars into first gear and taking them down with circumspection they managed to get the laden vehicles to the bottom without another bout of loading and unloading. The Spyker sometimes got up hills which had defeated the de Dions, since it had greater power and the special low gears which Jacobus Spijker had built in. When it would not go up forward Godard generally found that he could drive the car up in reverse, carrying its usual load. This gave the sick du Taillis some respite from the porter's work which was necessary all day for the others. He spent some of the time wandering in the woods—he had not seen woodland for nearly three months—and admiring the forget-me-nots. He picked blue buttonholes for each in the party, though he would not vouch that the thought was fully appreciated.

For the rest of the crews it was a wholly exhausting day. By half-past eight in the evening they had been forced to empty the de Dions some twenty times for the various mountain slopes, and they resignedly pitched a camp in the lee of their vehicles. They had bought nothing, in du Taillis's opinion, from the rich larder of the Stepanoffs which would absolve him from the duty of boiling some soup extract. And it was soup and corned beef that the cook presented to them.

The morning started glumly, with rain pouring on their bedding and equipment and making the task of packing much slower. It was Godard's turn to pilot the forces that day, and before very long he, like Borghese in the same sort of country, had run himself into a marshy 'quicksand.' Du Taillis was able to jump down and warn the others just in time, but when the following cars reached the Spyker on foot they found its wheels already completely immersed. It was resting on the flat resistance of its chassis.

So it was the Spyker which had to be unloaded now. Since it was impossible to bring too many workers on the undulating film of soil over the marsh, Cormier took his gun and went off to shoot bustard while the Spyker was stripped. Then, with jacks and crowbars working against the planks which they were carrying, and which were laid on the surface of the morass, the Spyker was raised and dragged back off the swamp in about two hours and a half. The party's navigation was now wholly unreliable, and after driving in great fanning sweeps to find the broad river Iro, which they knew they had to cross, they gave up the search and camped again for the night.

They found the Iro next morning, with a convoy of carts camped on the bank. But there was no sign of a ford. Bizac walked upstream to look for traces of one. Godard, impatient to get on, walked into the river until he was chest-high in the water, and realized that it might be possible to get the cars through at this point. Cormier persuaded one of the Mongolian cart-drivers to cross the river on his horse, and, working on the success of that demonstration, persuaded more of the cart crews to go off to find some oxen. Godard dismounted his magneto. The others merely protected their engines. Oxen were driven over from the other side, and, one by one, the cars were hauled through the river. The Spyker was the last to go, and there was a long delay on the other side. There was more to do than replace the magneto. With Godard's usual dash the Dutch car had been taken too hard over a V-shaped path which was too narrow for the wheeltrack and had forced the rear-axle housings out of line, producing a damaging knock on its back axle. Bizac and Collignon made an attempt to repair it, but du Taillis, who was at that period a slightly nervous passenger, was not wholly satisfied with their success. However, the route on the other side gave better going for the cars, and they made a higher speed, until they hit the soft sand-dunes before Kiakhta. Here Cormier bogged down, and it took another hour to release him. But they crossed the Siberian frontier before nightfall, and enjoyed the gay welcome waiting for them on the boundary line as the whole of the local *raid* committee cheered them into the Russian Empire.

Le Matin had obtained a special ukase from the Tsar absolving them from most frontier formalities. The only requirement that the Customs office demanded was an assurance that, since they had been excused from depositing a levy on their cars, they intended to take the vehicles out of Russia. Du Taillis confessed that that was, indeed, the purpose of the expedition, and they passed through. The crews received their permits to carry revolvers—indeed, they were encouraged to display weapons on their journey through Siberia, and to shoot first without asking questions in emergency. They also received a quiet warning that it was highly likely that they would be taken for spies by the local population, who were still very nervous of Japanese infiltration, and were quite ready to believe that the motorists came from Japan.

The Sinitzins recommended an inn to the travellers, and suggested that once they were installed they should come back for dinner with the banker's family. When they finally went back to bed Collignon, who had a room to himself, had no sooner dozed off than the door burst open and an extremely truculent Russian fell on to the bed. Collignon told him in a few short words to go away. The Russian tried to hit him. Collignon hit the Russian, and the dark shape of the intruder fell under the bed. Longoni, who was sleeping next door, burst into the room, with a candle in one hand and his newly licensed revolver in the other. Neither Collignon nor Longoni could find the intruder, but they eventually fell over his feet, brought him into the candlelight, and, drawing the obvious conclusions from the almost inflammable vapour of vodka rising in the room, placed him delicately outside, where he recovered in the morning and made smiling apologies. But the most serious shock experienced at the inn was felt by the delicate du Taillis. When the party were presented with the bill they were horrified to read that it was—for the equivalent of bed and breakfast—170 roubles, over 470 francs to them, or nearly £20 in English money at the values of the day. Since they then had no Russian money at all they excused themselves, ran to the bank to cash their remaining silver ingots and taels, and resolved to continue with their camping as often as possible.

The petrol ordered by the de Dion team, like that which should have been supplied to Borghese, had not been delivered in Kiakhata. But Cormier was put in touch with a merchant in the town who had a stationary engine. They relieved him of about 300 litres of his fuel on the understanding that he would take it back out of the supplies which they presumed would reach Kiakhta after they had gone. Such a credit transaction was very near to Godard's heart, and he was able to get himself included in the deal.

Getting petrol, changing money, and the social distractions that accompanied these duties occupied more time than they had scheduled—as did a council of war called by du Taillis on the matter of the hotel bill—and the three cars did not leave Kiakhta until the middle of the afternoon. They had driven little more than five kilometres into Siberia when they were waved down to a halt. They were reluctant to lose any more time, but the drivers stopped. They saw a table set on the grass under some trees, and the people by the roadside were offering them glasses of wine. In the pine-wood was a crowd of young people in traditional costume, and the girls in the party were crowning a bride with flowers. The 'raiders' were being invited to a wedding.

Violins and cellos were playing. Godard got down to dance, and Longoni soon followed him. Refreshment was pressed on them. Longoni had developed a passion for milk, and this particular craving was pandered to. Collignon, on the other hand, was a beer-drinker, and as soon as this was discovered a flurry of bottles was propelled in his direction. But Cormier sat in his car with his hands on the steering-wheel. After a brief dance and a drink the visitors got back into their cars to go and pitch camp in the chill of the mountains above. The next day Longoni's new addiction to milk grew so strongly that he asked for it in every village they passed. The Russian word for milk was easy to remember—it was *molocko*—and Molocko seemed an eminently suitable nickname to bestow on Longoni for the future. The 'raiders' were, indeed, in spite of the language bar, beginning to enjoy Siberia for the friendly contact they found it so easy to make with the people. Army officers billeted during manoeuvres would invite them off the road for a bottle of champagne: none of the party ever submitted to vodka. Villagers shyly mobbed them. And, at a night stop between Verkhne-Udinsk and Missowaya, where they put their cars into a private courtyard, accepting beds offered them by the owner, they were surrounded by a crowd of hero-worshipping girls, who followed them from the stables to their bedroom, kept touching them as if they brought luck, and set a number of demands to them through an inter- preter, a girl who could speak German. They wanted to know the full names of the party, where they could write to them, and, above all, they wanted pictures of the 'raiders.' They insisted on the men turning out their wallets for photographs. Collignon did carry a picture of himself, and they bore it away in triumph, with ecstatic cries of "Victor." When the motorists left, early in the morning, the girls had sentinels peeping over the wall to report on them. And as they drove away they were pursued with the thistledown of blown kisses.

The season in eastern Siberia was that of a delightful late spring. The pine-woods and the fields were bright with wild flowers. The foliage of the trees was delicate and young. But the time of year also meant that the rivers were in spate with the melting of the snow—which could still be seen on high hill-tops— and the strong streams made fording difficult, and hastened the destruction of decrepit bridges. The motorists were in the area to the east of Lake Baikal, and when they came to Missowaya they found a telegram from Borghese warning them of the impossibility of the land route round the lake and advising them to take a ferry if they could get it. There was no craft plying regularly from the dying port, and so the drivers chose the railway. But they did not drive along it. They put the cars on goods wagons. The fare by rail to Irkutsk was 24 roubles by car against 300 roubles quoted for a chartered ferry. And the passengers travelled free—though in the coffin structures allocated to the fourth class. They came to Irkutsk at six in the evening of the 3rd of July. And they were now hot on Borghese's heels. For he had left the city only at dawn that morning.

Awaiting them at the railway-station was the Governor of Irkutsk, his aide-de-camp, and Count Jacobleff, the president of the local Peking–Paris committee. Behind the deputation of honour were many scores of cyclists, and a noisy vanguard of motor-cyclists. The automobile teams were not allowed to go to their hotel. Instead a preliminary demonstration of welcome had already been planned at the Velodrome, the sports stadium which catered for a city that seemed quite mad on cycling. The visitors were then given a brief opportunity to make their toilet before they attended a dinner, which was followed by a reception, which was followed by an informal planning committee meeting to arrange a series of festivities for the future.

It was in this manner that Borghese increased his lead on Cormier by two days and his lead on Godard by three weeks. For something had happened to affect Godard's faith in the Spyker in its present condition. The magneto seemed to be developing a fault. It had already failed after getting wet, and he had dried it out again. The back axle was worrying him more seriously. The housing, already out of alignment, had been pierced at some stage by a sharp stone. The oil had leaked out, and the serious problem of an overheated rear axle had developed. Godard promptly repaired the hole with a plug of raw bacon, forced in with a wooden spigot and held by an iron bracket. He charged the axle with grease again, and continued, knowing that the repair was only temporary. But, in addition, he was convinced that he would never catch Borghese unless fairly soon in the race now he took out the low gears which Spijker had installed, and put in higher ones for speed across the steppes and in Europe—a continent where, though he could scarcely adapt himself to the thought, they had *roads*. With these preoccupations in mind he had taken the drastic step of re-establishing communications with Heer Spijker. From Irkutsk he cabled him confidentially, outlining his needs and requesting a mechanic to be sent out along the Trans-Siberian Railway to meet him at a point to be decided later with the complete components of a new back axle. Meanwhile he said nothing—nothing to du Taillis and nothing to the sporting Russians in this the last city he was likely to traverse for a thousand miles where he could reasonably expect to find enthusiasts, and therefore experts, on the internal-combustion engine.

At Irkutsk the order of the day was gaiety. It culminated on the 5th of July in a great fête at the Velodrome, where the military band blew all night and the daring cyclists of Irkutsk performed the most formidable acrobatics. In the middle of the show Longoni challenged Godard to a race on motor-cycles around the track. The foolish Molocko did not know that he was pitting himself against a veteran of the Wall of Death. Godard won the race with such a breathtaking display that Count Jacobleff took from his breast the gold insignia specially struck for the office of President of the Peking–Paris Committee and presented it to the professional. Godard was happy to let his hand close round gold again, after the sacrifice of his gold watch-chain to the tribesmen in the Gobi Desert. And he cheered all the more enthusiastically as the sporting ladies of the cycle club fluttered round the track on a circuit of honour, driving motor-bicycles with the utmost grace and skill, and setting an unforgettable stamp on the evening.

They left next morning over the long bridge of boats across the river Angara and surrounded by a circus of exhibitionist cyclists. Bizac and Collignon had been working on the de Dion-Boutons during the days of festivity. The passage through a number of high rivers had affected the engines, and had distorted the clutch-plates so seriously that they had to be renewed. Godard had done nothing to his Spyker beyond plugging the axle because he did not know what more to do. The one operation he could have done successfully was the installation of a new magneto—he had dismounted magnetos frequently enough recently. But he did not have a spare magneto for the Spyker. It was true that he had started out with a spare from the Trompenburg factory. But he had sold it in Paris to put towards the money for his fare to Peking. He regretted it. But, with luck, Spijker's mechanic would arrive in time. Spijker had, indeed, greatly relaxed his wrath against Godard, and had sent him the spare parts he had asked for. But the man who was bringing them let the cases of parts get out of his control in the guard's van of the North Express. The consignment was suspected of containing bombs for anarchists, and the envoy was held up for ten days in Moscow before he found the right man to explain the problem to.

The magneto went wrong on the day the Spyker left Irkutsk. The convoy had made good progress when, late in the afternoon, the car faded to a standstill. "Ignition playing us up," said Godard as Cormier and Collignon came up with him. They tested the engine. The magneto was turning all right, but there was no sparking. There was not going to be enough light for a detailed examination, and Cormier drove on to summon up horses. Two of them dragged the Spyker by eleven that night to Tcheremkhovo, a colliery town. The de Dions stayed with the Spyker. Next morning Bizac and Collignon were working on the engine at five o'clock. After four hours they confessed that they could not right it. Godard begged them to continue the *raid* while he made efforts to repair his car. Cormier and Collignon decided that they should go on. They left du Taillis with Godard, and drove off for Zimskaya, their next fuel point in a chain that was now functioning perfectly. As they filled their tanks and spare cans a troupe of strolling acrobats, exploiting the crowd which the cars had attracted, put on a show that brought them a bonus collection. Next day, as the de Dions passed through the river town of Tulun, the police stopped them with a message that the Spyker was on the railway, going to the west in a freight-car. Cormier misinterpreted the reason for this, and telegraphed *Le Matin* demanding that Godard should be disqualified for having taken the train, contrary to the rules. The sporting world in Europe, which was following the daily course of the *raid* with intense interest, was not informed of Cormier's private cables; and if they had had knowledge of Godard's private cables to Spijker they would have been extremely perplexed. But Godard's messages never got any farther than the Dutch Press. Godard was, in fact, issuing his own cover story, and deliberately not making it too coherent. As his train stopped at Nijni-Udinsk he sent a message which appeared garbled, and could be taken to indicate that at Nijni-Udinsk—the place where he filed his cable being impossible to disguise—he had been bogged in a mud pool, and was experiencing slight delay because the magneto was wet, and he had to wait for it to dry out. At Krasnoyarsk, however, one day later and 150 miles down the line—which indicated no mean progress for a brokendown Spyker—he telegraphed that the car was running beautifully, despite the mishap to the magneto he had previously mentioned. The car was, of course, running very well—on the Trans-Siberian Railway. From Tomsk, about 850 miles nearer Paris than where he had broken down, he sent picture-postcards of himself, the old shuvver Godard, posing in front of an apparently immaculate (though still tricoloured) Spyker, with messages such as "your car is the only one that has not needed any repairs since leaving Peking." The reason for sending picture-postcards was that telegrams were received too quickly, and were accurately dated, and Godard was now three days ahead of the de Dions in this amazing spurt.

The fact was that Godard was to stay in Tomsk for some time. Du Taillis had dropped off the train at Krasnoyarsk, where he was joined by the de Dion crews two days later. He explained to Cormier what Godard was doing. He had taken the Spyker to Tomsk because Tomsk had the best technical academy in Russia. If anybody could adjust, repair, or even redesign a magneto for his Spyker he was likely to be found in Tomsk. When he had obtained his repair Godard intended to take his car by train back to Tcheremkhovo, where he had broken down, and complete the whole of the course as he had set out to do. In the face of these facts Cormier could not sustain his claim for Godard's disqualification. And when he actually met Godard at Tomsk five days later the subject was tactfully not mentioned.

Du Taillis had made contact with the others at Krasnoyarsk because as the organizing representative of *Le Matin* he could not tie himself to a crippled competitor, but must keep up with the main body. He therefore had to request a passage on one of the de Dion cars. It meant dropping Longoni from the run, and Cormier, Bizac, and Collignon said good-bye to their good-natured Molocko with real regret. Cormier decided that he and Collignon would carry du Taillis on alternate days. It was no secret that the writer and the de Dion number one driver were not blood brothers. The first day they started out together from Krasnoyarsk was the 14th of July. Du Taillis, a simple patriot as well as a convivial soul, proposed a drinking-party in the morning. Cormier would have no part in a feast, and refused any elaborate celebration of the glory of the Republic. He did consent to accept one small glass from du Taillis—it was a terrible imitation of green Chartreuse—and then sat glowering at the revellers until the party was packed and ready to go.

The roads through central Siberia had been growing steadily more execrable. It was a bad season, and the rich black mud of the Moskovy Trakt was higher and more glutinous than usual. The party had all bought themselves Russian boots, and were a little more at ease in the village streets—the places where they had to descend most frequently, for the heavier cart traffic centred on the villages converted the track there into its most treacherously pot-holed and rutted state. The village streets were where the cars broke down most often, and the only advantage of such a *locale* was that there were usually plenty of draught animals for pulling them out of the village. In the country the track was occasionally a log road—infuriatingly impassable once a few of the logs had been removed by the peasants for more practical purposes than transit. But generally it was a barely recognizable path across the soggy earth or the black forest rides. It was often not recognizable because it was never used. The local people preferred to drive their carts on 'private' tracks through the fields. Lack of use could mean an agreeable lack of ruts, but it might also follow that holes, obstructions, and fallen trees had never been ameliorated. The most deadly and permanent enemy to traction was mud. Skidding for two hours to mount a slight slope extending 200 yards was a commonplace occurrence to all the 'raiders.' The frequent ferries were sometimes frail and always slow, but they improved steadily as the 'raiders' went west through Siberia.

No such improvement was noticed in the Russian inn, which grew steadily more inhospitable as the travellers neared Europe. There were two scales of hostelry. In the larger towns the hotel was a cluster of bedrooms built over a music-hall on the ground floor. The show went on for ever, and it was impossible for the French, for instance, to pull the sheets over their heads because it was not the custom in Russia to provide bedclothes. A traveller should carry his own. Foreigners? The Frenchmen should have been told before they left Paris.

In the rural areas the standard 'inn' was the *zemskaya*—a shelter the travellers had to resort to much more freely as the rain and cold continued and tents grew less inviting. The *zemskaya* was a truly public house. It was maintained for Government officials travelling on business and for anyone else who could get in. *Zemskayas* were crude buildings, occupied by a concierge with, usually, a family large enough to overflow into the few public rooms. And if the concierge decided that he did not wish to be disturbed he would firmly refuse to admit any traveller. The

French drove on sometimes from inn to inn, enduring a running fire of refusals.

Through rain and mud and unclothed beds the de Dion crews passed like a black smudge across the map of Asia. There were occasional peaks, like the welcome given them by Russian officers on manœuvres, when supper was served in the billet and the regimental band played warm serenades underneath the balcony. And the interval in Tomsk, where Godard had preceded them by a week, had its moments of agreeable civilization—shattered only by the crescendo of the *oom-pa-pa* of the music-hall beneath their bedrooms.

After Omsk the steppes hardened, and the de Dions began to achieve a better daily average distance. The longitude was lessening, and the weather was turning. On the 22nd of July the sun came out. It was a Sunday, and the swallows sat on the telegraph-wires and sang. The land dried. Dust edged back into the travellers' consciousness. Within two days the Frenchmen were passing through country where—incredibly to them—there had been no rain for six weeks. The wheat was dead on the stalk. Miserably undeveloped cattle were being slaughtered before they died. The English speculators, who had made £1,000,000 profit the previous year from the export of agricultural and dairy products, were cursing the turn of the wheel. And, as if to ensure that they would not even be able to sell the straw from their dry wheat, a succession of destructive prairie fires began.

The two de Dions, which had suffered from every other element in the alchemist's handbook, were destined to take their taste of fire as well.

They had passed through Omsk, which they had not found an inspiring city: it was the centre of the Imperial Government vodka-manufacturing monopoly, but the Frenchmen all disliked the spirit, and passionately loathed the condition of besotted dependence to which its unrestricted exploitation had reduced the majority of the peasants they had observed. The motorists were navigating to get to Kazan by way of Kurgan and Tcheliabynsk, and had crossed the river Irtych by a ferry which had its own tug to tow it. They were running by the side of the railway since they had to cross the railroad in about fifty kilometres.

They saw the fire ahead. It might well have been kindled by a locomotive spark. It was racing broadside down the line of the railway, like the edge of a guillotine advancing on them, and there seemed no escape to the right. The wind was almost undetectable, and the flames burnt brightly upward without streaming smoke. And yet the edge of the fire seemed to come on at extraordinary speed. They did not want to be forced back to the river, yet they could not risk driving at speed through the flames, and trusting to the scorched earth beyond being cool enough for their tyres. They were carrying too much free petrol to take such a risk, for they had refilled their tanks in Tomsk.

Bizac marched towards the front of flame on reconnaissance. The fire had taken a whole village in front of them. Wooden houses, thatched hayricks, were all going up in a furnace-draught together.

Bizac found a section of the band of flaming grassland that was comparatively narrow in depth. He ran back to the cars and called for spades and a helper. With a spade and the picks they cut a path for the cars through the heathland—irreparably scorching their Cossack boots in the process. Once they had cut the passage they threw earth from the centre on to the fire burning at the sides of it. Working quickly, they were soon able to signal the cars through. For a long time they were uncertain if they had improved their fate. It seemed that Bizac had chosen the narrow central neck of a figure 8 and they had merely passed from one ring of fire to another. But they drove fast, always towards the closing top of the 8, and though they went many miles out of their way, the de Dions did get ahead of the pace of the fire, and were able to swing round the rear of the conflagration into Petropavlovsk.

It was a week since they had left Godard, apparently idling in Tomsk. In the meantime he had completed his business, taken a train back for 850 miles to his point of breakdown, and was now engaged literally night and day in a race that was to spark with a strange encounter on the very site of the prairie fire.

14 ◉ ◉ Godard rides again

When Jacobus Spijker received Godard's telegram from Irkutsk—characteristically offering no excuses or reconciliation, but requesting that a mechanic should be sent by rail to meet him at Tomsk, with a new rear axle and a variety of replacements—the industrialist was in a mood to be courted. He had been surprised, after his earlier experiences with Godard, that the Spyker car had ever set out from Peking at all. It had been his conviction that the car would be sold so that Godard could pursue in Asia some facet of his shifty career. He had completely missed appreciation of the man's unconquerable determination to drive with glory on this Peking–Paris *raid*. As the reports of the expedition's progress came in Spijker changed his mind. Du Taillis had always been generous in his tributes to the Spyker's performance, and though much of his praise was removed by the subeditors of *Le Matin*, who understood the managerial intention that the primary purpose of the project was to boost the French automobile industry, enough percolated through to benefit the reputation of the Dutch firm considerably. Spijker therefore decided that the considerable expense of sending a man to Siberia was justified by the strong prospect of being able to get the car through.

The man he had in mind was a youngster of twenty, Bruno Stephan. He was taking an engineering degree at the Technical University in Delft, and he had been doing his practical training at the Trompenburg factory for over a year. Stephan knew the Spyker inside out, had three languages besides his own, and seemed to have enough resource to be able to handle the wily Godard. He therefore received an invitation to dine with Heer Spijker at the Bible Hotel in Amsterdam.

It was a good meal, as Stephan expected. A third in the party, nearer his own age, was Wellington, a young Englishman from the British Automobile Syndicate, who was making a last-minute effort to reorganize the financial and administrative chaos at Trompenburg. For a long time the conversation was directed to trivialities as the industrialist discussed his works, or the wine. Then, as the liqueurs were poured, he pushed back his chair. The eyes in the handsome, persuasive face of the older man focused on the apprentice's with deceptive casualness, and he asked, "How would you like to go to Siberia?"

It was a joke, of course, and the fair-haired young man, relaxed after his entertainment, replied in the same spirit. "I don't mind, now that they are sending the convicts by train. I don't think I should have fancied those terrible forced marches. Why? Have I done something very wrong?"

"I mean it," said Spijker. "How would you like to go to Siberia and service the Spyker in the Paris *raid*?" He explained the situation and ran through the list of Godard's requests. "If he wants higher gears fitted I shall trust his judgment. The special gears we fitted worked beautifully on the sand trials in the dunes here, but perhaps we gave too much importance to desert conditions and not enough to the other 12,000 kilometres. He says he fears his magneto will go. Well, I gave him a spare magneto, which he could easily have fitted, but we know now what happened to that. So there you are—the back axle, the gearing and a good set of spare parts. I have had them crated already, and they make a pretty bulky consignment. You'll want to let your family know, of course, but I'd be glad if you would agree to start for Moscow the day after to-morrow. I have arranged all the tickets. Now, about telegrams . . ."

Stephan, a high-spirited young man, smiled at the excitement of the prospect. "You have made all the preparations already," he said.

"I know my man," said Spijker. "And, anyway"—as he calculated—"it was a nice dinner, wasn't it?"

And so, at the time when Godard and Longoni were theatrically dicing with death on borrowed motor-cycles, on the track of the Irkutsk Velodrome—and before Godard was finally disabled with his magneto trouble—Stephan was taking the train to Russia. The long box containing the Spyker equipment was in the luggage-van. But before he got to Moscow he had lost it.

The Customs regulations of the day were far more stringent and detailed than they were to become, and all passengers to Russia, whatever their linguistic skill, feared the wearisome inspection on the border of the Empire. Spijker had consigned his spare parts with an impatience—once he had decided to act— which gave him no time to make contact with Paris for information on the relaxation of *octroi* and import duties which had been extended to competitors in the *raid* by the Russian authorities. He was not anxious to advertise his intervention in any case. Consequently Stephan, after a long verbal examination at the frontier, found himself asked to step aside to a waiting-room while the cumbrous Russian bureaucracy creaked into position to deal with his case. Before any final decision was made it was thought prudent to separate the passenger, who was probably a revolutionary, from his box, which was probably bombs. Stephan was therefore allowed to go on to Moscow, provided he reported to the police on his arrival. His box, he was informed, would be sent on separately under Customs seal, and he would be able to collect it after he had satisfied the farther authorities. It was a skilful method of avoiding any commitment, and, therefore, any subsequent reprimand, on the part of the officials at the frontier.

Stephan kicked his feet in Moscow for nearly a fortnight. He was not alone in his distress. A number of businessmen from Europe were also trying to trace their samples. Finally, after the intervention of the Dutch Vice-Consul, Ansoul, the box was brought in from the pound at Alexandrovno, and he continued his journey to Tomsk.

Godard, in the meantime, had broken down on his first day out of Irkutsk, and had been towed by horses to Tcheremkhovo. As soon as he had pressed Cormier and Collignon to continue the *raid*, after some hours of work the next morning, he had a council of war with du Taillis.

"I shall never be able to repair the motor myself," Godard told du Taillis. "We are not going to waste time here. I have been talking to engineers here, and none of them knows enough about electricity to attempt to handle the magneto. But there is a place along the railway line where they have the oldest university in Siberia. It is nineteen years old, I understand. Moreover, they are not just concerned there with Aristotle's *Odyssey* and Tartarin de Tarascon and all that crap, but with the important things of life, like engineering. They have a polytechnic institute there, which all the mining engineers in Tcheremkhovo swear by. So we'll put the car on the train, and take it along for them to have a look at it."

"What is the name of this place?" asked du Taillis.

"Tomsk."

"Tomsk! But that's not 'just along the line.' It is thirteen or fourteen hundred kilometres away."

"I never said I was any good at geography," said Godard mildly. "But you ought to realize that Siberia is a big place. Get used to the idea of distance, du Taillis. In Russia, Tomsk is just along the line."

"Have you any idea of the freight-charges to take the car 1300 kilometres?"

"I never said I was any good at arithmetic, either," said Godard. "Find out for me, there's a good chap. Anyway, there's nothing else we can do."

"Twenty-four roubles to Irkutsk ..." du Taillis began to calculate quickly.

"Very cheap, you know ..."

"We've got to think in terms of a thousand francs."

"Well, yes—two thousand," said Godard.

"Why two thousand?"

"We'll have to come back here and start the *raid* again. You don't think I'd cheat, do you?"

"And where do you think you will find two thousand francs?"

Godard looked expressively at du Taillis, and the journalist sighed with resignation. Du Taillis knew that he would advance the money from the *Matin* float, and Godard knew that he knew. But when the report of this transaction reached Jules Madeline, the paper's managing director in Paris, it proved the last exasperating straw to his accountant's mind, and the board of the newspaper moved into punitive action.

Godard and du Taillis got the Spyker to the station, and had it loaded on to a truck. They began the 850-mile journey to Tomsk, but du Taillis announced that he himself would have to get off at Krasnoyarsk. He could not withdraw indefinitely from the main stream of the race, and it would be Godard's responsibility to catch the party up. As soon as the Spyker was available du Taillis would rejoin it. It was a friendly agreement, to which Godard readily responded, and du Taillis bade him a warm good-bye on the platform of Krasnoyarsk, in a railway-station swarming with alert soldiers. For the city was retained most uncertainly against the forces of revolution, and all its tactical points were held by troops.

The train moved on westward at a depressing average speed of twelve miles an hour—even the Trans-Siberian Express was timed to average only twenty miles an hour. Godard relaxed in the spacious saloon—the broad Russian gauge allowed great width in their railway compartments—sipped a drink, talked to anyone who would listen to him, and set himself to solve the next problem on the journey.

This was the transport of the Spyker for the last fifty-five miles into Tomsk. The engineers of the Trans-Siberian had bypassed the city after the local magnates had declined to pay 100,000 roubles for the privilege of having the railway. When the contribution was refused the engineers discovered that the levels in the area were so sharp that a railway line could not be built. The nearest point they could serve was eighty-two versts away, and they built a station in the middle of the depressing forest country, and, since there was not even a village near, baldly named it Taiga—to make the unnecessary emphasis that it was just a neck in the woods. When Godard's train reached Taiga and the Spyker was unloaded the Frenchman had to hire horses to harness to it for the long haul into Tomsk. As soon as he arrived he went to the university to start his inquiries. He got into touch with an instructor in electrical engineering at the polytechnic institute. This man examined the engine with the greatest interest, removed the magneto, and spread his hands apart to indicate that the problem was already solved.

"Well, at least you have some spare brushes?" he asked.

"Brushes . . ." said Godard, hoping that before the end of the sentence he would remember what brushes were. "Brushes . . ."

"Yes. You know—*brushes.*"

"Well, no," said Godard, "—no brushes." He tried to recollect how much he had got for the sale of the spare magneto in Paris, and cursed as he realized it had hardly made the price of a round of drinks. "As a matter of fact, I have no spare brushes."

"H'm," said the instructor. "Contacts pitted. Brushes worn. You would have had no trouble at all if you had attended to this in time. But now the magneto is burnt out. It's useless, I'm afraid."

"Useless!" exclaimed Godard. "But this is impossible. Where can I get another magneto?"

"Oh, the magneto is all right," said the instructor. "It's the coil. It's burnt out."

"Burnt out."

"But you should have kept an eye on those contacts."

"Contacts."

"And I'm amazed that you didn't renew those brushes."

"Brushes," said Godard with enthusiasm, recognizing the word. "Er, no. I haven't any brushes."

"Well," said the instructor briskly. "We'll just have to rewind you one."

"A brush?" asked Godard gratefully.

"A coil. The coil is burnt out. Didn't you understand me?"

"Perfectly," said Godard.

"Well, there's no need to worry," said the instructor. "Just you leave it with me."

"How long will it take?"

"How long?"

"Yes—the duration."

"Oh, it shouldn't take long. I'd just like to show this to my students, though. Before I start. It should be very interesting for them."

"Can't you show it to your students now? To-day? To-morrow?"

"But it's Saturday."

"I have to get to Paris."

"Paris," said the instructor—"now there's a wonderful place. Tell me, is it true what they say about Mistinguett?"

"But I know her intimately," lied Godard, and launched into an exhaustive category of the qualities of the music-hall goddess. An hour later he left, having extracted promises of urgent attention to the magneto, and returned to his hotel, pausing on the way to select at a stationer's some picture-postcards to send to those of his friends who maintained a permanent address.

"Why not old Spijker?" he thought, and looked for a suitable card. Then he had a better idea. He beckoned to an assistant. In French, assisted by explanatory sketches, which he drew on blotting-paper, Godard asked where he could find a photographer. He begged that the man should be sent to his hotel. There he revealed the possibility of a substantial profit which the photographer could earn, at a commission of only 50 per cent. in advance for the idea. Next day the photographer took his apparatus to the polytechnic institute where the Spyker was. Godard had spent an energetic morning cleaning the car, and now sat in the driving-seat, beaming beneficently above all the glory of its red, white, and blue. A number of pictures were made, of which at least two were printed as postcards, and sent by Godard to Jacobus Spijker. On one card, posted on the 20th of July, he wrote, "Your car is the only one which has not had to change a single tyre since the start." On a second card, posted on the same day, he wrote across the picture, "This is the state of my Spyker after a tough crossing of the Gobi, the Walls of China, rocks, swamps, and Lake Baikal." On the back he wrote, "I can assure you that if I had been helped, and if I had had the petrol, Borghese would not have been the leader, although his car is 60 h.p." The official rating of the Itala was 35-40 h.p. The Spyker, at any rate, looked magnificent. With the bonnet shut there was no indication at all that it would not go.

Cormier, du Taillis, Collignon, and Bizac drove into Tomsk on the 18th of July, and spent the whole of the next day there. Godard met them at the hotel where they had stayed their first night—the uproar in the music-hall had been so disturbing that they moved out to a tent in the country for the following night. Godard proudly drove his Spyker to the hotel, for he had just collected the car, in working order at last, from the polytechnic institute, where he had been obliged to leave it for six days. On the next day, the 20th of July, the de Dion crews left for the West and Godard drove to Taiga to catch the train to the East. On that day Prince Borghese crossed the frontier from Asia into Europe. He was now ten days ahead of the de Dions and, allowing for the return to Tcheremkhovo, twenty-two days ahead of Godard. Moreover, he was but a day or two away from made roads, after the weeks of driving over open country, and should be certain to increase his lead dramatically. Godard gritted his teeth, and told himself that he must do something about that. It was a tragedy that Stephan had not arrived with the higher gears. The desperate young man was still in Moscow, waiting for the gears and spares, not even knowing that he was nearing the end of the ten-day delay to which the officials had sentenced him privately. Godard telegraphed to him in Moscow as he was about to leave from Taiga station and told him not to travel as far as Tomsk. He was now to book to Omsk, about 700 miles nearer Moscow, and to go to the poste restante for telegraphed instructions. It meant that Godard would have to drive at least 1500 miles using the gear-wheels that he wished to reject.

Godard reached Tcheremkhovo, detrained, drove to the point where his magneto had failed, and turned round. It was six in the morning of the 25th of July, and the first patches of prairie were smouldering before expanding into the great fire that was to threaten the men on the de Dions that day. Godard was alone, which he did not like, but he was resolute. He had enough petrol in his tanks and cans, he thought, to get to Krasnoyarsk. From that point on he could rely on du Taillis to have made arrangements with the stockists for the de Dion crews that a surplus would be retained and delivered—inevitably at du Taillis's expense—to Godard as he came up the line. Godard's only real misgiving as he started, apart from the loss of the speed which Stephan's replacements would have given him, was that he was so short of money that he seriously doubted whether he had enough to buy food for the journey. Well, the faster he could go, the fewer days there were in which to go hungry. He slapped the painted side of the car like a horse's flank, slipped the car into gear, and drove as fast as he could down the mud causeway to Tcheremkhovo.

Tacking in wide cross-country sweeps to avoid the belts of fire, the de Dion crews reached Petropavlovsk that night. They started unusually early next morning in the hope that they could accomplish in one day the 300-kilometre stage to Kurgan. Until the late afternoon they made excellent progress, running all the time some miles ahead of a storm front, and they were already congratulating themselves on being able to put up in a decent town hotel instead of the wretched village inns to which they had lately been condemned. But the storm overtook them. Exceptionally heavy rain made it difficult for the drivers even to see the way, and the surface was almost instantly converted to a treacherous expanse of mud. Skidding and sliding from side to side like skaters, the cars were making a negligible advance, and when a village came in sight the crews agreed that they must yield to the storm, hope for better terrain in the morning, and surrender themselves to the embrace of the post-inn in the village, which they ascertained was called Morevskoiy.

The Zemskaya Morevskoya offered no sign of welcome at all. The gate was barred, and the concierge resolutely refused to open it, in spite of the heavy blows directed at the door by du Taillis, his red face apoplectic over his blond beard as he danced furiously in the downpour, looking horrific in a streaming tropical helmet and an ankle-length mackintosh. Du Taillis stopped knocking, and went round to the yard gate. He burst it open with a shoulder charge, and the de Dions hurried in before the landlord could summon reinforcements to close the gate. But mine host still would not open the inn door. After five minutes' further hammering the men of the de Dions miserably decided to camp in the yard. 'Camp' was now a term of extravagance since they had jettisoned their tents to save the weight on the cars. It was pitch dark. They pulled up the cars by the side of a barn. Du Taillis foraged in the food-box and distributed tins of sardines, bottles of beer, and a little bread. Then he put up his camp bed in the barn while Bizac chose a stack of straw to sleep on. Cormier and Collignon went out to their cars, and, under the partial cover of the car hoods, slept in the front seats. Cormier soon awoke, shuddering in the cold. There was a hollow clanging echoing from the car, and there was a tumultuous scuffling across his knees. An army of rats had descended from the rafters of the barn. They were skidding on the car bonnet and fighting on his knees. Du Taillis was beating at his bed, where the elders of the colony were holding a parliament. Bizac simply slept on. Cormier drove his car to the middle of the yard, and found that he could sleep undisturbed. Du Taillis, who had no other shelter, continued to beat his blankets. And Bizac slept on.

Next morning they were away early, revving their cars to a tortuous level of sound as the only retribution they could bestow on the still-invisible innkeeper, and set off to Kurgan, where they refuelled. The country changed suddenly from the open steppes to the forested hills of the Ural Mountains. Having missed the good hotel at Kurgan, they were forced to put up that night at another *zemskaya*, to which at least they were admitted. They were in the district of Tcheliabynsk, a desolate area, which had been the marshalling yard for sorting out the concentrations of convicts and political exiles who assembled here for the long march into Siberia, staggering, before the railway came, in dreary column from one stockaded prison-compound to the next. Now Tcheliabynsk was the sorting centre for the Siberian immigrants, but the change had made no improvement in its miserable atmosphere. In the morning Collignon, who had been furiously rubbing himself, decided to investigate his flannel body-belt. It was swarming with lice. His companions took one look at the belt, and fled from the room into the yard. "Oh, what's the use," said Bizac. "We are all landlords now."

They went on now through days of rain, utterly exhausted by their skidding progress through the muddy hill-country, and considering that they had done well if they averaged six kilometres in an hour. On the 30th of July they awoke to find the sky blue again, but the ground a complete morass. They were so discouraged by the tiring sequence of the last few days that they considered waiting for some hours in the hope that the sun would dry the ground. But, at Cormier's insistence, they went on. The country was beautiful. Cormier likened it to the Tyrol. Very high above them they saw the Trans-Siberian Express pass on a lofty bridge. And then, ahead, they saw the frontier post. It was a simple wooden signpost whose arms said on one side Europa and on the other side Asia. They stopped their cars and jumped down.

Du Taillis fumbled for the one bottle of Mumm's champagne which he had reserved for this occasion. The cork popped, the wine was poured, they were about to drink, when Cormier felt it was the occasion for a speech. He sucked for a moment at his heavy black moustache as he pondered, and then he declaimed, "We are now at the frontier between two halves of the world. For the first time two motor-cars, starting from the centuries-old city of Peking, have crossed Asia from end to end and have now reached the Urals. They will cross this frontier and re-enter Europe. And it is we—we who have driven them there. Gentlemen, I drink to us."

They were lifting their glasses when du Taillis interrupted. "To the peaceful conquests wrought by progress!" he said. "To the fusion of all races and the fraternity of all peoples."

They drank, and drank again, and then went a little mad. Du Taillis stood like a schoolboy, with one foot in Europe and one in Asia, saluting the French flag which flew from the first de Dion, and Collignon photographed him in the pose. But the low clouds of a fresh storm were driving towards them, and with a last *"Vive la France"* they got up again and pushed on to Zlatoust. In this market town of the jewel mines of the Urals they saw in the shop-windows topazes, beryls, aquamarines, and chrysolites, and bought some for souvenirs. Then, after refuelling, they went on again. The fierce rainstorms trapped them on a muddy hill, from where they could not advance until the water had cleared, and they spent the night in their cars. After another day of struggle they reached an inn, where they hoped for a better rest. They did not get it. Soon they knew that they were infested, but in the dark they could do nothing. In the morning they found their sleeping-bags alive with bugs. They threw the bags away, threw petrol on their beds of canvas stretched on steel, and resigned themselves to facing the rest of their journey without blankets.

But they were able to refit at Birsk, a pleasant town mingling the blue domes of Orthodox churches with the slender white spires of the minarets which abounded to serve the Mohammedan Tartars who largely lived there. At Birsk they got their first taste of the civic welcome which the cities of Europe were preparing for the 'raiders.' A squadron of Cossacks, riding stocky horses, and with their revolvers carried always at the ready in their hands, escorted the de Dions into the city. But when the official welcome was over and they walked through the town to buy strawberries in the market the children fled in terror at their wild and dirty appearance and tousled beards. "If we can even frighten the Russians," said du Taillis, "it is time we tidied ourselves up." And they stayed three nights in Birsk relaxing from old tension.

When they started again the rain returned, and for three days they fought it with all the reserves of energy they had accumulated in Birsk. On the 7th of August the day dawned clear again, and they thought they would have a fair run to Kazan. Cormier came to a bridge under reconstruction, and halted for Collignon, who was some two miles behind, to come up. A man approached him. Before he spoke Cormier said quickly that he did not speak Russian. "Mais vous parlez joliment bien le français," replied the man. He was the overseer for a French firm manufacturing reinforced concrete which had secured the contract for highway reconstruction in the area.

"This rain must have been the very devil for you," he said. "I saw Prince Borghese go past some days ago, and the weather was so good that he was kicking up clouds of dust as he passed."

A few miles farther on there was a sudden change in the sound and rhythm of the cars' progress. Du Taillis, who was sick and dozing, glanced over the side and then looked quickly towards Cormier. The driver's face was creased in an ecstatic grin. They were travelling on a metalled road. It was smooth, well engineered, seven metres wide.

"It's just like France!" said Cormier.

"Look!" yelled du Taillis. "There's a steam-roller!"

They accelerated towards the roller, which was finishing an intermediate stretch. They bumped as they hit the rough again, and the grit flew up into the mudguards. The workmen shook their fists and cursed because they had not slowed, and they were back on metal again, all the way to Kazan.

A good hotel at last. "And now for a night's sleep," sighed Cormier. But at four in the morning there was the most unmuffled roar they had ever yet heard emerging from four cylinders. The Frenchmen lurched out of bed, and ran to the balcony. Below, with its headlamps burning through muddy glass and tarnished brass, the Spyker shuddered, carrying two men who might have been dead. The driver had collapsed over the wheel, his arms hanging down to the floor. The passenger lay back with his chin in the air as though he had been shot. The driver turned his head up to the balcony, and in the light of lanterns some ostlers were holding it looked thin, grey, hollowed, unrecognizable. But it was Godard. He had kept his word. He had rejoined his companions.

Just fourteen days had passed since Godard set out from Tcheremkhovo, the point which the de Dions had left thirty-two days ago. Godard started at six in the morning of the 25th of June. On this day 20-year-old Bruno Stephan of Delft, reunited at last with his psychologically explosive box of spare parts, gingerly boarded the Trans-Siberian Express bound east from Moscow. The two men were some 4000 miles apart, and Godard in the car was to close the distance at a faster rate than Stephan on the train. Stephan had a rough idea of Godard's progress through the telegrams which they exchanged, addressed to principal stations on the railway. When Stephan arrived at a major stop he sent a telegram and got his answer at the next stage.

On the 25th of July Godard drove until ten o'clock at night to reach Nijni-Udinsk. The next day he drove for seventeen hours and slept at Kansk. On the 27th of July he drove from three in the morning until eleven at night and arrived in Atchinsk. After less than four hours' sleep he started at three, passed through Tomsk at five in the afternoon, and carried on for another 100 kilometres, completing about 630 kilometres in the day.

Stephan had now reached Omsk, and knew that he must leave the train. He hired a cab—a victoria with a body of pulped cane, drawn by three horses. He loaded his crate and baggage and resolutely instructed the cabby by signs to drive east. Stephan had no Russian at all, and the cabby at first thought this was a minor trip to some hotel in the outskirts. As they emerged from the town he looked inquiringly at his passenger. Stephan grimly pointed east. The afternoon ripened, and Stephan was still gesticulating along the trakt. Night fell, and the horses were weary. Stephan jabbed his finger forward—forward.

On the 29th of July Godard crossed the Obi at Kolyvan and

started his great sweep across the steppes. He drove all through the day and all through the night. In the early light of the 30th he stopped in a small village to seek some sort of refreshment. The curious peasants came out of their cottages. They surrounded the Spyker, the first automobile they had ever had a chance to study in their lives. In their absorption they did not notice the victoria cab slowly advancing from the west. Out of the mist the stumbling horses dragged the coach, their driver cushioned from the full bite of his poisonous ill-temper only by the wadding of sleep. Godard stared along the village street. This could only be Stephan. With a new energy of exhilaration he rushed to the cab, introduced himself to the passenger, brusquely demanded help from the villagers to transfer the precious box of spare parts, and drew tactfully aside while Stephan settled the account of his highly disgruntled driver. Then he bundled Stephan into the Spyker and drove full out for Omsk. He reached the city at eight in the morning. In twenty-nine hours of non-stop driving he had completed a cross-country journey afterwards calculated to be 865 kilometres. Both this and the previous day's efforts were better twenty-four-hour records than the trip from Urga to Kiakhta, but their terminal points were never exactly known.

In Omsk the two men collapsed into bed. But they could sleep for very few hours. Stephan had to get to work. As quickly as he could he mounted the new back axle and thoroughly overhauled the machine, fitting it with all the new spring-leaves he had brought in his box. Then the two went back to bed, and at five in the morning they roared anew across Asia. The Spyker was most definitely roaring now. The first thing Stephan noticed about it was that the silencer had disappeared. Soon he realized that he had not brought as many spares as Godard could use. In the exuberance of having had a refit, Godard hit a bump at speed and broke a front spring. They had to crawl fifty kilometres to Petropavlovsk to have a new spring forged. When the carriage-blacksmith had finally fashioned it they fitted it to the car and began to lower the jack. The jack came down to its normal low position and was still carrying the full weight of the car. The spring flattened as they continued to lower the chassis, until one of the frame-members was resting on the front axle. The steel used for horse-carriages was clearly not strong enough for the weight of the Spyker. They jacked up the car again and fixed timber between the spring and the frame-member, and had to retain this wooden buffer until they got to Moscow.

The broken spring had cost them almost a day for an advance of only 250 kilometres. At dawn on the 1st of August they were off again and Stephan had his first taste of Godard's night driving in a non-stop session which lasted until seven the next morning. Godard repeated the dose by starting out that same evening, so that they crossed the Europe-Asia frontier in the dark without knowing that they had done it. That night the last stock of carbide for the headlamps was consumed, and Stephan walked for hours in the Urals, with a white towel tied to his back so that Godard could follow in the Spyker. Finally they came to a monastery, where they slept, and drove off again at daybreak.

All the competitors noticed that as soon as they entered Europe the attitude of the peasants changed from amusement to anger at the approach of an automobile. The Siberian peasants had been mainly tolerant and often convulsed with laughter at the horseless carriages. The terrifying roar of the Spyker did nothing to ingratiate the crew with the local population of Russia. Sometimes the men and women would stampede along with the animals in a panic flight from the explosive vehicle. Sometimes, when they thought they might corner it while it was bogged in a morass, bands of men would approach menacingly, and could often be kept off only by revolver shots. Once, in an area where the motorcar was believed to be the weapon of the revolutionists—because they could plant a bomb and escape quickly, leaving an innocent if sympathetic community to suffer the reprisals—the Spyker was ceremonially banned from a village. The car was met at the village gate by the pope—Russian villages had their own pope— with his acolytes. He raised his gilt cross in the air, exorcized the devil, and bade it depart without coming in. This was a serious obstacle in a countryside where the road ran through the village, which had a palisade fence running, with a circumference of miles, as a common enclosure for grazing cattle: it was a long and difficult task to get round.

The Spyker came thundering up behind one cart with such

frightening effect that the horses bolted, and easily outdistanced the motor-car as they galloped ahead. The cart had no driver and Godard hooted urgently to draw the attention of some one in the fields. There was no response. But after some distance a bundle dropped from the careering cart and rolled along the ground. Godard just missed running over it, made an exclamation and stopped, and asked Stephan to get down to pick up the baby. Stephan came back to his seat with a bitterly crying, stiffly swaddled, very small child. "What do I do with it?" asked the boy.

"You're built wrong," said Godard irritably. "You can't do anything with it. Just hold it."

The cart had completely disappeared during the time that the Spyker had stopped. Godard gave an extravagant groan. "Here we are in the middle of the Peking–Paris race, and we get stuck with a baby. I bet it's one of Borghese's."

"Atalanta?" suggested Stephan.

"Never been there. What the hell are we going to do with this kid. Hey, there's a village ahead. You'd better dump it."

"Slow—slower!" said Stephan. But it was useless. At the noise of the car the village street had emptied, and the inhabitants had barred themselves in their houses.

Godard stopped, with the engine running. "Leave it on a doorstep," he said.

"I can't. They'll kill it. They'll think it's a devil we've spawned."

"You soft-hearted git," said Godard. "Ah, come on. We'll try somewhere else."

"The next village. And we stop outside."

The Spyker was driven cautiously to the gate of the next village. Stephan went into the street, carrying the baby. A woman was coming towards him. She walked in a wide circle to avoid him, but the Dutchman darted to her, thrust the baby towards her and smiled. The woman reacted convulsively. *"Niet—niet!"* she screamed, as if she had been irrevocably insulted. And she pushed the baby back in Stephan's arms. As he stood in bewilderment another woman came out of a house to see what was going on. With a courtly gesture Stephan offered her the baby. She shook her head violently and ran back inside. The street was now as deserted as the last village had been, but through the shutters dozens of eyes were straining to follow the fair young man. He walked out to the gate, back to the Spyker. "The church. Other end of the village," he said hoarsely.

Godard started the car, and drove with a certain decorum to the church by the farther gate. Stephan got down with the child again.

He was stealing up the steps of the porch, and had almost reached his objective when the pope came out of the church door. Quite nonplussed, Stephan stood for a second with the child in his arms, then dumped it in the priest's arms, turned, and ran like a stag. He hurdled into the car. Godard rammed in the gear lever. The Spyker accelerated to freedom.

Godard's hands were now blood-raw from continuously driving the bucking car, and he could no longer operate for twenty-four-hour sessions. Stephan, knowing everything about the engine and chassis, was not a driver. They were therefore forced—and Stephan was most grateful for it—to put up occasionally at an inn. At an inn in the Urals soon after they had passed the frontier there was a peremptory knock on their bedroom door one night. A large lady in several thicknesses of old, but expensive, clothing was revealed. She would have spoken perfect French if she had not been almost speechless with drink. Godard gathered that she was a countess, that she lived in a château quite near, but that she would never go back to it—never, unless Monsieur Godard would take her on a stage of his journey next morning. Godard politely explained that it was impossible, asked to be excused owing to his exhaustion, and shut the door.

When they emerged to start their car early next morning the Countess was still outside their door, on a seat, with a bottle. "I insist," she said tearfully. "I have sworn that I shall not go back to my estate. It was wrong of me to swear. I am bound in my own chains."

The innkeeper looked soulfully at Godard to see if this cross could not be removed from his own neck. Godard shrugged his shoulders, and smiled. "As you wish, Countess," he said with a slight bow. And then, to Stephan, "Stephan, she's got to go on your lap."

Before a kilometre was completed Stephan was in agony. So was the Countess, but noblesse obliged her to make no complaint. It took ten miles before the irregularities of that bumpy road finally beat the Countess. At the sixteenth verst she was sick—over Godard. He stopped, and allowed Stephan to arrange her on the ground. "Countess," said Godard, "it is clear that motoring is not good for your health. It would be better for you if you walked back." And he drove on.

With diversions like this, but under increasing tension, Godard made his eastern journey. The strain hit Stephan first. At Ufa, in the Urals, Godard cabled to Spijker that the lad was seriously ill and would have to be left behind. Stephan, however, recovered from his deep exhaustion, though, like du Taillis, he retained his dysentery; and he stayed in the *raid* for much longer. He had left Amsterdam a month before he picked up Godard, and he travelled for nine days with him on this breakneck drive to Kazan, continuing for fifteen days altogether to get to Moscow. The stage into Kazan, where they met the de Dion team, was another all-night trip, since they had been able to buy more carbide in Birsk.

When they had arrived at four o'clock that morning they had completed, in well under twenty-four hours, a stretch that had taken the de Dions four days. In all, Godard had moved across the map by fifty-five degrees of longitude—from 103° E to 48° E at about latitude 55° N—in fourteen days. He had probably covered—he had no milometer—about 3500 miles, of which the last twenty-four kilometres had been on a metalled road. If he had repeated the distance he could have driven past Gibraltar and on to the ferry and into North Africa. He completed in a fortnight what Borghese had done in three weeks, and the de Dions had covered in nearly five weeks. There was some excuse for his hands being skinned to the flesh.

During the days that Charles Godard was passing through the fire in this test of sheer driving fortitude he was sentenced in his absence by a Paris court to eighteen months' imprisonment and a fine of 5000 francs for obtaining money from the Dutch consular officials in China by false pretences.

15 ◎ ◎ The Advance to Moscow

No General Staff could have got more intellectual pleasure from experiencing the unrelenting pressure of a planned advance than Prince Borghese drew from his nightly calculations before writing his journal. The factors which lifted Borghese into the lead were many. The most important was the power of his machine, but the virtue in having entered it was wholly Borghese's. The great controversy before the start of the *raid* had been between the supporters of light and heavy cars. Would the heavy car bog down irretrievably in bad conditions? Would the light car have the power to get out of even mildly unfavourable conditions? Borghese had decided unhesitatingly on *power*, believing that speed would get him out of more difficulties than lightness of weight. He had a good car and an excellent mechanic, who gave it complete daily service. He was a driver of skill and stamina himself. His planning was more extravagantly cautious than anybody's: since even the Itala company had tried to persuade him to keep their car out of the race he had drawn the appropriate conclusions from their lack of faith, and had almost the components of a duplicate car available to him as replacements at various stages. (But, like the other owners, he said after the *raid* that he had hardly had to touch a thing.) As captain of his crew his day-to-day attitude of calmness and efficiency and almost self-conscious unflappability had their effect. But he was working on easy material. Guizzardi was his devoted personal servant, and Barzini was in the position, through his newspaper, of being a paid-up partner who made no claim on policy decisions.

Even Borghese's professional modesty—he was described after the race by a Paris journalist as "the English-gentleman type with ingratiating Italian manners"—had faltered sufficiently for him to bear a placard on his car besides the Italian flag he proudly flew. At Irkutsk he had got a sign-writer to paint on each side of the car PECHINO–PARIGI in letters that stretched from the wing tank to the side of the bonnet. The script was a little too untidily decorative, and Barzini declared it looked like a shop-sign. The first grandstand audience who might have admired it *en route* unfortunately missed it, because they were all asleep; and because they were asleep they missed arriving at their destination.

They were the passengers and crew of a huge public mail-coach. A sort of Pickwickian omnibus—which was coming towards them along the Siberian trakt. At the sound of the approaching Itala the three horses who were drawing the coach wheeled in the path, turned completely round, and began to draw the coach back on the way it had come. The driver and guard and all the passengers were asleep, and they even stayed sleeping when the Itala, at low speed for the sake of the horses, passed the coach and went ahead. When the Italians looked back from a long hill several miles farther on they could see that the coach was still slowly moving in their direction.

Prince Borghese said at the end of the *raid*—following the natural compulsion to tidy up the warts from the finished portrait—that he had never had any doubts about getting to Paris, because he had never thought about Paris. "The secret of our success was this: that we never thought of the final goal, never admitted that our end was Paris. Every day when we awoke we concentrated on nothing but getting the day's stage done well." But it would have been as unnatural for them never to have thought of Paris as it would have been for them never to have despaired, and, in fact, both these venial sins were committed.

There were two moments of profound despair. The conditions caused by the rain and mud of that terrible—and apparently genuinely exceptional—Siberian summer were at the core of both of them. They had come into the taiga, the interminable forest stretch with the trakt forced through artificial clearings—an isolated and melancholy region even in the eyes of Russians, and trebly so for soaked motorists trying to negotiate a path which alternated clear pools and thick mud. They had declined an escort of armed soldiers which the Chief of Police in Kansk had urgently pressed on them. Revolutionaries had recently made an open attack on the Krasnoyarsk barracks, captured a store of arms and ammunition, and released forty prisoners from the gaol. These convicts were now roaming the taiga, robbing travellers in order to survive.

The rain was falling in sheets. The 'black earth,' the residual mould from thousands of years of fallen forest leaves, was a skid-pan from which the wheels threw up a continuous spray of black mud. It settled on their clothes and faces, as viscose as oil. The car was bogged. The rain stopped, but they still had to wait for the land to drain before volunteers among the foresters could help them to dig it out. As soon as the sun came out they were attacked almost to the point of nervous collapse by the great gadflies and mosquitoes of the area, against which the local people continuously wore chest-length black veils in the summer. They were utterly discouraged, and Barzini even committed to print in the *Daily Telegraph* the admission, "I must confess that for the first time a vague shadow of doubt is clouding our hopes of victory."

By the time they neared Tomsk the log roads laid down in some parts of the trakt were slowly knocking the Itala to pieces. Their luggage-straps were continually breaking as the chassis hit the back axle, pounding away remorselessly at the differential casing. But Borghese kept to his policy of using speed to stop their being buried. At every ditch he accelerated for the extra impetus to get through the deep mud at the bottom. The car would run up the opposite bank like a shying horse, with its front wheels in the air. Then the back would crash down on the crest. They had to stop when at one hurdle the rear petrol-tank was stripped from its supports by the impact. They roughly repaired the damage, and went on. They came to a wide swamp, at the bottom of a large dyke, which they could not avoid. Borghese got down, and even on foot found himself almost stuck in the mud. Again they must rely on speed to get through. Borghese backed the Itala, and catapulted it at the swamp. The car bounded in a series of equine springs, but suddenly stopped in a fog of exhaust smoke. They were ditched again.

Borghese walked away for help. An hour later he came back with woodmen and horses. The horses could not shift the car. The woodmen had first to fell trees to lever the machine upward. They went on again, and finally caught their first glimpse of the gold-and-green domes of Tomsk. They came out of Tomsk escorted by a troop of galloping Cossacks, with bells jingling on their bridles. An imperious voice halted them. A local photographer, deter-mined to record them for history, had set up a huge camera on a tripod at a turn on the road, and would not let them pass. "Regardez ici, Messieurs. Ne bougez pas." ("Look this way, please. Quite still.")

"But we're in a hurry."

"Moi aussi." He exposed several plates, and then saluted them.

"C'est la gloire. Adieu!"

They crossed the Tom and then the Obi on rope ferries pro-pelled by horses circulating round a large wheel on the shore. On the other side of the Obi they were piloted through the twenty-five miles of swamp stretching between the river and Kolyvan by a carriage to which three horses were harnessed radially, as in a troika. The coachman set off through the marshes at amazing speed, changing horses at stages which had been pre-pared every six miles. At Kolyvan the whole town was waiting to welcome them. The Chief of Police was at their head, with the text of a speech of welcome in his hand. Unfortunately, the arrival of the Itala coincided with the evening return to stable of all the town's oxen from the common pasture outside the town gates. Guizzardi's open racing exhaust had its usual effect on the live-stock. Several hundred head of cattle stampeded, taking the shortest way through the reception committee. The Chief of Police had been allowed a few well-rounded sentences. Then he disappeared in a cloud of dust, and the speech with him.

As the country broadened out into the steppes the Itala began to notch a better constant speed again. The car had no speedo-meter. One of the crew used to stand with a watch in his hand, timing the verst-poles as they passed. A verst is 3500 feet, 1166 metres. They reckoned that on the steppe they could reach 30 m.p.h. and average 25 m.p.h. The steppes gave them their record run hitherto of 250 miles into Omsk in just over twelve hours. This included the time spent on putting out a fire, which started in the brake-block. Their unaccustomed speed, and the position of the fire, which was fanned straight under the car by the flywheel, caused the floorboards to catch fire only a few inches from the reserve petrol-tanks before they noticed the blaze. They ran to the ditch for water, but in the steppes the ditches were dry. They threw Borghese's fur rugs on to the flames to extinguish them, and ripped out the smouldering floorboards to scrape the red-hot wood away with knives. When the fire was out Guizzardi detached the footbrake action, since it was the inefficient return of this block that had caused the trouble, and drove the rest of the way to Paris on the handbrake alone.

They came into Omsk on a Sunday afternoon, when all the citizens were strolling on the wooden sidewalks. The quays along the river were stacked with thousands of American ploughs and cultivating machines, which were being sent up and down the river Om to the new farms of the Russian immigrants into Siberia, who were coming in by batches of up to 10,000 people to till the virgin land. An export trade managed principally by English, Germans, and Norwegians was already sending away a refrigerator-train each day loaded with butter for the English market.

In Omsk an attack of delayed exhaustion affected the Italian crew. Even Borghese, who took a special pride in never appearing tired before strangers, would collapse as soon as his many visitors had gone. Barzini fainted quite suddenly in the street. As he was passing out he signalled to a hackney carriage, but he had collapsed before it drew up. He came round some time later to find himself still on the sidewalk, with the driver waiting patiently at the kerb and passers-by politely stepping over him. The population of Omsk had assumed that he was drunk, like everybody else on occasion, and he would be best left to recover in his own time.

At Omsk they tidied the footbrake and changed the tyres of the front wheels, which had lasted since Peking. Both Borghese and Barzini declared that though they would have liked to change both the wheels and the springs, the large consignment of spare parts which Borghese had ordered to be sent to Omsk had been held up by the Austrian Customs, and never arrived. On the other hand, when du Taillis arrived at Omsk he was told in circumstantial detail by both mechanics and police officers that enormous crates of spares, on which the Customs duty payable was 700 francs, were awaiting the Itala, and out of these spares "a completely new Itala" was built. But du Taillis hedged his report by saying that all Siberians are liars.

They came out of the steppes, and reached a stretch of difficult sand-dunes which marked the approach to the Urals. In a village a group of troikas were awaiting them in the charge of richly dressed coachmen, with the long hair and beard of the mujik. A Siberian mine-owner had sent them to request the pleasure of the party's company at luncheon. They left the car for the fast, light troikas, and dashed for miles behind the jingling bells of the beautiful black horses, until they came to the mine-owner's villa. They lunched in the open air in ancient state that might have been copied from an early Tolstoy novel. The ladies wore French clothes of a fashion half a century old. The men wore silk embroidered shirts, with great silver-mounted belts. The children were dressed in traditional Siberian costume, the boys wearing their hair long. Barefooted family servants crowded round to watch the masters eat. The banquet was lengthy, and Borghese had to beg for the troikas to be summoned for the return to the car. Next day they were in the Urals, in the elegant city of Ekaterinburg, the market centre for the mines of gold and of coal. The rich merchants entertained the Italians with the most lavish hospitality, in the flush of the last surge of security that their class was ever to know. Eleven years later, in that same elegant town, the Tsar and all his family—except Anastasia?—were shot to death in a cellar. And Borghese was the head of a mission in St Petersburg trying to save something from the wreckage.

As the Italians drove deeper into Europe and came to Perm they became seriously alarmed that a delay of several days was threatening them. The left rear wheel was breaking up. It was creaking badly, and the spokes were displaced in their sockets. They unshipped the wheel, bound the spokes with string, and stuffed string into the cracks of the rim. All that was left to do was to soak the wheel overnight. But there was neither bath nor tub in the whole of the city big enough to hold the wheel.

A sympathetic local magnate, who had been watching the operation with great interest, interrupted them: "Excuse me, do you want to soak your wheel?"

"Yes."

"Then why don't you send it to the public baths?"

Prince Borghese analysed the man for drunkenness with his usual faint diplomatist's smile.

"The public baths?"

"The hydro. All you have to do is to hire a private cubicle, put your wheel in the bath, and leave it there until you call. Why go yourself? I'll call a cab and tell the cabby to put the wheel in the bath."

It seemed an excellent idea. The wheel came back next morning, and was fitted to the car. But by eleven o'clock the spokes had come completely adrift, and the car could not move. They tied it all together temporarily, and drove very slowly to a carriage-maker whom a passing workman had recommended. He called his workmen to hew new spokes from a weathered pine-log, fixed them to the rim, and screwed them to the hub with a craftsman's accuracy. By luck—for the carriage-builder was reputed to be the best in the province—Borghese had avoided the necessity of riding to a telegraph-station, ordering a new wheel, and awaiting its delivery, which might have taken a week. Instead in eight hours he had a wheel which was at least good enough to take him to Moscow.

And so, sixteen miles from Kazan, they came to the hard white carriage road that was to delight their rivals. They swept along it, down the valley of the Kasanga river, and ahead they saw the long, bright line of the great Volga. The sky was blue, and a haze from the change of weather hung over the horizon. Out of its translucent mist they saw rising the gold domes of sixty churches and the pearl spires of a dozen mosques. In a moment of time they had left the lands of omens, of forest gods and fear, and a peasantry that had hardly changed its way for centuries. They were in a wide and gracious town, bustling with the accepted signs of modernity—humming electric trams and the brittle clop of elegant carriage horses. Kazan! It might have been Paris in the Balkans.

A lady of local society sat in her carriage on one of the boulevards, and as the Itala passed she followed its progress with a self-possessed stare. She was wearing a man's Homburg hat, like Edward VII. She was smoking a cigarette. She gave an order to her coachman, and he touched the reins, pulled out after the Itala, and caught it up. The lady coolly regarded the crew, fixed on Borghese, leaned over to him, and drawled, "Are you from Peking?"

"Yes, madame."

"Oh! And where are you off to now?"

"We are going to our hotel."

"Do you know the best?"

"We want the Hôtel d'Europe."

"Yes. Do you know the way? Would you like me to show you?"

"With pleasure, madame."

And Kazan's most enterprising hostess led the way to luxury.

Kazan, on the Volga, was one of the great ports of the world, sending liners for thousands of miles on inland waters, through an empire where the river traffic was far more important than the rail. Its quays were hedged with masts as the Italians crossed the brimming river next day in a steam ferry sighing with the sound of the balalaikas that the Cossack migrants played. The route onward lay roughly along the line of the Volga, and ahead lay Nijni-Novgorod. Outside this city a group of carriages was awaiting them, and as the Itala slowed there were loud shouts of "*Evviva!*" The Italian colony had come out to welcome their compatriots. They had brought champagne, and they had brought the mail from home. There was time only to read the most desired letters before the checked excitement of the meeting surged. With anecdotes and gossip and rare unself-conscious exuberance the roadside party developed, until the night was falling, and they had not yet penetrated the city.

The sun had almost set over the ancient capital of Russia, but on the hill of the High Town its rays still caught the eleven square towers of its Kremlin, and the white crenellated walls creeping up the slope still glowed. A rose gleam lay on the golden cupolas, in whose shade so much massacre, war, national renaissance—all that men called history—had been witnessed, and where now a quaint and noisy car passed that might also, the idealists thought, be the instrument of history. It was in the High Town that the Governor of Nijni-Novgorod had organized a garden banquet for the 'raiders' of peace. Barzini hurried to write his copy before he dressed to go. But in the middle of the banquet he was called to the telephone. The telegraph office had refused to send the wire because it was not written in Russian. Barzini had had trouble of this nature before, and had not always overcome it. But at a meeting of the highest dignitaries of the province he could not fail to find some one to telephone brusque orders to the office. "I can tell you why they were making things difficult," the grandee explained as they walked back to the table. "They thought the telegram was too long. They prefer easy jobs like death announcements, not Press messages."

The banquet ended. The guests sank into welcome sleep. But Barzini was awakened by a knock on his door. "What is it?" he asked the maître d'hôtel.

"Did you send a telegram?"

"Don't tell me they haven't dispatched it!"

"Calm yourself. It has gone. The clerk merely wants some information."

"Yes?"

"It is because you are from Peking. Should the words of your telegram be read down the page or across the page? And if across the page, from right to left or vice versa?"

"My telegram was in Italian. It is written across the page, and reads from left to right."

"Thank you, sir. The telegraph clerk will be most interested. I shall let him know at once."

"But he has already sent it, you said!"

"Oh, yes, sir."

"Which way did he send it?"

"Reading down the page, sir."

In the morning the Italians breakfasted in some style, looking down from the hotel terrace on to the wide, sandy plain between the two great rivers, the Volga and the Oko, where Nijni-

Novgorod's great annual fair of St Peter and St Paul was held. It was two days before its official opening by the Archbishop and the Governor of the Province, but the merchants were already in full activity, and the crowds were thronging across the river.

In a rectangular space measuring about a mile by 1000 yards, 5000 shops were symmetrically sited. Their rents brought to the Government 1,000,000 francs a year. There were no shop-windows because the plain was used only during the period of the fair, and during the winter the empty buildings were flooded to their first storeys. The area of the shops was divided into zones specializing in tea, carpets, silk, wool, furs, and every other sort of ware. Merchants from as far as Persia, India, and China had gathered for this annual market, which half a million people attended. As the goods were sold fresh supplies were unloaded from the barges lined along the quays of the two rivers. Above the uniform line of the shops the roofs of theatres and churches rose. In the streets the costumes of every Russian nationality could be seen as the buyers pressed along the straight-ruled lanes, between the sentinels of mounted Cossacks, who kept a rough order. Monks and nuns stood at every vantage-point with money-boxes that never failed to extract a copeck from the unsophisticated bypassers. Quack dentists were barking out their prowess at curing toothache. Quack doctors were telling confidential tales to credulous women of the power of their fine white powder, costing hardly anything, to cure the drunkenness of husbands. And everywhere the acrobats, escapists, buskers—and pickpockets—flourished.

Past these crowds the Itala rumbled in low gear after crossing the river on the route to Moscow. Tartars, Circassians, Armenians, Persians, all gazed excitedly at the men who had come from Peking, and then the car was out of Nijni-Novgorod. The road was fair, but construction work at bridges delayed the car considerably—a transport bulletin which could be repeated in every year since 1907. They passed through Vladimir, and began the last lap to Moscow. But now the road was too good. They had been asked particularly by the Peking–Paris committee in Moscow not to arrive before two in the afternoon because a timetable had been worked out for their reception. As they checked their schedule they saw that they would reach Moscow by ten in the morning if they did not stop. They were therefore obliged to stop at Bogorodsk, and to sit down in the hotel there for breakfast, for which they ordered champagne.

Two hours later they got back into the car. At a point almost twenty miles from Moscow Cossack guards on horseback were posted in pairs at hundred-yard intervals all the way to the centre. Soon the Italians were met by a great convoy of motor-cars carrying the Press and some personal friends, along with the committee. Amid the carnival tooting of motor horns, the sincere official welcome, the hard, pointed interviews with journalists, and the more intimate reunion with friends it was a somewhat prolonged period of emotion. The President of the Moscow Automobile Club presented them with gilt-and-enamel club badges, which they pinned into their head-gear—they were now wearing peaked caps back to front like true northern motorists. There were more presentations, speeches, questions; and then they were urged on into Moscow. It was a city of white and gold again, like so many Russian centres they had passed through, though here they saw factory chimneys on the outskirts. They were in the inner zone now. The traffic was stopped as the police passed the long convoy through. The passengers in the tramcars stood and waved their hats and cheered. The line of cars climbed the slope of the noble approach to the Kremlin, and drew up outside— what? The Tsar's palace? The Hôtel Métropole. Porters scurried out to take the luggage of the honoured guests. There was no luggage to give them. Even Borghese's imposing furs had gone to quench the fire in the brake-block. Prince Borghese stepped out of the car and strode into the hotel, looking the reverse of a conquering hero. Even his suit did not fit any more. He had lost twelve pounds in weight on the journey.

He was now about to be given the chance to recover his figure in the most exhaustive series of celebration breakfasts, luncheons, and banquets that he had ever been called upon to endure.

16 ◎ ◎ A Very Sporting Reception

Prince Scipione Borghese and his crew arrived in Moscow on a Saturday afternoon, and stayed three full days there, leaving on the morning of Wednesday the 31st of July. They were in Moscow while du Taillis was at the salute astride the border between Europe and Asia, and while Godard and Stephan were introducing themselves to each other under the eyes of a desperate cab-driver.

There was not a social or sporting event in Moscow that Borghese and Barzini were not begged to attend, nor a smart hotel or restaurant they did not visit—the Hermitage, the Mauritania, set in the middle of Petrovsky Park, the Yard, a night resort that was lively until dawn.

But Russian club and café-concert life always did embrace dawn in its rhythm. And when, at four in the morning of July the 31st, the Itala left the garage of the Hôtel Métropole for its last 2500 miles Borghese was not stealing away from genial hosts who had banqueted him in an effort not to wake them, as he had tried to do at Urga, Kiakhta, Irkutsk—so many places that he might never see again. This time an escort of friends was following in cars to accompany him out of the city. And the fashionable quarters of Moscow were still rustling with people who, if not friends, were friendly towards him as they ended their social day in the deep peace of knowing that they need not work for their breakfast.

Club men came out on to their balconies as the fleet passed. Starched shirts a little dented, white ties a little askew, they offered a subdued chorus of good wishes as genteel as a parliamentary cheer. The carriages were bringing people home from the restaurants, the horses stepping smartly after standing too long. From farther out, from the Petrovsky Park, the horses had run past their nervous activity, and were clopping much more quietly home to match the mood of the hour. The gentlemen and ladies inside them, perhaps a little sleepy, a little tight, put down the windows, and waved languidly at Borghese.

He drove into St Petersburg Avenue, which was not the exit for Paris that any planner would suggest. But Borghese was not going straight to Paris. In the middle of the banqueting his hosts had represented to him how eagerly their friends in the capital were hoping to see him; and because Borghese owed the Peking–Paris committee in St Petersburg a great debt of gratitude—they were the fathers of the *raid* as far as the Russian Empire was concerned, and their Ministers and sportsmen and capitalists had done more than anyone to organize its success—he agreed to add the considerable distance to his route mileage in order to see them. But he emphasized that it was his firm intention to arrive in Paris on Saturday the 10th of August—at 4.30 P.M.

The Nobel organization improvised a further supply of petrol on the St Petersburg road and out of Russia—which they did not extend to the following de Dions and the Spyker. Borghese arrived too early at the rendezvous outside St Petersburg. A massive caravan of cars had been organized to escort him in, and while some of them were arriving the first comers invaded the railway-station buffet of Tsarskoye Selo, and ordered a case of champagne. Captain Windham, an Englishman who had driven out from the capital to join in the welcome, approached Borghese in the buffet, and asked him, as an old motorist and a member of the Automobile Club of Great Britain, whether the Prince had any message for the British.

"Yes," said Borghese. "I am very disappointed that there are no English competing, and I hope that if ever there is another journey of this sort the English will take part."

A number of the Italian colony had been unable to take part in the early welcome. They had hired a large motor-omnibus, but as a reminder that not all automobiles could "go anywhere," it had broken down *en route*, and lay skewed across the road as the party finally drove into the capital. But the passengers cheered louder than any, and kept up the shouting until the convoy was out of sight.

The banquet lasted until 1.30 in the morning, and the Italian motorists, who had had to attend in their travelling dress, were on the road again three hours later. By ten o'clock the rain was falling—they had had none at all in Moscow—and in the middle of the storm they broke a back spring. Guizzardi substituted another, which was not very efficient. And although they had greatly lightened the load on the car by leaving all their tools and chains and even tow-ropes behind in Moscow, they considered that they must once more fill the back seat with their spare tyres and luggage instead of suspending them from the rear. Barzini was once more ejected from the place that had been designed for him, and took up his seat on the floorboards with his foot on the step.

As they drove into Kovno (now Kaunas, Lithuanian S.S.R.) they were intercepted by a breathless officer. "Prince Borghese!" he gasped. "Please! The Governor's wife is expecting you at the Red Cross Charity Fair."

The Governor's lady had had the brilliant idea of exhibiting the Itala, and the Prince, at her garden party for an admission fee of ten copecks. The Prince could not agree.

Next morning, the 4th of August, 1907, they came to the little bridge that marked the frontier between the Russian and German Empires. The Russians completed formalities with speed. The car advanced across the bridge. The white uniforms of the Russian guards yielded to the field-grey tunics and spiked helmets of the Germans. A braying of car hooters announced an excited welcome from the Königsberg branch of the Imperial Automobile Club. The German Customs routine was imposed and the Prince paid his deposit as indemnity if he sold his car in the Empire. And the authorities graciously gave him a German driving-licence without insisting that he should take a test.

Next day they came to Berlin in the midst of a fleet of Itala cars which the Turin firm had brought in for the use of the many journalists who were covering the progress across Europe. The Press of the world seemed to have produced dozens of photographers, who formed themselves into a battery at a country-inn lunch before the triumphal entry, and quite exhausted the Italian crew with their demands of "Look here," "Keep still," "Look up," "Keep still," "This way," "Keep still," until all their film was exposed. They came into Berlin by the Berlinerstrasse, Frank-fürterallee, Königstrasse, Unter den Linden, to the square before the Bristol Hotel, which was kept clear by the Imperial Guard. The banquets began—and the Itala firm stole the veteran car, and put it in their showroom on the Lindenstrasse. When Borghese learnt of it he angrily ordered his car to be with-drawn and returned to him.

On Wednesday the 7th Borghese left Berlin, now tailed by three more Italas which were gaudily advertising *Le Matin.* They drove through Potsdam, on to Brandenburg, and made for Magde-burg. The countryside was swarming with units of the Kaiser's army on manœuvres. The Itala came up with a battery of horse artillery, and kept pace alongside the gun-teams in their shining brass spiked helmets. They met a patrol of Uhlans, motionless, with the points of their long lances piercing the ground so that the enemy should not see the fluttering black-and-white pennants at the point. In Magdeburg they had to halt while a full regiment of German infantry went by on the march. Barzini was strangely moved by the pageantry of their passage. "The soldiers were singing a war hymn in strong unison, and in the depth of our hearts we felt the wonderful impact of this forceful, solemn music that was the formidable voice of an army." They went on to Her-ford, and passed the spa where invalids were taking the waters. The cripples hauled themselves up in their bath-chairs, and gave a feeble cheer from the weak to the strong.

The next day they were banqueted for luncheon in Cologne, and passed across the frontier into Belgium. The speed-limit in Belgian villages was low—low enough for one old woman to threaten the innocent Italians for money. "I know you—you swine," she yelled. "You're the one who ran over my hen last Thursday. Pay up!"

"Last Thursday," observed Prince Borghese conversationally, "we were in St Petersburg."

In another village a Belgian policeman stopped Borghese and

prepared to book him. "Who are you?" he asked, taking out his notebook.

"Prince Scipione Borghese."

"You a prince? That is not true. You are a Belgian chauffeur. I know you. You are a Belgian chauffeur, and you are breaking the law because you were going too fast. You know the regulations—ten kilometres per hour. Your name and address."

"Prince Scipione Borghese, Palazzo Borghese, Rome."

"That's enough of a joke. Show me your papers."

The policeman studied the papers. "They are not yours. You are a chauffeur. Why do you try to pass as a prince? In that costume! Are you ashamed of being a chauffeur? Every one must earn a living at something. Where do you come from?"

"From Peking."

The message was through. The policeman assumed an attitude of profound regret. "Passez, Monseigneur, et bon voyage."

On the 9th of August the Itala passed into France at the frontier point near Agimont. In the No Man's Land between the frontier posts a crowd of French journalists were waiting—with champagne. They finished the bottles, and went on to the Customs point. They were in Reims at lunch-time—inevitably for more champagne in the centre of the champagne vineyards. In the afternoon they came to Meaux, thirty miles from Paris, where they were to stay before their formal entry. A cinematographer was waiting for them. They groaned. They had had enough photography that week. But in resignation they looked in his direction and kept still.

"No, don't keep still! Move! This is a movie. Move more— much more! I must have movement."

But his camera was static. He could not take the car in motion. And the only things that could be moved were their necks.

By the next morning Meaux was seething with motor-cars— belonging to the Press, the Automobile Club, sportsmen, and sightseers. The ceremonial procession was not to move off until after two o'clock. When, at last, they started, the continuous cheering from the onlookers packed in the road for the last eight miles so overcame Borghese that—Barzini noticed—for the first time in sixty days he smiled spontaneously and with obvious enjoyment instead of his habitual, enigmatic diplomatist's smile. The women thought he was wonderful, and blew kisses and shouted endearments to him.

The rain began. The weather at the finish in Paris was to match the start at Peking. The Itala was stopped at a check-point. A thirty-seater charabanc was directed to go before it. It was decorated with the Italian and French flags, and it carried a full brass band. The band thundered into the Triumphal March from Verdi's *Aïda*. And that is the style in which the Itala came back through the centre of metropolitan Paris as the leader of the Peking 'raiders.'

The crowds were dozens thick. L'Avenue du Trône, Boulevard Voltaire, Place de la Republique—Boulevards Saint-Martin, Saint-Denis, Bonne Nouvelle. Boulevard Poissonnière. Borghese had never really known where the *Matin* offices were since he had never attended a committee meeting. The road outside was kept clear by the Garde Républicaine, but only intermittently. The bright-helmeted cavalry had to sweep the crowd away in continuous rushes, and each time they cleared a space the hardy photographers rushed in to take pictures before the horses kicked them. On the lesser balconies of *Le Matin* cinematographers were cranking their apparatus and imploring "Look up at the lens!"

Smiling really warmly now, but very conscious of the need for casual precision, Prince Borghese gave a graceful sweep of his whole right arm over the steering-wheel. This brought the Itala round in a fast U-turn, angled accurately so that the motor-car jumped up the kerb, continued its line, and stopped dead in position, in front of the red velvet stage where it was to be displayed. Guizzardi, Barzini, and the Prince were carried shoulder-high into the *Matin* building. He kissed his family and friends—his uncle and aunt were there, but not Princess Anna Maria. The champagne was poured. The speeches came. And Prince Borghese replied before he went on the balcony to show himself to the people.

"Gentlemen, you have exaggerated," he said. "We were not heroes, we were simply patient. Yes, our only virtue was patience. Perhaps we had one other—perseverance. The secret of our success was this: that we never thought of the final goal, never admitted that our end was Paris. Every day when we awoke we concentrated on nothing but getting the day's stage done well. And—as each day the obstacles to overcome were very like those we had already conquered, and the fatigue was much the same—so we came to the end on the strength of the habit we had created between us."

The speech, as was to be expected, was delivered in impeccable French. So was the address at the banquet that night—while in the soaking Jardin des Tuileries thousands of the *Matin*'s public braved the rain to attend a grand fête followed by cinematographic projections of the entry into Paris. The next night the banquet was at the Restaurant Zucco on the grands boulevards. Among the presentations to Prince Borghese—he had a trunkful already after his trip through Europe—was an allegoric cup representing the race through Asia, Russia, and Europe. It was in the form of a gold driving-wheel, surmounted by a lion holding a palm between his hind-legs, and with the arms of Savoy above. The driving-wheel rested on two camels' heads. On the base of Carrara marble there were designs of laurel and oak, with a map of the route. On the cup was the inscription, "To Scipione Borghese, to the triumph of Italy and of Italian automobilism: the Italian colony in Paris, 1907." Barzini's presentation on this occasion was an inkstand in the form of a globe crossed from pole to pole by a pen and surmounted by telegraph-wires.

Two days after his entry Borghese told the *Matin* directors that he wanted his car off the stage outside their office immediately, since he was going to take it to Italy. The newspaper had to apologize to all the people it had persuaded to come to Paris to see it, and offered them instead "every evening on the screen the arrival of Prince Borghese in Paris." By Friday the 16th of August Borghese was in Milan, driving the Itala round the arena in an official welcome attended by 300,000 people, who broke through the barriers, and carried the crew to the tribune. Bruised by this experience, Barzini declined to go on next day for similar treatment in Turin, but stayed in Milan, where a banquet was given for him and Guizzardi by the Italian journalists.

Before he left for Italy Prince Borghese gave a newspaper interview—characteristically not to *Le Matin* but to *Le Figaro*. He confessed that he had got to the point where he had had enough of the *raid*. He declared that by his calculation he had covered 16,000 kilometres, 10,000 miles, not 8000 kilometres, or 13,000 kilometres, as had been suggested. (By comparison the rail distance between Vladivostok and Paris may be given: it was then officially 7283 miles.) He said that the tyres he had used were Pirelli standard products, and he had used fourteen tyres altogether, thirteen of them on the front wheels. (All versions of the tyres used, though varying, were about this number: Barzini said they used twelve outer covers, "which, with the other four taken on board at Paris, make up a total of sixteen tyres in all, and of these sixteen, the four with which we reached Paris were in such good condition that we further travelled with three of them as far as Milan. The front right wheel came from Peking to Paris, changing tyres only once at Omsk." If this last sentence is difficult to reconcile with Borghese, Barzini should be rejected: he was always mixing up the front wheels with the back in his cables.)

Prince Borghese also denied in the interview that he had spent anything like the 250,000 francs that he was said to have poured out on the *raid*. "I have spent 30,000 francs, including everything, not much more than if I had travelled by ordinary means." (This is a low figure since Godard owed over 10,000 francs before he had left Peking, and Godard had only one person to support and pay passage for whereas Borghese had four. Moreover, Godard had not had to buy a car. The 30,000 francs may represent Borghese's expenditure after he had "sold a piece" of the expedition to *Corrierre della Sera*, who brought in the *Daily Telegraph*. His attitude to sponsoring commercial products, including the Itala car, was markedly negative. But nobody now knows the accounting arrangements with the Nobel organization.)

Finally Borghese said this to *Le Figaro*, "It was a very sporting reception. I have a slight apprehension that if the same *épreuve* had ended in Italy—say, Milan or Rome—and the first home had been a Frenchman my compatriots would have given him a pretty cool reception. They would certainly have considered it a battle lost. But in Paris every one appreciated what had been done, and applauded it from the bottom of their hearts, without wanting to know *who* had done it."

This was a sincere and very generous tribute. But Prince Borghese could not know the sort of "sporting reception" the directors of *Le Matin* were at that very moment preparing for Charles Godard.

Godard lay over his steering-wheel in the inn yard at Kazan, until the Frenchmen bullied him inside, half carrying him, for the cold had stiffened his limbs. "After a drive like that we wouldn't let a horse stand without a blanket, so don't think we're going to watch you die," said du Taillis with cheerful cruelty. It was always Godard's fate, having caught up with his friends, to have no time for recovery, but to press on again with them. The de Dions were to leave next morning.

Stephan, in a complete whirl after the successive hardships that he had had to share with Godard, was pathetically delighted that he was even allowed to go to bed. The de Dion crews found him a likeable young man. "Phew!" he sighed, shaking his head. "I'm not used to this business. Since I got in that car I haven't eaten or slept. I'm not sure that I'm still alive. We were always hurrying, to lose no time on these terrible roads. If I had known what this Peking–Paris trip meant I should have stayed at home."

Stephan was, in fact, suffering from dysentery, and completed the journey to Moscow with great difficulty. Du Taillis had another bad bout of the sickness, and could not travel the next day. He stayed in the hotel, and went by boat to Nijni-Novgorod. When he arrived he was still sick, and after five days he finally joined the party at Vladimir, the stage before Moscow.

He therefore missed what all the veterans declared was positively the worst section of the entire route—the 400 versts from Kazan to Nijni-Novgorod. Cormier said bleakly that there was no road at all. On the Russian military maps he could read two firm lines indicating a first-class road between the cities. He stated emphatically that any army, and particularly its artillery, would be bogged down under the first rainstorm.

On the first day they achieved their all-time minimum for a day's travelling. They accomplished thirty-six versts, under twenty-four miles. There was no inn where they finished. They found refuge in a monastery. Collignon had encountered his greatest hardship in the *raid*—he was out of cigarettes. But the French-speaking daughters of a Russian colonel living near by learned of his deprivation, and managed to obtain a stock of tobacco for him.

The rain fell throughout the four days. Godard and Stephan were stranded in the Spyker at one spot for three hours without the least protection. They were soaked and shivering when at last they moved on. They stripped and tried to dry off before a huge fire built by telegraph linemen. Godard, with his incredible toughness, recovered, but Stephan's condition was pushed farther towards breakdown.

But they came through to Nijni-Novgorod, refuelled, and swept straight out of the town. Now they were on a *road*. The rain seemed unimportant. And by the time they came to Vladimir the sky was blue, the sun was strong, and they declared they could not drive better on a billiard table.

On Wednesday the 14th of August they arrived in Moscow, escorted by a fleet of cars more impressive even than Borghese's convoy, for the de Dion organization had moved into Russia in strength. And in the Hôtel National Georges Cormier took his clothes off for the first time since he had left Peking 65 days before. There were sheets on the bed, even a pillow; and a bathroom next door had taps which gave as much water as you wanted!

Four de Dion-Bouton mechanics set to work on a feverish overhaul of the works cars, for the party was to leave in two days. After renewing the front spring Stephan was absolutely satisfied with the condition of the Spyker after a good cleaning and greasing. Its Hutchinson tyres were down to the cord, but they had done their duty well. Gaston Leroux, a *Matin* journalist who had arrived in Moscow to report the last haul home, telegraphed ecstatically that not only had the tyres not been changed, they had not even been blown up since the Spyker left Peking—they were clearly made of crocodile-skin, not rubber! Leroux was a magnificent colour-writer, but not an acknowledged expert in technical matters. Du Taillis, however, another 'poet' in the eyes of the motoring journalists, but one who had been with the Spyker for most of the time, said, "the Spyker's tyres have done 9000 kilometres without the least tear. Godard's confidence in Hutchinson seems to have justified him in his decision not to carry any spare tyres, but only the set of wheels he stood up on." (But there had been, of course, the little necessity of raising cash in Paris.) The de Dions ran on Dunlop throughout, and the Spyker changed to Dunlop in Moscow.

On the 16th of August, after a memorable celebration banquet, the party set off to the west. Stephan had been summoned to go by train to Posen and report personally to Jacobus Spijker. John Coucke, of *De Telegraaf* of Amsterdam, accompanied Godard for part of the way, though there was some ploy at musical chairs as Coucke moved occasionally into another Spyker being driven down by a director of the Amsterdam firm. Du Taillis was greatly attached to Godard and fervently loyal to the Spyker, and he travelled on it whenever he could. Godard, with his superior speed, was happy, in any case, to act as the advance agent of the convoy and to go ahead and arrange accommodation and petrol supplies for the group following.

After Moscow the tension seemed to have dropped completely. There were *roads*, not always first class, but certainly an improvement on the swamps of Siberia. They could *buy* petrol—not, indeed, in the *ad hoc* pits which Nobel had set up for Borghese, but at least in chemists' shops in the main centres through which they passed—it was Godard's job to ascertain which cities had sufficient supplies. Consequently the mood of the *raid* was continuously gay. John Coucke played incessantly on a trumpet, giving wild fanfares as they approached any habitation. Du Taillis sat beside his friend Godard, hands in his pockets, a cigar in his mouth, and exerted himself only to remove the cigar for a few bars of *La Petite Tonkinoise*. They slept the first night in a five-storied coaching inn, with great stables and barns ranged round the courtyard. They lounged in a high room furnished in oak and leather, and Godard staked a claim to a magnificent sofa, as he still had no bed. At Warsaw they arrived with a hangover after a wild night with the officers of the Polish Dragoon Guards in Siedlce. They were fêted by the newspaper *Courrier de Varsovie*—the ladies decorated the Spyker with flowers while they celebrated—and next day they reached the German frontier.

In a Spyker on the other side Jacobus Spijker was waiting for the reunion with Godard after five very eventful months. It was almost immediately reported that Spijker, in fury, threw Godard out of the car, and put in a mechanic to drive the Spyker to Paris. The facts are completely different.

Spijker was already reconciled with Godard. There was a large financial account to settle, but the prestige Godard had earned for the car would compensate for that if Godard never paid his debts —which Spijker was worldly enough to assume. Spijker had, once he accepted Godard's bohemian nature, given the maximum assistance the driver had asked for—which was very little compared with the aid made available by the de Dion resources. There was just one nagging disagreement to settle: *why had Godard not gone ahead to beat the de Dions?*

It would have given the Spyker firm enormous standing to have come in ahead of the de Dions. Once Borghese had broken the convoy there was a clear case for lone-wolf tactics. The de Dions had treated Godard as a lone wolf since the Gobi Desert, making no alterations of plan to suit him: but du Taillis, in his personal capacity, had eased Godard's petrol difficulties in the lonely journey from Tcheremkhovo to Kazan. There was justification for the three cars having travelled together from Kazan to Moscow. But why had Godard not then shot ahead to Paris? It was the stretch in which he had most advantage. The roads were good. He had more power. Except for eight litres of petrol he owed nothing to de Dion-Bouton. Why could he not clinch a Spyker triumph among the medium-power cars?

The answer lies in Godard's character. He was no longer bound to stay in convoy. The agreement reached in Peking, and published by Barzini in the *Daily Telegraph*, was valid only as far as Irkutsk, though it was violated long before. Bizac and Collignon had spent some hours on his engine when the magneto failed just past Irkutsk, but the delay had cost them nothing. And from

Moscow, at least, no one expected that any obligations existed. Indeed, the Dutch Press had already been speculating on the great race from Moscow to Paris, confidently declaring that the Spyker would win.

Instead the Spyker went ahead as a scout car, as it had been hoped the Itala would act in the desert. Having completed the tasks of organization, Godard waited for the other crews. Godard was faithful to his companions after his fashion.

When Spijker interrogated Godard on the German frontier this was the only explanation he was given. And painfully he accepted it. The *raid* would finish as a team event. Godard would even give up his bonus for second place, the agreement on which was still a firm bargain with Spijker.

Spijker accepted it. But did Cormier and Collignon know that he had accepted it? Above all, did the board of *Le Matin*—and particularly M. Jules Madeline, the managing director—have faith that from the German frontier Godard would not streak ahead? They had already noted that the convoy had not broken at Moscow. The Dutch Press had had to climb down about the immediate race to Paris. Instead John Coucke reported that the cars would travel together *as far as the German frontier*.

If Godard was a clear winner over the de Dions one of the major objectives of the *Matin* project would have failed. The organization of the *raid* had two purposes—to publicize *Le Matin* and to boost the French automobile industry. The first was indubitably achieved. The second was reaching a certain success through the blatant imposition of a black-out in *Le Matin* on any comment on the Spyker's performance beyond the fact that it was there; but the exercise would fail if the de Dions finished behind the Spyker, and especially if the boastful Godard, speaking French, was available to publicize the performance of a Dutch car driven by Tartarin du Gobi.

It would be a step in the right direction if Godard were removed.

The managing director of *Le Matin* therefore had him arrested.

At Küstrin, the stage before Berlin, plain-clothes German policemen approached Godard and informed him that he was to be held for extradition to France on a charge, already heard, of false pretences in China. It was a frame-up. Godard's friends had already instructed a lawyer, who had appealed. A sentence *in absentia* could not be enforced if the defendant had not been formally charged. There was plenty of room for legal argument, and Godard soon argued himself into release. But the object of the arrest was achieved. Godard was out of the race, and discredited.

Spijker, who was prepared for a last-minute blow by *Le Matin*, had brought his best works drivers up from the rear and swiftly handed the Spyker to one of them, Frijling. With Stephan and other associates he returned immediately to Amsterdam in disgust. Du Taillis ostentatiously rode in the Spyker. He was proud of the car and its old shuvver. But he was still under the pressure of being paid by *Le Matin*. Would Frijling make a dash for Paris when Godard had declined? The complicated publicity schedule in Berlin, in which the Spyker firm were deeply involved, probably prevented it; but du Taillis rode on the Spyker into France. Afterwards he wrote:

The brave driver, who had everything but luck, did not drive his car in the entry into Paris, for *the moral prestige of* "Le Matin" *does not permit the newspaper to receive Godard*—the man whose incredible odyssey and marvellous performance is not enough to wash the memory of one or two fairly crafty expediencies from the minds of people of principle.

I had to fight hard to have the Spyker given the honours due to it. It reached Paris not only without having had any of its parts changed (the famous magneto was not, in the end, replaced), but without any mechanic having to be asked in eighty days to check its gearbox or tighten a nut. This car ran with outstanding regularity, and its endurance and power were unsurpassed.

I saved the Spyker from the boycott to which people wanted to condemn it. But I interceded in vain for my companion in distress in the Gobi, whose courage was unfailingly mantained at a point beyond all praise.

Nothing I could do could make the Boss change his mind.

The three cars drove to France. The de Dions were now being

dogged by a farcical series of breakdowns, which brought the mechanics rushing from the rear. The party had to spend three hours at the French frontier, with a table laid for a *champagne d'honneur* visible over the border, waiting for Cormier to emerge from a repair. None of this was reported in *Le Matin.*

It would not be true to say that the arrest of Godard damped the triumph of the 'raiders'' return. They were men. Life was dangerous. Accidents happened. The survivors got on with it. And their own very dear Paris lay ahead.

The *Matin* organization had decreed that the triumphal entry into Paris—for which every trick in their considerable *savoir-faire* in publicity had been planned—was to take place on the afternoon of Friday the 30th of August, twenty days after Borghese's arrival.

The crews took their lunch in a restaurant hidden in the woods of Montlignon, near Enghien. They were harassed fugitives from the constant public acclaim they had already received in the towns of France, and this place had been carefully selected as a hide-out before the last ordeal. A few local residents, however, had recognized the cars and spread the word, and a small crowd was standing round the vehicles as the crews rejoined them, after a long and cheerful meal.

Cormier, who had not shaved for eighty days, had a wild black beard. On his head was a tropical helmet. "It amuses me to put it on again."

"But you lost yours in Siberia. Don't tell me you've bought another!" said du Taillis suspiciously.

"Ready?" asked Cormier, and the three engines were swung. They moved off, but had to stop at Enghien. In this little spa, only eight miles from Paris, the last of the preliminary receptions was to be given. In the courtyard of the *mairie* they were toasted in champagne, overlaid with eloquence, had sandwiches and cakes and enormous sheaves of flowers pressed on them. Cormier could hardly get into his car for two bouquets he was carrying. Bizac, Collignon, and Frijling went to the starting-handles. A laughing, excited crowd waited to see them go.

"Ready?" asked Cormier.

There was a quick ripple in the crowd, and a man came charging through. He almost fell to the ground as the resistance of the onlookers stopped. He ran to the Spyker and jumped into the empty driver's seat.

"Ready!" yelled Charles Godard.

Bizac and Collignon swung automatically, and their engines fired. Frijling hesitated, looked at Godard in the driver's seat and du Taillis beside him, and did nothing.

"Swing her!" roared Godard in nervous fury. The Dutchman started the car.

Godard turned to du Taillis. "*Ça va?* All right?"

"*Ça va!*"

Godard leaned and smacked his hand on the bonnet of the car as if it were the neck of a horse. "My brave Spyker!" he said. He shouted over to Cormier.

"*Ça va?*" And he put up his thumb.

Cormier did not alter his expression as he considered the situation, the flowers bursting over his shoulder. Then he jerked his head upward in amused resignation, and his white teeth showed against the black beard as he yelled.

"*Ça va!*" And he put up his thumb.

There were two men at the open side of the Spyker now—two of Madeline's men. They had been travelling in the publicity section of the motor fleet, in de Dions placarded PEKIN–MATIN, which Madeline had made the slogan of the moment.

"Get out!" they said.

"―――――" said Godard, in an epithet straight from the Wall of Death.

"Get out, or you will be dragged out." The two men had become four. They were inexpressibly menacing. The atmosphere in the courtyard had changed swiftly. The kindly hosts of Enghien had stopped laughing. These men had nothing to do with festivity. They had none of the tolerant comradeship of sporting motorists or working journalists or any of the people who have lain side by side in the labour ward of ambition, and been delivered in agony of a something—a nothing—that could not be sold because it had no value, except that it was there.

These men believed in value, expressed as francs. They were promotion men, not poets. They could bestow value on anything

—even poetry—given time and money. And they knew how a new-minted image of value could be tarnished by untidy presentation.

"Get out!" said one. "This is business."

"Leave the chap alone," ordered du Taillis. At that moment Godard moved his hand to put the car in gear. The promotion leader brought the side of his hand sharply down on Godard's wrist.

"Get him out," he said to the others.

Du Taillis took off his gold-rimmed glasses, and got out of the car. One of the promotion men ran round and held him from behind and told him not to be a fool. Cormier sat in his driving-seat and watched the struggle intently. Collignon watched with his face turned another way, as if he did not want to be caught looking.

The promotion men tried to drag Godard out of the Spyker. It was a difficult angle for them, and they could not reach him effectively, but one man kept Godard's right fist held away from the gear lever. Another climbed up behind and half strangled Godard with a forearm lock. Godard was heaving and yelling, but he could not last. When he was exhausted they prised him out of the driving-seat and pitched him on the ground. Then they raised him and held him.

Two policemen came up. They had not understood the struggle, but they felt confident now that there was an obvious loser. "Put him in the cooler," said the promotion man authoritatively. "He's mad. He's trying to stop the show. He's mad. You won't have to hold him for long."

The policemen understood this. They took Godard. He was still shaking with the fury of his struggle and the tension that had led him to it. His lips and chin were gleaming with saliva, and—there was no doubt about it—the man had been weeping.

"Du Taillis!" he called.

"Godard!"

The writer was still being held from behind by a promotion man, who spoke to him urgently again. "Don't be a fool. Du Taillis, Jean, old chap, this is nothing to do with you. It's not your business."

"Business!" shouted du Taillis. "God wither business!" He shook himself free from the promotion man, and stood swaying, looking at Godard. "And I work for this lot!" he said thickly. He walked away across the courtyard of the *mairie* of Enghien, with its bunting and roses and geraniums, besashed mayor, and silent spectators. It seemed he was leaving them all. But he turned. He came back straight towards Godard with his arm out and his thumb up, as their rescuers in the desert had done.

"Eh, Godard."

"Eh."

"One of us had better do it. If it can't be you it will have to be me. I'll take her in."

"What?"

"I'll take her in to Paris. What's the gate for the gears? In 10,000 kilometres I never learnt it."

Godard was recovering himself in his interest at what du Taillis was saying.

"You'll take my Spyker into Paris?"

"Yes. Just tell me the gears."

"Like hell you will. I'm not going to have you sugar up that old lady. What the hell do you think you are—a driver?"

"No," said du Taillis. And he wiped Godard's eyes with both his thumbs, and got into the Spyker and nodded to Frijling.

"Ready?" called Cormier.

The victory parade began to move into Paris.

"*Are you Godard?*" asked one of the policemen.

There was hysteria and band music and exhibitionist displays by cycle teams; there were people knocked down and flowers cascading everywhere and genuine pride for France. After the last speech of the day had been delivered at the scheduled banquet the company settled itself for 'projections'—lantern slides of the many photographs which du Taillis and Cormier had sent to Paris *en route*.

It had been a good dinner. Gaston Leroux, who was reporting it for *Le Matin*, was feeling mellow after leading punishing raids on a Château Léoville and a Volnay 1893 before launching a general attack on the champagne. Idly he felt for paper, and scratched a phrase or two in the dark.

"It is satisfying, as the Latin poet has said, to watch from the shore the efforts of others fighting against a stormy sea. It is satisfying to sit in a spacious banqueting-hall, belly to the table, and gaze at the perils to which others have exposed themselves."

Epilogue

Prince Scipione enjoyed his triumph in Italy, and settled down to the activities necessitated by his editorship of the Radical Journal *Il Spettatore* and his position as deputy in the Italian Parliament. His Itala motor-car was put on exhibition in various countries: with the two de Dions it was a feature of London's 1908 Motor Show at Olympia. It was later due to be shipped from Italy to the United States, but rolled into the dock at Genoa, and after being salvaged, badly damaged, was virtually abandoned. It was finally rescued, restored, and put into the Museo Nazionale dell'Automobile, in Turin, where it is still to be seen.

When the First World War involved Italy Prince Scipione Borghese rejoined the Colours, and served as an artillery captain on the Udine front. Later he was recalled to diplomatic service, and made two journeys to Petrograd, as St Petersburg came to be called before the final change to Leningrad, in 1917 and 1918.

For some time Borghese was estranged from his wife, Princess Anna Maria. She continued to live in the family estate on the Isola del Garda, from which both their daughters—who are still living —were married. Princess Anna Maria, an imperious, somewhat eccentric, but well-liked woman, was widely known in the Society of London and Paris as well as Rome. But it was on the Isola del

Garda that she mainly dispensed her memorable hospitality and indulged a passionate interest in horticulture. On a November day in 1924 she went with her favourite wolf-hound to plant some acorns she had received from America in a garden she had created on a shelf of rock overhanging the lake. Late in the evening the dog was found at the spot, standing by her handbag, gloves, and trowel. The Princess was never seen again, and it was presumed that she had fallen into the lake at this, one of its deepest parts. Prince Scipione hurried home from Hungary, where he was attending a family wedding, but although he organized extensive searches he could not find the body of his wife.

Two years later Prince Scipione married a widow, Teodora Chilesotti, *née* Martini. His health had been bad since a stroke in 1923, and he lived only seven months after the marriage, dying at Florence in March 1927. He was succeeded in the title by his diplomatist brother Livio, who had helped him with the organization in Peking. Livio's second son, Prince Valerio, became a famous figure in the Second World War, leading the Tenth Light Flotilla of the Italian Navy, the organization whose piloted torpedoes and explosive motor-boats severely hit the Royal Navy and the British merchant fleet in Alexandria, Malta, and Gibraltar.

Luigi Barzini became the most famous special correspondent in Italy: the noun *barzinismo* was coined to describe his characteristically colourful style of writing. He reported the First World War from the French and Italian fronts. In 1922 he left *Il Corriere della Sera* and went to New York, where he founded *Il Corriere d'America*. He returned to Italy in 1932 and edited *Il Mattino* in Naples. He died in 1947. His son, also named Luigi Barzini, was born in 1908, and also became a special correspondent for *Il Corriere della Sera* of Milan. In 1945 he founded the journal *Il Globo* in Rome. He is still living, an author and Member of the Italian Parliament. Ettore Guizzardi died in Rome in 1963 at the age of 83.

Cormier celebrated the end of his Peking–Paris ride with a hunting trip, and resumed his work for de Dion. Du Taillis, after the Atlantic seaside holiday he had promised himself with his wife, and forecast the time to a day, continued in journalism.

Charles Godard did not serve a prison sentence, but he was

ordered to make restitution of some of the money he had acquired from the Dutch diplomatists. In order to raise the cash he persuaded a manufacturer to enter him in *Le Matin*'s sensational new *raid*, the contest for the *Coupe du Monde* in which the competitors had to drive from New York to Paris—via Japan! He was engaged to drive a Motobloc, and took with him a nineteen-year-old ciné-cameraman Maurice Livier, who had held a job in London as bioscope operator at the Empire Theatre, Leicester Square. Though Godard started with his usual panache, and panniers of champagne among his luggage, he retired from the race with mechanical trouble before he reached the Pacific coast of America. He arrived in San Francisco by train with his car aboard, but was disqualified. Auguste Pons also entered this race, driving a Sizaire-Naudin, but he too was forced to retire before leaving America. He settled down, married, and became the father of Lily Pons, the opera singer.

Godard's great Peking–Paris achievement in the Spyker and the robust performance of the machine itself did nothing to save the personal fortunes of Jacobus Spijker, who had backed Godard so generously, with the receiver's money, at the essential moment. Three weeks after the Spyker's entry into Paris an extraordinary general meeting of the shareholders of Spyker Cars removed Jacobus Spijker from the board. If Hendrik had lived matters might have been very different. On the 1st of April, 1908, the company went bankrupt. But four months later, after paying a dividend on debts of 25 per cent., Spyker Cars was reconstructed under fresh directors, and almost overnight became solvent and flourishing. The firm produced aircraft during the First World War, and finally folded in 1927. Bruno Stephan became a professor at Delft, a director of Fokker Aircraft, and adviser to the Turkish Defence Ministry. In 1964, aged 77 and a consultant engineer at The Hague, he drives—a Volkswagen.

Never since 1907 has the motor ride from Peking to Paris been achieved. Luigi Barzini junior unsuccessfully tried to negotiate a repeat of the *raid* to mark its fiftieth anniversary. It is not now absolutely true that "As long as a man has a car he can do anything and go anywhere—*anywhere!*"

◎ ◎ Index